Notes & Apologies:

★ Annual subscriptions to *The Believer* include four issues, one of which might be themed and may come with a special bonus item, such as a giant poster, free radio series, or annual calendar. View our subscription deals at *thebeliever.net/subscribe*.

★ Dispersed throughout the issue is a microinterview with poet, essayist, and editor Kevin Young, conducted by Nick Hilden. Young is the poetry editor of *The New Yorker* and the author of fifteen books, including, most recently, *Night Watch*. He spoke to Hilden over Zoom from his apartment in New York City.

★ Bay Area, come join us at Litquake's daylong book fair on September 28, 2025, at the Great Lawn at Yerba Buena Gardens, in downtown San Francisco. We'll be there from 11 a.m. to 4 p.m., alongside a jolly fleet of other small presses and indie publications. We don't yet know what deals we'll be offering, but we expect them to be considerable.

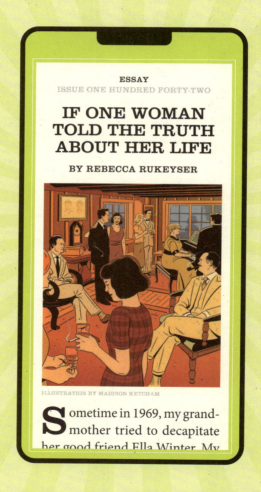

DEAR THE BELIEVER
849 VALENCIA STREET, SAN FRANCISCO, CA 94110
letters@thebeliever.net

Dear Believer,
Like Nora Lange ("Resurrector," Summer 2025), I loved *Weekend at Bernie's*, and I tried to excuse my laughter at its macabre premise by reminding myself that "the actor who played Bernie Lomax was not actually dead." But, Nora, I have some bad news. Even though the actor, Terry Kiser, wasn't dead, he did not emerge from the film's production unscathed. Apparently, he suffered nerve damage from being thrown around so much—and his stunt double actually broke a few ribs in that boat scene you mention (which, admittedly, made me laugh too).

We're still forgiven, but unfortunately, less forgiven than we were before. Sorry to add more discomfort to the laughter.
Lily Nguyen
New York, NY

Dear Believer,
I was charmed by Paul Collins's piece on the world's (formerly) largest broadsheet newspaper ("The Last Mastodon," Summer 2025). I went down a rabbit hole starting from the 1993 newspaper that displaced *The Constellation*'s claim on the Guinness World Record: a June issue of the Belgian newspaper *Het Volk*, which sold fifty thousand copies (!).

In my research, I discovered a related category of Guinness records: the curiously separate distinction for "Largest single copy of a newspaper," which belongs to the Chilean newspaper *El Mercurio de Valparaíso*. *El Mercurio* appears to be among a small number of newspapers attempting this publicity stunt in the twenty-first century. It re-created its December 3, 2015, issue at eighty-one times its original scale—about six times larger than Collins's mastodon. In a remarkable display of journalistic bias, the issue's top story featured its own attempt to break the record, accompanied by a (supposedly incidental) picture of a fireworks display. The headline also suggested it was breaking a record held by the British tabloid *The Sun*, which was set in 2005.

Now that another ten years have passed, I think it's high time that you all at *The Believer* continue the pattern and dethrone them!
Jackie S.
Chicago, IL

Dear Believer,
I appreciated Sheila Heti's reflection (Interview, Summer 2025) on the productive value of complete, total aloneness for her writing. It brought to mind Byung-Chul Han's *The Burnout Society*, in which he describes how modern life has produced a state he calls "hyperattention" that leaves us scattered and dispersed. What Heti's pointing to isn't just being alone in space, but a kind of deep attention that is being increasingly displaced by the phenomenon Han describes. Thank you for bringing these ideas to life through dialogue.
Jacob Thorpe
New York, NY

Dear Believer,
Lyle Lovett's song "If I Had a Boat" was an anthem of my childhood, but I hadn't heard of "Pants Is Overrated" until I read his interview in the last issue (Summer 2025). Alongside its takedown of pants, the song celebrates alternatives like socks, shirts, and kilts, suggesting we broaden our sartorial horizons in pursuit of the good life. It's the same casual absurdity that we see in "If I Had a Boat," where Lovett lets his imagination wander, starting from a utopian premise. There's an ageless purity to these tracks, which is why I couldn't help feeling a bit impugned by Lovett's assertion that they "should be children's songs."

I have always been grateful that my parents played Lovett for me as a kid, along with our other mainstays like the Talking Heads, Sade, and Sting. They never liked so-called children's music, and the one time we tried listening to a Raffi CD in the car, my dad hastily ejected it and threw it onto I-95. My parents' choice to expose me to "adult music" early on gave me a head start on developing my own taste, instead of patronizing my young ears with "Baby Beluga."

But maybe this lack of exposure to children's music has made me less critical of its tropes—and ironically makes me feel compelled to defend Lovett's oeuvre on behalf of the artist himself. Anyone of any age can dream of riding a pony on a boat or eschew the wearing of pants—so long as the music moves you.
Chelsea Popescu
Washington, DC

THE INDEX
to issue one hundred fifty-one

A	PAGE
Abigail Keel	45, 49
Ada Nicolle	118
Afrofuturism	103
Alchemy	29
Alice in Wonderland	31, 59
Anabel DeMartino	74
Anagrams	65
Ancient	6, 22, 27–29, 40, 62, 110
Andrea Bajani	114
Andrea Settimo	74
Anne Boleyn	63
Anne Rice	8
Annunciation	51
Apples	110
Arabic	94–96, 98–100
Arsenal	9–10
Artifacts	51, 76, 79–80, 85–86
Artificial insemination	21
Ash Sanders	34
Austere	50, 96

B	PAGE
Benjamin Tausig	118
Bigfoot	53
Birthing pool	11
Blast-beat	20
✶ Blondie	87–92

Bloomsbury Group	13–15
Blues	28
Borges	31, 100
Boxing	14, 54, 59–61, 97
Brian Barth	113
British modernism	14
Bronski Beat	20
Burning Man	44
Buster Keaton	68–70
Byung-Chul Han	3

C	PAGE
Cacophony of screams	74
Caitlin Van Dusen	120
Calexico	36
Cambridge	13
Cannes	25
Cantankerous	88
Carrie Brownstein	19

Cat	48, 54–55, 110
CCTV footage	10
Cervantes	31, 95
Chase Bush-McLaughlin	12, 69, 89, 117
Chekhov	10, 68, 111
Chicago	3, 101, 103–106, 109–111
China	23, 28, 32, 46
✶ Chris Stein	87–92

✶ Chung Seo-kyung 22–33

CIA	89, 110
Cities of Salt	96
Cobbler	111
Collectivization	50
Crash Zone	113
Crime	8, 11–12, 30, 75, 97
Cryptic	65, 75
Cupola	74, 82

D	PAGE
Dan Gutenberg	32
Dante	55, 95
Debbie Harry	87–92
Denizens	88, 112, 120
Dilapidated	74, 78–79
Dinosaurs	96
Disability	73–79, 81–86
Duncan Grant	13–18
Dungeons & Dragons	8
Dust	15, 36–38, 40–42, 50, 78, 81, 84, 94–96, 113

E	PAGE
Edibles	48

Elizabeth Jane Howard	9, 11
Emma Ingrisani	88
England	13, 63
Evan Trimbur	21
Excel	99
Exodus	48
Experimental	15, 115

F	PAGE
Facade	74, 95
Faulkner	9, 59
Faux	95
Film	3, 22–27, 30–31, 33, 40, 55, 66–70, 88, 103–104, 115
Flamenco	38, 48
Florida	54–56, 58–59, 83
Forest Denka	62–64
Format	90
Frank Sinatra	37
Fraudster	111
Freedom	29, 37, 41, 69, 104
Freud	9–12
Front Street	113
Fugue state	19

G	PAGE
Gabrielle Bates	110
Gawking	86
Gender	16, 88, 90, 102, 105, 115
Genius	54, 114
Gertrude Stein	115
Ghost	15, 18, 40, 43, 64, 75, 78, 115
Gibberish	65, 94
Glitter	89, 100
Glue	8, 97
God	10, 36, 41, 81, 91–92, 124
Gorilla	120
Grandfather	46, 98, 109–110
Guillotine	92

H	PAGE
Hackberry	64
Harauld Hughes	66–68
Haunters	75, 79, 81–85
Healing	56, 101–102, 105
Heather Christle	13
Hibernating	102
Hinderparts	69
Homeless	113
Hong Sang-soo	23–24
Human design	103
Husband	11–12, 56, 111–112

I	PAGE
"Ignore the Explosion"	92
Incestuousness	89
Ingredients	51, 106
Inheritance	106, 111
Intelligence	89
Interstitial	103, 107
Iris Murdoch	9

Italian	19, 39, 101, 110, 114

J	PAGE
Jagjaguwar	102
✶ Jamila Woods	101–107

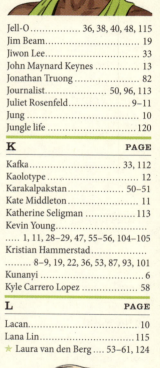

Jell-O	36, 38, 40, 48, 115
Jim Beam	19
Jiwon Lee	33
John Maynard Keynes	13
Jonathan Truong	82
Journalist	50, 96, 113
Juliet Rosenfeld	9–11
Jung	10
Jungle life	120

K	PAGE
Kafka	33, 112
Kaolotype	12
Karakalpakstan	50–51
Kate Middleton	11
Katherine Seligman	113
Kevin Young	1, 11, 28–29, 47, 55–56, 104–105
Kristian Hammerstad	8–9, 19, 22, 36, 53, 87, 93, 101
Kunanyi	6
Kyle Carrero Lopez	58

L	PAGE
Lacan	10
Lana Lin	115
✶ Laura van den Berg	53–61, 124

Le Corbusier	14
Leftist	96
Lenin	51

4

Compiled by Chase Bush-McLaughlin and Simon Traub-Epstein; portraits by Kristian Hammerstad

Lepidopterist	65
Lettuce	36, 114
London	10–11, 13–14, 91
Lukewarm Dasani	74

M	PAGE
Machinery	22, 27
Magic: The Gathering	8
Malodor	19
Manchester United	10
Manflower	69
Manifesto	40, 45, 124
Marital bedsheets	10
Mark Twain	12
Meghan Racklin	112
Melismatic	92
Memory	17, 24, 49, 55, 57, 77, 85, 99, 106, 112, 115
Methodology	97

A BREAKDOWN OF THIS ISSUE'S CONTENTS
(by number of pages)

- Essays (45 pages)
- Interviews (39 pages)
- Poems (3 pages)
- Columns (15 pages)
- Reviews (4 pages)
- Departments (3 pages)

MI6	89
Michael Snyder	50
Middle school	23
Mona Kareem	93
Monstrosity	11
Mourn	15, 111
Mrs. Dalloway	13–14, 17
Mullet Island	36–37, 49
Musicianship	89–90, 92

N	PAGE
Natalie So	23
Nathaniel Rich	62
Navy	89, 109
Nebraska	121
Needlepoint	18
Nick Hilden	1
Nick Hornby	7, 9
Nightmare	36, 49, 56, 74, 121
Nikki Giovanni	101, 106
Normal	25, 59, 66, 70, 92, 121
Numerology	107

O	PAGE
Octavia Butler	101, 106
Oeuvre	3, 13, 22
Ogre	110
Oliver Egger	74
On the Calculation of Volume	112

P	PAGE
Palm Springs	36, 42
Paranormal investigations	74–75, 78
Park Chan-wook	22–26, 33
Party	14, 17–18, 38–40, 42, 45, 47–48, 50, 100, 110, 121
Passover	38
Pennhurst State School and Hospital	74–76
Performance art	38, 41, 89, 90
Personality	14, 60
Peter Orner	109
Philanderer	10
Philosophy	23–24, 26, 28, 30, 37, 40, 44–45, 48–49, 56, 95
Photographer	88, 109–110
"Pigeon Man"	102
Plasmon	12
Plump	69
Poetry slam	90, 102, 104
Poland	11, 117
Polymath	101
Portal	18, 105
Postcoloniality	115
Power-lifting	60
Princess Diana	9
Pristinus	62
Profundities	102
Progress	20, 26, 31–32, 51, 78, 96, 109, 120, 124
Puzzle	65, 118, 124
Pynchon	8, 117

R	PAGE
Reality	9, 57, 59, 112
Revenge	26
Revolver	111
Ricardo Frasso Jaramillo	114
Richard Ayoade	66–70
Rilke	9
Riviera	36–37
Robbie Arnott	6
R. O. Kwon	21, 54
Rome	50, 114
RVs	38, 40

S	PAGE
Saffron Maeve	115
Salton Sink	36–37, 49
Salvation	26, 36, 97
Sam Sax	102
Sappho	100
Scapegoat	27
Scarcity	54, 61
Scheme	93
Secret	26, 56, 70, 89, 96
Septology	112
Sherlock Holmes	33
Smuggling	63
Social justice	105–106
Soham Patel	100
Solvej Balle	112
Sombrero	111
Spanish Civil War	16
Squares	18, 65, 88
Steampunk bunny mask	77
Stephen Grosz	9–10, 12
Steven Duong	8
Stranger Things	76
Suffering	8–9, 11, 83, 120, 124
Suds	19

T	PAGE
Tableaux	70
Talking Heads	3, 56, 91
Tanizaki	8
Tarzan of the Apes	120
Tea	6, 13, 16, 36, 48, 96, 98
Tess Wayland	111
"The Asylum"	74
The Autobiography of H. Lan Thao Lam	115
The Book of Homes	114
The Crying of Lot 49	117
The Flamingo	109, 111
The Method	91–92
Therapy	56, 79, 83, 104
Thrillers	54, 59
Translation	95, 100

U	PAGE
"Ugly laws"	84
Unidentified Vietnam No. 18	115

↖ **"THE LAST RESORT"** *by Ash Sanders*
(page 34)

V	PAGE
★ Vanessa Bell	13–18
Vertiginous	114
Vijay Khurana	65
Virginia Woolf	13–14, 17

W	PAGE
Wallace Shawn	67
Whitman	36, 95
Wile E. Coyote	43
Wink	99

X	PAGE
Xenogenesis	106

Y	PAGE
Yoon Suk Yeol	23

Z	PAGE
Zealotry	20

Photo by Ash Sanders

THE ROUTINE: ROBBIE ARNOTT
AN ANNOTATED RAMBLE THROUGH ONE ARTIST'S WORKDAY

4:30 a.m.
Daughter (2.5) jumps on neck. Convince her we live in a forest populated by talking crabs. Go back to sleep.

4:30–11 a.m.

7 a.m.
Read a page (any page) of *The Peregrine* by J. A. Baker. Breakfast, Yorkshire tea, parenting.

9 a.m. → **9:30 a.m.**
More tea. Read over yesterday's writing. Grimace. Write.

Trail above house

12:30 p.m.
Lunch at home (boring). Brisk and aimless walk around foothills of kunanyi (mountain above my house).

11 a.m.–12:30 p.m.

Pub (longed for)

12 p.m.
Consider lunch at pub with friends (fun). Resist.

1:30 p.m.
Radio interview over phone. Emails. More tea.

2:45 p.m.
Shift from laptop to notebook. Try to come up with ideas/notes for current manuscript. Fail.

12:30–4:30 p.m.

Desk made from old church pew

4:30 p.m.
Pick up kids + wife. Parenting, laundry, cooking dinner.

5:30 p.m.
Back to desk.

4:30–7 p.m.

7 p.m.
Read books to daughter until she falls asleep. Sing to son (three months) until he falls asleep.

Stunning and fun?!?!?

7–9:30 p.m.

8 p.m.
Watch *Slow Horses* with wife. Try to write more notes. Fail again. Drink large glass of red wine.

9 p.m. → **9:30 p.m.**
Read a few pages of *Seeing Stars* by Simon Armitage. Fall asleep on couch listening to ancient-history podcast.

Photos by the author

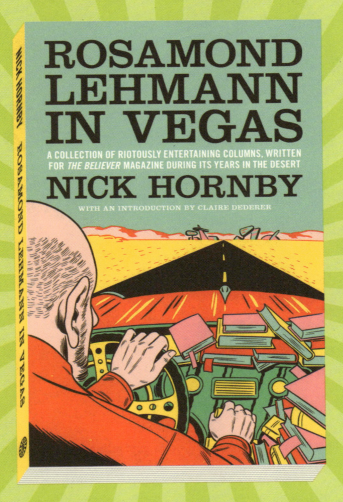

UNDERWAY

WE ASK WRITERS AND ARTISTS: WHAT'S ON YOUR DESK? WHAT ARE YOU WORKING ON?

by Steven Duong

Note from Lucie
My partner, Lucie, left this tiny card on my desk two years ago. It's still there. The drawing makes me think of that Bright Eyes song. "Here it comes, that heavy love. You're never going to move it alone."

"Macaron Hello Kitty" Figurine
This particular incarnation of Ms. Hello Kitty was gifted to me in a "blind box" by the writer Yasmin Adele Majeed. She's holding a birthday card, but I like to pretend it's a very slim novel manuscript.

Clip-On Dog Treat Pouch
You never know when your dog is going to do something treat-worthy.

Galadriel, Elven-Queen
My brother got me a bunch of Tolkien-inspired Magic: The Gathering cards for Christmas. Galadriel is here as a reminder for me to write about what matters most: scary, powerful women.

1968 Brother Montgomery Ward Signature 440T
Over the last few months, I've been fixing up cheap typewriters from Facebook Marketplace. It's nice to have a machine with one purpose and no delete function.

Dungeons & Dragons Miniatures
I paint these using very tiny brushes. This is my friend Sam's character, Princess Maris Carillo. I need to glue her shield-arm back on.

Pile of Novels
Lately I've found myself reading a few novels at once. Right now I've got a Pynchon, a Tanizaki, and a particularly smutty Anne Rice, initially published under one of her pseudonyms.

I'm currently working on a short story about a recovering addict who, when his Buddhist parents refuse to put down their very old, very clearly suffering family dog, decides to attempt DIY euthanasia with the help of his former dealer.

I'm also writing a novel. It began a few years ago as a short story about a poet navigating an unexpected influx of attention, praise, and professional success after publishing a poem addressed to the victim of a violent hate crime. In expanding it into a longer project, following the poet as he ends his estrangement from his family and reenters their lives in search of subject matter, I'm starting to write more deeply into the relationship between sincerity and cynicism—how contemporary artists and writers leverage qualities like honesty and vulnerability in service of career advancement, and how examining cultural projections of sincerity with a more cynical eye might offer us a new (and hopefully more compelling) path forward. ✭

Illustration by Kristian Hammerstad

STUFF I'VE BEEN READING

A QUARTERLY COLUMN, STEADY AS EVER

by Nick Hornby

BOOKS READ:
★ *Love's Labour: How We Break and Make the Bonds of Love*—Stephen Grosz
★ *Affairs: True Stories of Love, Lies, Hope and Desire*—Juliet Rosenfeld
★ *The Light Years*—Elizabeth Jane Howard

BOOKS BOUGHT:
★ *Working the Room: Essays and Reviews, 1999–2010*—Geoff Dyer
★ *Zero at the Bone: Fifty Entries Against Despair*—Christian Wiman
★ *Uncle Willy and Other Stories*—William Faulkner
★ *Cue the Sun!: The Invention of Reality TV*—Emily Nussbaum

It's Epigraph City out there. Just about every nonfiction book I have started over the last couple of months begins with at least one of the little bastards, often two. *Love's Labour* by Stephen Grosz goes with a Rilke and an Iris Murdoch:

> For one human being to love another: that is perhaps the most difficult of all of our tasks, the work for which all other work is but preparation. (*Letters to a Young Poet*)

> Remember that all our failures are ultimately failures in love. (*The Bell*)

Juliet Rosenfeld, in *Affairs*, plumps for one Freud and one Princess Diana:

> We are never so defenceless against suffering as when we love.

> Well, there were three of us in this marriage. So, it was a bit crowded.

You have to say, Diana has done well to work herself into this company. Her laconic line has become a classic, and she deserves her place alongside the greats of European literature. Hats off to her. You really couldn't see it coming when she was working as a nanny for that posh American family in the early days, but she found a cutting epigrammatic style when she needed it most. Few of us can say the same.

Both Juliet Rosenfeld and Stephen Grosz are psychotherapists; both have chosen to write about love, and the mess we make of it, in their latest books. I like to presume I know a little bit about you, dear reader, having spoken to you from this pulpit for over two decades. And yes, very few of you have said anything to me in reply, nor have I afforded you many opportunities to do so. It's been a very wordy one-way conversation, and I get to change the subject whenever I feel like it. This works great for me, and I can't imagine what wouldn't work for you.

Anyway, one of my presumptions is that you are interested in the subject of love. It comes with the territory of *The Believer*, no? You might not agree with Iris Murdoch that "all our failures are ultimately failures in love." (I am writing this after the disappointment of Arsenal's trophy-less season, for example, and this failure was ultimately a failure in personnel recruitment, particularly up front, in the summer of 2024. But maybe Iris wasn't much of a sports fan.) Any interest in the arts, it seems to me, presupposes an interest in matters of the heart.

Illustration by Kristian Hammerstad

That's what most of the best art is all about, especially if we count God or gods, as I think we must. People love Him or them or Them. The point is, I think you're likely to want to read both *Affairs* and *Love's Labour*, and I suspect you'll be provoked and stimulated by both.

Stephen Grosz is a beautiful writer, a clear, compelling thinker, an observant, wise, and deeply empathetic human being. Like *The Examined Life: How We Lose and Find Ourselves*, his previous, much-loved book, *Love's Labour* is a series of case studies, stories of patients that he has come across during his career as a shrink, focusing exclusively on their romantic travails. He has changed the details of their situations so they cannot be recognized. And that's where I trip up a little bit.

I grew up in the suburbs with my mother and my sister. I have an autistic son. My first book, about my relationship with Arsenal over the first three decades of my life, was successful, and changed my professional trajectory. That's me. I mean, not all of me, obviously. I'm also a picker, a grinner, a lover, a sinner, a joker, and the author of several novels and screenplays. But start messing with any of those details, and am I myself anymore? Or am I someone else? If my son had been diagnosed with cerebral palsy rather than autism, my life would have been profoundly different from the one I ended up living. The same would be true if I had written a book about cricket, or Manchester United, or if I had grown up in Kensington with a brother. The narratives and problems I would have presented to a psychoanalyst (and I have kept the entire London branch of the profession fed and clothed for decades) would not have been the same. So what are we reading here? In what way were the patients anonymized? Is it even possible that they could get to *this* point from *there*?

But "this point" is never less than extraordinary, and you can't stop reading. Dr Ravi M. is a forty-three-year-old mathematics lecturer. (Except, of course, his name isn't Ravi and he might not lecture in mathematics and…) He tells Grosz that his wife, Sonal, is having an affair, but he never wants to confront her about it, because he is terrified of the consequences of divorce. He has two young daughters, and cannot bear the prospect of being separated from them. Ravi knows who Sonal is sleeping with. Her lover is a lawyer called Rakesh, who lives on the same street. Ravi knows the exact time that Sonal and Rakesh have sex, because Sonal has started changing the marital bedsheets on a different day. She has started leaving diaries, receipts, and bank statements lying around, so that Ravi can see that nothing untoward is happening. She has bought new clothes, new underwear. And Ravi retrieves her panties from the laundry basket every night on the hunt for a surfeit of pubic hairs: One Friday, the day he knows the adulterous couple sleep together, he finds four, including a darker one that clearly must once have belonged to Rakesh. Ravi puts it in an envelope. "I'll bring it in and show you," he tells Grosz.

Grosz learns that, if he wanted to, Ravi could confirm his suspicions—his *certainty*—that something is going on by examining the CCTV footage available to him on his home security system. Ravi refuses to look. The only evidence that would dispel his jealousy, the jealousy that is eating him alive, is of no interest to him. The affair is, as you may have guessed, all in his imagination. Grosz explains, with elegance and acuity, the purpose it's serving, and where it's rooted. And he does this over and over again, with equally compelling case studies. "Think Carver, Cheever, Calvino, not Freud, Lacan, Jung," said Grosz's agent when *The Examined Life* was submitted to publishers. Therein lies the beauty of *Love's Labour*, and perhaps the problem too.

Juliet Rosenfeld found her subjects through advertisements in *The New York Review of Books* and the *London Review of Books*: "Have you had an affair? Published author and psychotherapist keen to interview under strict anonymity for case studies in this underexplored aspect of behaviour." "I cannot emphasise enough," Rosenfeld says in her introduction, "that the central motivations for affairs relate to all our own infantile, forgotten selves." It's an uncompromising stance, and one of the objections one might raise is that, according to therapists, just about everything we do relates to all our infantile, forgotten selves. Every artist of any kind knows this better than anyone. *Look at me! Look at what I've written/made/painted/whatever! Please! Mum! Dad!* Ahem. Anyway. *Affairs* will make you think about Freud, Lacan, and Jung rather than Carver, Cheever, and Calvino. Rosenfeld chooses a psychotherapeutic rather than a Chekhovian lens for her case histories, but it is of course no less gripping than *Love's Labour*, not least because the affairs under inspection are not the common or garden variety. Whatever marital crimes you may have committed, *Affairs* will provide some perspective.

Neil, a senior partner in a big law firm, holds his wife, Serena, under her armpits in a birthing pool while she gives birth to his first daughter; he already has twin sons from a previous marriage. Forty minutes after Amelia has entered the world, Neil is having sex with his girlfriend, Magdalena, in a flat he rents for her. See, guys… you probably haven't done anything like that, right? So there you go! You can feel better about yourself!

Magdalena is younger than his wife, and his wife is younger than him. Magdalena is lonely, unhappy, uneducated, utterly dependent on Neil. In the end she goes back to her native Poland. Neil has two more children, but he also has other lovers, on and on into his seventies, while apparently cherishing his relationship with Serena. Psychoanalysis unearths a painful, difficult childhood; but at the end of the chapter, Rosenfeld, who has spoken to Neil on Zoom, spots him in a London street. She follows him for a moment. He meets up with a young woman at coffee shop, and the author observes physical contact between them.

Eleanor and Miller are attracted to each other more or less instantly. They meet at Eleanor's workplace; both of them are married. So far, so ho-hum, right? But… Eleanor is a therapist and Miller is her patient, and by Miller's third session they are helpless, giggling, squirming wrecks. Eleanor ends up losing her license—she set up the practice with her husband and a couple of other colleagues—and both her career and her ability to support herself vanish. Miller and Eleanor are still together.

There is damage in her past that led to the adult catastrophe, inevitably, but Eleanor's conviction that she made the right choice, that she has found the love of her life, complicates the picture and the book. Her willingness to cross a red line that cannot be negotiated away under any circumstances is of course both curious and troubling. In classical Freudian psychoanalysis, the relationship between Miller and Eleanor is called the "incest taboo," such is the gravity of the professional crime. "We are never so defenceless against suffering as when we love." The suffering in both of these smart, absorbing books is everywhere, and though it may be occasionally horrifying and frequently perplexing, it always illuminates what it is to be human and to love.

There is adultery in Elizabeth Jane Howard's *The Light Years*; let's face it, there's adultery in a lot of great novels. *The Light Years* is the first volume of Howard's *The Cazalet Chronicles*, beloved by Hilary Mantel, Penelope Fitzgerald, and the Duchess of Cornwall, among many others. (If you don't know your Cornwalls from your Kents, your Yorks, and your Sussexes, the current Duchess of Cornwall is Kate Middleton, William's wife.) People have been telling me to read the series for years, and during a recent bout of illness I decided that the Cazalets would be my comfort read, even though I had no idea whether they would provide the comfort I was seeking. I wasn't ill enough for long enough to read my way through the lot. *The Light Years* alone is a hefty five hundred–plus pages, so I'd have to have been a Victorian consumptive to polish off the lot. But I am converted, and will read on, possibly by water somewhere during the holidays, and hopefully in good health.

The Cazalets—Hugh, Rachel, Edward, and Rupert—were born at the end of the nineteenth or the beginning of the twentieth century, and the events narrated in *The Light Years* take place in 1937 and 1938. Three of them are married, but Rachel is, unbeknownst to her family, gay. The adultery here is a pretty standard 1930s variety, so I'm not sure either Juliet Rosenfeld

---

MICROINTERVIEW WITH KEVIN YOUNG, PART I

THE BELIEVER: You've been in the poetry and publishing worlds for some thirty years now. What changes have you seen in that time?

KEVIN YOUNG: I think poetry itself has broadened and deepened. What I see, having edited *The New Yorker* anthology, is the way that poetry really, in the past forty years, has exploded in terms of who's publishing and who's able to publish and the outlets for publishing. At the same time, it once felt like there was a different kind of robust, smaller-press life, and you had these different outlets and magazines, some of which I miss. But in general I think there are a lot of people writing who were always writing, but who are now getting published more. ✶

or Stephen Grosz would find much to write home or write a book about. Edward has a mistress. His wife, Villy, does not like "the bed side of life." "Sex was for men, after all," according to Villy's interior monologue. "Women, nice women, anyway, were not expected to care for it." I should point out that the book was published in 1990, so Howard is describing a prewar English middle-class mind-set rather than attempting to speak for all women. Villy doesn't enjoy sex, because she's been prepared never to enjoy it, and she tolerates her husband's joyless and mercifully brief rutting because that's what she is supposed to do. Freud's *Civilization and Its Discontents* is only eight years old when the book takes place, after all: Before Sigmund came along and complicated and explained everything, the infidelity Howard describes was, it seems, straightforward and brutally inevitable.

Meanwhile, Rupert, who, unlike his brothers, does not work at the family firm and is struggling to square his artistic aspirations with his domestic responsibilities, has married a younger woman too hastily after the death of his first wife. Zoe is a reluctant stepmother, and restless; she allows herself to be seduced—the word *rape* isn't used, but it would be now—by an older man. I don't know what happens in the subsequent volumes of the sequence, but I am hoping and praying that at some point a woman has a sexual experience that isn't thoroughly miserable.

But *The Cazalet Chronicles* are not about sex, or marriage. Or rather, they are not only about these things. All British upper-middle-class life is here. Children and their parents, children and their relationships with one another. Families. Work and ambition. Money. And, hanging over it all, the enormous dark cloud of the impending war. Children and adults are afraid. The adults remember the carnage of the Great War, and Hugh still bears the wounds and the trauma, and Chamberlain's negotiations with Hitler are followed by a fear you can taste and smell, even though the Cazalets are following the news from an idyllic, big, rambling house in the countryside. Howard is not, perhaps, especially good at characterizing children, as in making each one (and there are many) distinctive.

But she is brilliant at conjuring up different stages of childhood, the terror and the wonder, the anger and the vulnerability, the cruelty and the stupidity. I fear for them all, because I'm pretty sure 1939, and then 1940, are just around the corner. I am happy that I have so much more of the Cazalet saga to look forward to—*and I forgive them all their poshness*, usually the English literary crime I cannot ignore. Our affairs, our marriages, our romantic lives have all become more understood, and certainly much more visible, since 1938, but the central question remains, and will never be answered: What the hell are we supposed to do about it all? ✶

MARK TWAIN'S FAILED INVESTMENTS AND BUSINESS VENTURES, IN ORDER OF MAGNITUDE

✶ The Paige Compositor, a mechanical typesetter (1880–94): invested $300,000, or about $8,000,000 today
✶ A commissioned autobiography of the pastor Henry Ward Beecher, who died of a stroke before writing the book (1887): invested $105,000, or about $3,500,000 today
✶ A memoir of Pope Leo XIII (1886): invested more than $100,000, or more than $3,400,000 today
✶ A chalk-engraving process called Kaolotype (1883): invested $42,000, or about $1,300,000 today
✶ An early protein powder called Plasmon (1900): invested $32,000, or about $1,200,000 today
✶ A revolutionary new steam pulley (circa 1882): invested $32,000, or about $1,000,000 today
✶ The Hartford Accident Insurance Company (1874): invested $23,000, or about $650,000 today
✶ The International Spiral Pin Company (1904): invested $10,000–$12,000, or $360,000–$430,000 today
✶ The New York Vaporizer Company (1877): invested $5,000, or about $153,000 today

—*list compiled by Chase Bush-McLaughlin*

VANESSA BELL IS NOT AT HOME

THE ARTIST, LONG DISMISSED FOR HER DOMESTIC INTERPRETATION OF MODERNISM, IS FINALLY GETTING HER DUE. BUT CAN HER QUEER ARCADIA BE REPLICATED IN THE CONTEXT OF A MUSEUM?

by Heather Christle

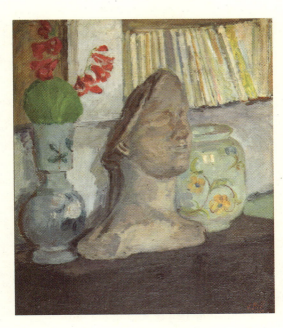

In Virginia Woolf's novel *Mrs. Dalloway*, which celebrated its centennial in May, the title character remembers a friend mocking her years before; the young Clarissa had the makings, jeered Peter Walsh, of the perfect hostess. Both Woolf and her older sister, Vanessa Bell, knew well the dangers of becoming stuck in that role, forever passing tea and buns about the room, never speaking beyond decorum's limits. As female members of a respectable upper-middle-class Victorian family, they were trained in the domestic arts, excluded from the Cambridge education provided to their brothers and half brothers. Forced by the oldest of their siblings, George Duckworth, into attending society gatherings, the sisters dreaded the life he imagined for them as Peter Walsh's perfect hostess. When left to their own devices, they practiced their other future vocations: writing for Virginia, painting for Vanessa. Once, the young artist took a piece of chalk and began writing on a black door, "When I am a famous painter…," before setting the chalk down and erasing her clause. As it turned out, Vanessa Bell would manage to occupy both positions, that of a famous painter *and* that of a perfect hostess, though in forms neither George Duckworth nor Peter Walsh would have been capable of imagining.

In enthusiastic reviews of the largest-ever solo exhibition of her work, *Vanessa Bell: A World of Form and Colour*, which ran from October 2024 to February 2025 at England's MK Gallery in Milton Keynes, critics lined up to complete her chalked sentence. After decades of appearing as the lesser half of the sisters, or as the subordinate artist to her lifelong companion, Duncan Grant, Bell is enjoying a moment of attention as a major modernist figure in her own right. Her oeuvre is large and varied, from her experiments in abstraction to her decorative work for the iconic Omega Workshops; from her bright, splotchy portraits of fellow members of the Bloomsbury Group to the instantly recognizable book covers she designed for her sister. The exhibition's title feels apt. The impressive catalog spans nearly six decades of artistic creation, and the gathering of over 150 works tells a story of more than a single life; together, they make a whole world.

But here I must make a confession: When I initially heard of the exhibition, I did not feel entirely celebratory. Part of me was indignant, proprietary. You might call me anxiously attached.

My first in-person encounter with Vanessa Bell's art occurred in September of 2021 at Charleston, the old English country house dubbed a "queer arcadia" by its current head of collections and research, Darren Clarke, and which is now a public museum. It was here that Bell and Duncan Grant lived—with intermittent time spent in London and elsewhere—painting everything from the usual canvases to the walls, the lamps, each other's beds. Bell loved Grant deeply, though she was married until her death to the art critic Clive Bell, with whom she had two sons. She and Grant had a daughter, who was not told of her biological father until she was an adult. Bell also had a serious affair with the painter and critic Roger Fry. Grant, meanwhile, mostly had relationships with other men, including the economist John Maynard Keynes (who would later have his own bedroom at Charleston), and the writer David Garnett,

Still Life with Plaster Head, 1947 by Vanessa Bell. Oil on board. 53.5 × 44.5 cm. © Estate of Vanessa Bell. All rights reserved, DACS 2025.

who lived with Grant and Bell during the years of the First World War. The house *teems*, not only with the colorful paint and fabric of Bell's and Grant's prolific making, but with a network of human relationships. Even now, that network feels radical, offering a potential model for other ways of imagining life: open, curious, slipping out of the straight and square world's attempts at a disciplining gaze. Charleston (if you will permit me to anthropomorphize the house's unmistakable personality) does not care that critics once sniffed at Bell and Grant's interest in interior decoration, marking it as inferior to their own preferred vision of modernism as a heroic, masculine movement. Those critics esteemed Le Corbusier and his claim for the right to "health, logic, daring, harmony, [and] perfection" "in the name of the steamship, of the airplane, and of the motor-car." How could Vanessa Bell look at the sloppy domestic circles she painted around her fireplace and think she could compete? (Art historian Christopher Reed has written brilliantly on this subject.)

Perhaps because I was exhausted by the pandemic's endless onscreen grids and their boxing-in of bodies that I longed to touch, when I finally arrived in person at Charleston in 2021, I was primed to fall in love. I was enchanted by its glorious mess of colors and patterns, its promiscuous layering of years, its demonstrations that art and life could be—indeed *must be*—intertwined. I came home and painted my own table. I renewed my artistic vows. The personal devotion the house inspired in me meant that when I first saw an image from MK Gallery's exhibition— a photograph of the two bedroom doors Bell painted for Grant, hung up on a blank museum wall—the word *sacrilege* bloomed in my mind like spilled communion wine on thick liturgical cloth. Put them back! I thought. They don't need this! Elsewhere on the museum's website, I spied a painted fireplace surround, which, unlike the ones I'd worshipped at Charleston, framed not a place for burning, but rather a flat, empty space. If you hang a fireplace on a white wall, I fretted, don't the flames go cold? I booked tickets so I could find out.

I like to think of art as a social occasion: a cocktail hour, a playdate, a dinner party. An artist is a host who fashions space and time for others to enter. Some are shy hosts and absent themselves. Some bully you through the house, forcing you to notice their symbolic decor in a predetermined order. Some register your presence and smile before wandering into the kitchen, where they are trying to repair a dripping faucet. Some stare at you with aggravation, certain you were not invited. I enjoy the metaphor in part because it lets the artist occupy a position easily dismissed as frivolous and feminine. Think back to *Mrs. Dalloway*, the light-hearted party preparations with which the novel famously opens: Clarissa Dalloway "would buy the flowers herself," and "the doors would be taken off their hinges." When the novel was first published, some critics sniffed at the insignificance of its subject, willfully ignoring the book's wide-ranging concerns. Yes, from one angle it's the story of a party thrown by a socialite, but—if we consider the idea that artists are themselves hosts—it would be impossible not to notice that at Woolf's party she has arranged war and death alongside the flowers.

Two opposing stories exist about Vanessa Bell as a host in the most literal sense. In one, she is formidable and remote, fiercely guarding her artistic practice. After years of sharing studio space with Duncan Grant at Charleston, she retreated to paint in the attic, which even now is closed off to visitors.[1]

If one were to knock on that door, would she answer? In Bell's younger years, while she was still living and working in London, she once fought off a phone call from her half brother: "I am afraid Mrs. Bell is out," said the artist.

"But you *are* Mrs. Bell," said the caller. "I am your brother George."

"I am afraid Mrs. Bell is out," the artist repeated.

"But, Vanessa, I know your voice," insisted George.

"I am afraid Mrs. Bell is out." She would speak no other sentence. Sir George Duckworth hung up.

In the other story of Vanessa Bell as a host, she is the quietly powerful social figure around whom Bloomsbury (and British modernism) grew. It was she who insisted on the need for a weekly salon to discuss visual art, to complement her brother's more literary gatherings. It was Bell who chose to approach marriage with nonmonogamous flexibility, opening space for a burst of lines between lovers in Bloomsbury's messy circles. And it was Bell who made Charleston a place with room for those who shared her nontraditional

---

1. Its door, I should add, has been taken off its hinges and added to a variation on *A World of Form and Colour*, which was on view at Charleston's new Lewes branch through the summer.

instincts. (Duncan Grant and David Garnett began their lives there working the farm, so that, as conscientious objectors, they would not be conscripted into the First World War.)

Recently, I was put in touch with a woman whose mother, Constance Bull, had been a guest at Charleston back in 1941, and I felt a little thrill at catching a new glimpse of Bell's life as a host. On a hot summer day, Michael Bagenal—who'd grown up playing with Bell's children as the son of another Bloomsbury artist—brought Connie, then his new girlfriend, to visit Charleston. It was a dusty, sweaty walk from the train station. When Connie and Michael arrived, they found Duncan Grant and others swimming naked, as usual, in Charleston's pond. Only twenty years old, and an aspiring artist herself, Connie had been thrilled at the prospect of meeting these great and famous painters, but when the nude Grant hopped out of the pond to shake her hand and introduce his dripping self, she was shocked and overwhelmed. She mumbled her excuses and ran into the house. Inside, she bumped into Vanessa, who had not yet joined the others in the pond. Connie stammered that she was looking for somewhere to change, to which the painter replied, "Oh, fancy that. I'm going to do that as well. Why don't you come into my room and we can both get changed together?"

When they stepped back out again, Grant must have laughed. He asked Vanessa, "Why are you wearing that?"

"I like swimming in my costume," she said calmly. "Come on, Connie, let's go into the pool."

When Connie's daughter told me this story, she marveled at Bell's

Vanessa Bell's painted living room at Charleston. Photograph by the author.

kindness. "You know, it's [the act of] the perfect hostess, isn't it?"

"It is, it is," I agreed.

I timed my visit to the MK Gallery exhibition to coincide with a daylong conference devoted to Bell's work, eager to gather more of the stories around and behind what she made. In a fantastic talk on Bell's painting *A Conversation*, which features three women leaning toward one another conspiratorially, the scholar Grace Brockington guided attendees through a careful analysis of its yearslong composition, during which "the sky changed color several times." The world changed too: Between 1913, when Bell began work on it, and 1916, when she finished, her country entered the First World War. This historical moment, argued Brockington, would have influenced Bell's decision to change the rightmost figure in *A Conversation* from "a man holding a cane" to "a woman with her arms folded in her lap." In 1916, Britain introduced conscription, Brockington explained, meaning that "large numbers of men were visibly absent," and so "there is a narrative logic to her decision… to paint over the man in the room, leaving him a sort of ghostly presence in an all-female society." The overall mood of the painting changed as well. The bright colors and patterns in the curtains, in one woman's dress, and even on the frame itself—painted at a moment when "the British avant-garde [was] at its most ebullient and experimental"—gave way to the darker, solid tones of mourning.

"The hostility of the general public," wrote Bell, "was real now; no longer a ridiculous and even stimulating

Conversation Piece, 1912 by Vanessa Bell. Oil on board. 58.5 × 76.5 cm. © Estate of Vanessa Bell. All rights reserved, DACS 2025.

joke." Questioning received notions of art, nationalism, gender, and home—as she and others had done so joyfully and publicly in 1913—had become, by 1916, dangerously unpatriotic and degenerate.

Brockington's talk stayed with me when I returned to the exhibition the day after the conference, moving slowly through the first room, a gathering of Bell's earliest works. I stopped before *Nursery Tea*, a domestic scene from around 1912 in which two nursemaids sit at opposite ends of a table whose other sides are occupied by Bell's two young children. I could not help but grieve what Bell did not then know: the fate of the boy on the right. Her older son, Julian, would be killed in 1937 while driving an ambulance for the anti-fascists during the Spanish Civil War. If I wished, I could do what Bell could not: consciously prolong the approach of that year and its loss. I could choose to walk over to the wall display of the playful set of fifty dinner plates that Bell and Duncan

16

Grant created together between 1932 and 1934, each of which depicts a "famous woman." The roll call includes the two artists themselves, troubling the imagined divide that the word *woman* implies. I fantasized about what a joy it would be to host a party with these plates. Or to throw one, perhaps, at a fascist.

Unsurprisingly, after my many years of reading Virginia Woolf, I especially delighted in the exhibition's display case of Bell's designs for her sister's book jackets, evidence of the lifelong collaboration between the great painter and the great writer. Bell's cover for *Mrs. Dalloway* echoes the novel's presentation of death and war at the party: A bouquet of flowers lies at the bottom of her illustration, while just beyond, surrounded by scalloping suggestive of lush curtains, a balcony looks out onto blackness. It is from such a height, and into such a void, that Septimus Warren Smith—Woolf's shell-shocked veteran—leaps to his death, just as Clarissa Dalloway's party begins. Clarissa is angry and dismayed when news of his death interrupts her gathering, but Virginia Woolf is a wiser host, arranging whatever pieces come her way.

My favorite object in the exhibition was a painted trifold screen that hovers between representation and abstraction. The left panel begins with a vertical off-white rectangle covered in Bell's signature "leopard" splotches, here in green and blue-gray. Strong black lines in the shape of a V cut through fields of pale blue and bone to lead into the second panel's stack of rectangles, upon which sits a decorated brown fan. The suggested interior continues into the right panel, where—and this is what

Self-Portrait, c. 1958 by Vanessa Bell. Oil on canvas. 45 × 37 cm. © Estate of Vanessa Bell. All rights reserved, DACS 2025.

thrills me—a detailed and delicately colored wallpaper design on the top half slowly transforms into cruder shapes and bolder colors as it reaches the floor. Bell blurs the distinction between interior design and fine art, between the thing itself and its depiction, *and* she reminds us that it's all happening at once on the same surface. The work feels mischievous and joyful, fluid and alert.

Despite this pleasant stimulation, I still had my reservations. I could not quite shake off the memory of my instinctive recoil from the picture I'd seen on the museum's website. It was easy enough to encounter works I'd not seen in person before and feel their fresh vitality, but what about my fire? I turned to the right to look at the surround on the wall. Something was off, its lines and circles far tidier than those I'd remembered from Charleston. A nearby explanatory text revealed why: This was a design made

Installation shot of Vanessa Bell: A World of Form and Colour. *Photograph by Rob Harris for MK Gallery.*

on commission, for the house of Lady Dorothy Wellesley, and so the looseness of the casual, affectionate work I'd seen around the fireplaces of Charleston had stiffened under a more tightly controlled brush. The museum wall didn't matter; the fire I'd thought I'd been attached to was never truly lit. My phone's screen (how frequently it does this! when will I learn?!) had raised in me an unnecessary and trivial outrage. Bell may have built a subversive life for herself and others at Charleston, but she was also an artist working to earn money, and so would occasionally straighten her marks into a smoother state. This, too, is part of her story, and one that apparently does not mind appearing in public.

Having made that peace, I felt ready to turn toward Duncan Grant's bedroom doors: far more intimate works than the commissioned fireplace. What would (or even *could*) they do beneath the museum's cold lights? I feared that, removed from the lively fullness of the place that occasioned their creation, they would lack depth, *literally*: pinned flat and inert against the white wall. A door is to open, I thought. I sat on a bench in front of them. Their shapes and colors were familiar; I remembered the lower panels' matching splotchy circles, the upper panels' different vases of blooms. I longed to send them home to Charleston, to return them to their softly lit, more colorful surroundings. Grant's bedroom must miss them, I thought, its numerous and amorous ghosts upset by the unaccustomed lack of privacy. Indignant again, I felt my blood rise on their behalf. Then my eyes moved to the frames built around the doors, holding them to the wall, and despite the formality of the gallery and the polite murmurs of strangers, I suddenly relaxed, so tickled that I could not help but laugh aloud.

The imperfection of the doors' angles—not at all perpendicular, wonderfully askew—meant that the museum's framers had had to abandon T-squares and work with the actual corners at hand. The result was beautiful, disorderly, and it unlatched in me a new realization, one I never would have reached had the doors been left unmoved. At Charleston the doors were held ever open, so one knew what lived on either side: the grain of the floorboards, the needlepoint on the chairs. Nothing could be more particular. (The ghosts, I suppose, must be accustomed to waiting for night and to letting darkness do for them what the painted wood refuses.) Here in the museum, the doors remained in an unusual closed state, which paradoxically transformed them into portals, invitations to imagine an unseen beyond. What existed there?

Shall I mention war? Death? In the age of this second Trump administration, I am often desperate to connect with other ways of being, with voices that can sing past fascism's stupefying shout. *The hostility of the general public is real now.* Sitting in that gallery, I sensed that the other side of the doors contained all possible futures, from those I dread to those I desire. *We can live*, said the paintings on this side of the wall, *another way. Or die*, said headlines flashing on my phone. I turned it over, not forever, but long enough to find something to carry back to my own home. I opened my eyes to Bell's colors, their darkness and their light.

We can begin, I thought, with flowers. We throw a party. (How very gay!) We take the doors right off their hinges. We lock no one in or out. We take care, make art, make room. ✶

ASK CARRIE

A QUARTERLY COLUMN FROM CARRIE BROWNSTEIN, WHO IS BETTER AT DISPENSING ADVICE THAN TAKING IT

Send questions to advice@thebeliever.net

Q: *I'm an adult. I bathe. And yet people keep giving me soap. My mom slipped a bar into my Easter basket this year. My best friend gifted me a bourbon-scented soap for my birthday. My dad found some artisanal soap at a Ren Faire, and my sister gave me some made by monks in Italy. These are all thoughtful gifts. But I'm starting to wonder if they're also… pointed.*

What began as a quirky gifting trend is beginning to smell like an intervention. I want to ask if there's some unspoken insinuation—but if the answer isn't a hard no, isn't it basically a yes?

So tell me: When does a friendly gesture become a red flag?

—Fraser Grant, Columbus, OH

A: There are lots of red flags here, but I think we differ on what they signify. I suppose it speaks to your humility—and a hint of self-deprecation—that you've concluded the problem lies with you. My admittedly less generous take is: What is wrong with these people, and why are their gifts so basic and uninspired?

At best, soap is an innocuous gift, likely to end up in a guest bathroom or perfuming a linen closet for the next three years until it's thrown out. At its worst, soap suggests a last-ditch effort, right below key chains, mugs, or their de rigueur equivalent, the tote bag. Sure, soap might be considered thoughtful if the recipient needs some rest and relaxation, and if it's bundled with other items to aid with rejuvenation; then again, bath products artfully placed in wicker are the edible arrangements of gift baskets. In fact, to help avoid this blunder, I've come up with an aphorism: "A bar of soap is but a cantaloupe."

Now, let's say the recurring soap gifts can't be blamed on the giver's penchant for the dull and cliché. I still believe your surfeit of suds may not be directly related to body odor. For instance, what if the soap's scent is less about disguising malodor and more a nod to your interests and hobbies? Think about it: Your best friend knows you like bourbon, and thus assumes you'll want to exit the shower reeking of Jim Beam. Or maybe the gifts reflect upon the giver and not the recipient. Your dad misses those father-and-son Ren Faire days of yore, and yearns for you to be reminded of his pleated ruffs every time you step into the shower. As for your sister, I bet she left that Italian monastery in a blissed-out fugue state, convinced she should spend less time on her phone or quit her job to help those in need. At a loss for how to begin her new life, she bought soap instead.

OK, Fraser, I can't avoid this any longer. So far my answer has been a thought exercise, and it's time I addressed your question head-on. What if you're right? What if you do smell? Unfortunately, I'm unable to determine or verify this via letters. I do know we can't always detect our own sour breath or body odor. And, yes,

Illustration by Kristian Hammerstad

I'd say when someone you're standing near in a tight space hands you gum, it's definitely a pointed gesture. Does this also apply to soap? As I've outlined above, not necessarily, so I think it's worth ruminating on the other possibilities. But the only way you'll know for certain is to come right out and ask, if not your friends and family, then perhaps your physician. If, in the end, you discover your instincts were right—that these gifts were imploring you to clean up your act (and by "act" I mean bits and bobs)—I'll offer up another pithy phrase so that others might avoid this torturous fate: Not unlike a mint, soap is a hint.

Q: *My friend has been trying to convert me into a metalhead. It started subtly with some pop-punk nostalgia playlists and a few moody grunge tracks—stuff we both listened to in high school. Then came the "heavier pre-grunge essentials," then screamy post-hardcore, and now we're in full-on blast-beat territory.*

I know this is just his way of sharing what he loves, but I've come to realize there's a whole system behind it. A kind of covert syllabus or sonic boot camp. He gets this look of approval on his face whenever I say I like slightly heavier music, like he's proud of my progress in his five-step plan.

I don't dislike metal, and, admittedly, my friend's influence has opened me up to the genre a lot more. But I also like other types of music, and I've started to feel like those don't "count" to him. His enthusiasm seems more like insistence, like he's trying to swap out my tastes for his own.

He means well. I know that. But it's gotten me wondering: Is it possible to lovingly manipulate someone's taste? And how can I convince my friend that my musical taste doesn't need fixing?
Sonny B.
Portland, OR

A: Is your friend a Spotify algorithm? Because it sounds like you're describing most people's relationship with their music streaming service. Offers subtle recommendations. *Check.* Sprinkles in a few nostalgic tunes to give you that warm glow: *Hello, Dan Fogelberg!* Makes you daily mixes that both understand your taste and introduce you to a few new artists or songs. *Wow, turns out my habits aren't as stale and ossified as I'd thought!* But then, once you're lulled into believing you'll never have to flip over an LP or create another playlist again… *boom*! The algorithm oversteps its bounds, proving itself reductive, prone to generalizations, and incapable of nuance. I promise you, Spotify, no matter how many times I listen to "Smalltown Boy," Bronski Beat is not my favorite band. Nor should they be a default gateway to Haircut 100. And if I go down a Lady Gaga rabbit hole after hearing her interviewed on a podcast, it doesn't mean I want my laundry folding soundtracked by a dance remix. One time I made the mistake of listening to a comedy album on a road trip, and suddenly my mixes vacillated between the Replacements and jokes about CPAP machines. So, yes, I empathize with feeling like you're in a compulsory sonic boot camp. As for the ability of someone or something to manipulate your musical taste? How's this for an example: I was making a playlist of early-2000s songs, and every time I went to make a selection, I'd notice my choices had some of the fewest streaming numbers. These were songs I'd put on countless iPod and CD mixes back in the day, without a single thought about whether my favorites aligned with anyone else's. But here, with the evidence enumerated before me, I started to doubt whether these were objectively good songs. I hesitated, and debated how to proceed. Eventually, I went with my gut, denying the social and behavioral pressure that was surprisingly difficult to ignore. But it could have gone the other way, and with bands I know little about, I'd definitely choose their most popular songs. This is how we drift toward a numbing mediocrity, our tastes and interests dictated by consensus and averages. Even more disheartening, many artists themselves start creating for that mind-numbing middle.

Sonny, I know he's your friend, but you must resist. If you can't stand up to a sentient human being, you won't stand a chance against the machines. Unlike an algorithm, he probably just wants to share his obsession and zealotry with someone else, so thank him for his efforts but let him know you're done. If you're wondering what to say, how about: "I oppose obedience masquerading as free will and refuse all forms of mind control and manipulation." Say this while making devil horns with your hands. As a metalhead, your friend should not only understand, he'll be proud and know his work here is done.

Q: *My roommate has a very clingy French bulldog named Rutabaga. I've always let him hang out in my room and even sleep on my bed, despite his snoring, wriggling, and frequent* let me out *door-scratching in the night.*

Recently I started dating someone new. She isn't so keen on Rutabaga or his antics, much less the idea of him sleeping in bed with us. She's asked, politely, if we can have some dog-free evenings when she comes over.

That seems reasonable to me, so I've started leaving Rutabaga in my roommate's room when my girlfriend visits. But now my roommate is clearly annoyed. She makes passive-aggressive comments and there's been some unmistakable sulking.

I want to keep things good with both my girlfriend and my roommate, but I feel stuck between them—and the dog. How do I navigate this tension without making anyone feel shut out (or shut in)?

Rebecca P.
Brooklyn, NY

A: At the moment, I'm particularly attuned and empathetic to your predicament. Namely, the difficulty of simply letting other people have their feelings. The second I detect another person's discomfort about something I've said, I want to rectify the situation by taking everything back. *Never mind! Don't worry about it! My bad!* Just the other day, my therapist asked me, "What would happen if you simply asked for what you need, or said exactly how you feel, without retreating, rescinding, or apologizing?" In other words, could I stand up for myself?

Honestly, who knows? Because I've been too nervous to try. But that won't stop me from attempting to help *you* break the cycle. We (you!) can do this! Together! (Alone!) I'll now attempt to answer your question through the rubric of *You are not responsible for other people's feelings!*

Let's put a pin in that to talk about your roommate's dog, Rutabaga. What a name. Perfect for a breed that wouldn't exist without human folly. (The Frenchie traits we deem desirable—narrow hips; giant, babylike heads—mean the breed's continuation is reliant upon artificial insemination and C-sections.) But poor genetics be damned, I love all dogs, Rutabaga included.

I'm also fine with dogs being on furniture. My own pup, Banjo, who has plenty of his own antics, sleeps on my bed in the crook of my knee. And despite this arrangement—where I'm a veritable human dog bed and heating pad—I've managed to maintain a long-term relationship. The reason I've yet to be dumped over attachment-parenting a dog is that Banjo goes onto the floor and sleeps on his own bed when asked. So, bravo to you: I absolutely think you've done the right thing by honoring your girlfriend's reasonable request.

As for your roommate—and this is where we circle back to the "other people's feelings" part—my sense is she's doing a whole lot of projecting onto Rutabaga. Rutabaga is sad you're not around as much? Rutabaga is upset you've shut him out of your room? Unless your roommate has been reading Rutabaga's diary, I think we can assume it's the human who's having a hard time adjusting to the new dynamic. Her feelings are understandable. The two of you had a good thing going: coparenting a dog-child; your lives revolving around Rutabaga and each other; rituals, routines, and markers of domesticity from which we derive comfort and stability. But, Rebecca, things change, and that's OK. If it isn't a paramour, maybe it's a new job, or a new city, or just a desire to live on one's own. This is where you sit with the discomfort, knowing you're doing your best to acknowledge everyone's needs, and you let your roommate have her feelings. I promise she will come around, or adjust, or simply accept.

By the way, Rutabaga also sent in a question: He wants to make sure your new girlfriend is at least a dog person. ✶

CONTEMPORARY AUTHORS WHO WRITE IN LONGHAND

✶ Amy Tan
✶ Elin Hilderbrand
✶ James Patterson
✶ Jennifer Egan
✶ Jhumpa Lahiri
✶ Anne Carson
✶ Stephen King
✶ Joe Hill
✶ Joyce Carol Oates
✶ Mary Gordon
✶ R. O. Kwon
✶ Ingrid Rojas Contreras
✶ Percival Everett
✶ Julie Hecht
✶ Anne Tyler

—list compiled by Evan Trimbur

CHUNG SEO-KYUNG

[SCREENWRITER]

"I THINK THAT IN ORDER TO WRITE, YOU HAVE TO GO THROUGH THE DOORS, GO THROUGH THE HALLWAYS, GO UP THE STAIRCASE, AND ENTER THAT SMALL, INNERMOST ROOM WITHIN YOURSELF."

Questions Chung Seo-kyung asks herself while writing scripts:
What does the character value as much as themselves?
What is the ancient force behind the story?
What makes the machinery of a character move?
Could this story have happened to people one or two thousand years ago?

Chung Seo-kyung may be an unfamiliar name even to those who are deeply familiar with her work, which includes cult-favorite Korean films like Lady Vengeance *(2005)*; I'm a Cyborg, But That's OK *(2006)*; Thirst *(2009)*; The Handmaiden *(2016)*; and Decision to Leave *(2022)*. That might stem from the fact that the screenwriter's role is often obscured, if not diminished, in an industry where the director reigns supreme. But if one takes a close look at the oeuvre of her longtime collaborator and cowriter, the director Park Chan-wook, it's clear that Chung has left an indelible mark: After Park's first two films, Sympathy for Mr. Vengeance *(2002)* and Oldboy *(2003)*—both of which Park has admitted "pushed women to the periphery"—the patterning of his movies took a distinct swerve, their centers of gravity shifting toward more complex and sometimes seemingly deranged female protagonists with multifaceted, indecipherable psyches; this centering of women is something he credits to Chung's influence.

Illustration by Kristian Hammerstad

"Usually, whenever we're writing a woman character, I try to make her as cool, chic, and smart as possible," Park said in an online interview in 2022. "She [Chung] always tries to give something faulty to the character or tries to make her a little bit unethical."

Chung Seo-kyung was born in Gwangju, South Korea, in 1975. Initially a philosophy major, she switched to screenwriting in college, where she studied under the celebrated filmmaker Hong Sang-soo. In 2003, Chung met Park Chan-wook when he was a juror for a short-film competition she had entered. He liked her work—he thought her short film *Electricians* was strange, which was allegedly a compliment—and asked her to cowrite the script that would eventually become *Lady Vengeance*. She's cowritten all his feature films since then. Separately, she has written other films, including *The Truth Beneath* (2016) and *Believer* (2018), as well as the acclaimed Korean TV dramas *Mother* (2018) and *Little Women* (2022). Her newest TV show, *Tempest*, a political spy drama which dramatizes the tensions between North and South Korea, airs in September on Disney+ and Hulu.

When Chung was writing *Tempest*, she initially thought its content might seem foreign or irrelevant to viewers. But in December 2024, the week after the show finished filming, political turmoil roiled South Korea, with then-president Yoon Suk Yeol declaring martial law and banning all political activities, including rallies and strikes. Even though the president retracted his declaration shortly thereafter, the country was already in upheaval. Suddenly, *Tempest* no longer seemed entirely like a fiction, born of a freewheeling imagination, but rather something more prescient. Now Chung is more certain that the show will resonate with viewers.

I spoke to Chung for two hours, via a translator. She dialed in from her bedroom in South Korea, wearing an elegant black turtleneck sweater. A fast talker, she rarely needed even a beat before answering my questions, often responding with a nugget of wisdom or insight that refracted the topic at hand in a new and compelling way. We discussed truthfulness in writing, shirking conventional approaches to storytelling, the breakneck pace of writing a Korean drama, and more.

—*Natalie So*

I. "YOU HAVE FOUND THE PATH"

THE BELIEVER: I want to ask you about your childhood. Were there any pivotal moments that made you want to be a writer or to work in movies? What experiences shaped your point of view as a writer?

CHUNG SEO-KYUNG: I initially believed I was just like any other kid. I assumed I didn't have any special experiences that could contribute to my identity as a writer. But after having my own children, I realized that kids are all very different, and that I was actually a pretty special kid as well.

Back when my older kid learned how to read, he would wake up every morning to read a book. That made me remember that when I was younger, I would read a book as soon as I returned home from school. I had assumed I did this because I was lonely or didn't have family around to spend time with me. But now, looking back, I realize that even as a child I was inherently drawn to literature. Even though I didn't assume I'd be the writer I am now, I knew that as someone who was always reading, I would naturally end up writing as well.

BLVR: Did you enjoy watching movies as a child? What was your relationship to movies and TV shows?

CSK: Actually, neither medium left a big impression on me when I was younger, but I remember that when I entered middle school [in the late '80s], Hong Kong movies and war movies were very popular in Korea. I watched a lot of them at the time, and I still remember that being such a vivid experience—sometimes it almost felt as though I myself were there, in the war.

I remember three war movies in particular. One was Steven Spielberg's movie [*Empire of the Sun* (1987)] about an English boy living in China during World War II. Another one, also about World War II, but set in the Soviet Union, was called *Come and See* [1985], and then there was a third, a French film, *Au revoir les enfants* [1987]. I watched all three in the same season.

BLVR: Do you remember your impressions of those war movies?

CSK: I initially thought I remembered those movies so vividly because I watched them during middle school, which is inherently such a sensitive time. But looking back now and seeing that all these movies dealt specifically with young people living through World War II or the Holocaust, I think my memory of them is so vivid and particular because of my parents' experiences—my parents were part of a generation that experienced war in Korea. And as a result, I grew up very familiar with the subject of war.

When I went to the Taipei Golden Horse Film Festival in the fall of 2024, I had the opportunity to interact with Taiwanese youth, and I realized they are also drawn to World War II in the same way I was, because their families had similar experiences, historically speaking, and perhaps harbored similar sentiments as Koreans did toward the Japanese.

BLVR: You studied screenwriting in college, but initially started out in the philosophy department. What led you to switch majors?

CSK: It's quite simple. I started studying philosophy in college, not necessarily with the idea of getting a job, but because I wanted to learn about how people think of and view the world. But I didn't have enough credits, and it was difficult to graduate, so I decided to switch tracks and actually major in something that could get me a job.

BLVR: I see. One of your teachers in college was the director Hong Sang-soo. I'm curious if there were any lessons from him that influenced the way you write or approach your scripts.

CSK: I studied screenwriting with Director Hong from when I was a freshman all the way to when I was a senior, and he was a very talented instructor. His perspective toward screenwriting was almost religious; he treated it like it was something sacred. Sometimes it felt like, in teaching us, he was bringing fire to cavemen. Thanks to that approach, his students devoted themselves to screenwriting with all their hearts.

However, over the years, I think my respect for him has perhaps diminished. Nevertheless, as someone with a twenty-year writing career, I still recognize that he was the first person who awakened inside me my passion for writing, and to this day I maintain the attitude toward writing that he instilled in me from the start.

BLVR: Was there anything in his approach to movie-making or script-writing, philosophically speaking, that you carry with you?

CSK: He always emphasized the importance of truthfulness in writing. It's a concept that's hard to express in words, so obviously it was also very difficult for students to put it into their writing. Whenever he gave feedback on our writing, he would point out what felt truthful and what didn't feel truthful. So naturally, as students we spent all day and all night, even in our dreams, searching for truthfulness. That process sometimes felt religious, as I mentioned earlier regarding Director Hong's approach to film.

Still, for the four years that I studied screenwriting, not everything I wrote was always truthful. It was only in writing my thesis project, the last script I wrote in college, that I finally discovered truthfulness in my own writing—it's almost like looking directly at your own face without the help of any other tools or mediums. As soon as I finished that script and looked at it, I realized, Oh, so this is the truthfulness that the teacher has been talking about. This is the truthfulness I've been searching for this entire time.

I'm pretty sure Director Hong felt the same way, because without any other words, he simply told me, *You have found the path.*

II. THE SCHOOL OF PARK CHAN-WOOK

BLVR: What was the name of your thesis film?

CSK: It was the screenplay for a feature film called *My Poor Baby*. In 2024, I actually published two of the screenplays I wrote for my thesis in college, so that students learning to write can reference them, but they haven't been published in English yet.

BLVR: When I first contacted you for this interview, I asked to watch a couple of the short films you made in college, and you said you destroyed them. Why did you do that?

CSK: I never had plans to direct; I've always just wanted to write. That's why I majored in screenwriting. But while I was at school, the graduation requirements suddenly changed: Initially I only needed to write a feature script, but then they told me I also needed to make a short film. So I went into making the film without any preparation or research. I was very inexperienced, so it was a painful process. I don't want anybody to see that anymore. But it did screen at film festivals. And the crew members that worked on the film enjoyed it a lot.

BLVR: And that was *Electricians*, the short film that director Park Chan-wook first saw, right?

CSK: Right.

BLVR: I'd love to know more about that first experience of collaborating with Director Park on *Lady Vengeance*. When he asked you to write a first draft, did he give you guidelines and parameters for the story, or did he just tell you to start writing?

CSK: When I first met Director Park [in 2003], he wasn't as busy and famous as he would be later on, because he hadn't yet won the award at Cannes [Editors' note: Park would go on to win the Grand Prix at the 2004 Cannes film festival for *Oldboy*]. So I just thought, Oh, he's a rising filmmaker who's really good at what he does. Until that point, I actually hadn't watched any of his films.

On the day I was going to meet him for the first time, I watched *Oldboy* in the morning and met him in the afternoon. After watching *Oldboy*, I thought, Wow, that's a fun movie. He's a good filmmaker. At the meeting, he gave me a choice: I could work on a movie about either a vampire or a kidnapper. I decided that writing about a person [as opposed to a supernatural creature] sounded a little more doable.

So he gave me a quick overview of his idea for *Lady Vengeance*—which was around four or five sentences—and there was one particular scene he described that really stayed with me. It was the scene where Geum-ja [the female protagonist], after being released from prison, goes to the house of the child whom she helped entrap, an act that eventually led to the child's death. To repent for her sins in front of the child's parents, she cuts off her own finger. That's the scene I fell in love with, because I really like characters who value their actions more than words. This scene was very easy for me to imagine.

BLVR: When you started working on the script, did you immediately have confidence in yourself, or did that take some time to develop?

CSK: At the time, I wasn't even sure if I could write a script; I certainly didn't know the proper way to write one. Director Park had told me we were going to make a new movie together, something that nobody had ever seen, but even that concept [of a "new" movie] was so unfamiliar to me—I wasn't sure what made a movie "new" or different.

Around that time, Director Park won his award at Cannes, and he suddenly became very busy, traveling all over the world. So I was left with this major task of writing a movie that nobody had ever seen before. During the day, I gave my all to my writing, but at night, I was filled with anxiety about whether I could actually finish the job properly. I didn't even spend the money I was initially paid, because I wasn't sure if I would have to give it back to Director Park in the end.

BLVR: Despite feeling anxious, how did you push yourself to complete that first draft and show it to Director Park?

CSK: I was twenty-eight years old at the time, which is quite young, but I already knew I was a writer, so I had to do it, and I knew I was ultimately going to end up writing it. I think that was the mindset I had while working on the script, and fortunately, Director Park was somebody who really accepted failure. Even if I came in with something weird or bad, he was never surprised; he would simply tell me to start over. For instance, if I wrote eight scenes, he would like only one or two scenes out of the eight, but he would just allow me to feel as though it was completely normal to write eight scenes and salvage only one or two out of all of those. So I was left with the task of wondering and figuring out for myself: Why did he like these one or two scenes? What was good about them? The whole process was just writing a lot and then throwing a lot of it out, and then writing again.

BLVR: It sounds like you received something of an education from him very quickly.

CSK: Yeah. Now, after thousands and thousands of iterations of that process, what he wants and what he likes have been downloaded into my brain like a computer program. I would say I was a student at the Park Chan-wook School and I learned a lot about writing from him.

III. "WHAT IF THERE IS NO OBSTACLE?"

BLVR: When I first watched *Lady Vengeance*, I was very drawn to the character of Geum-ja. I also really liked the way the movie explored notions of innocence and experience, of good and evil. I know that Director Park had given you the seed of the idea for Geum-ja, but I'm curious how you further developed her character. What were you thinking about as you were writing her?

CSK: When I develop characters, I don't start from an external point of view. What I mean by that is I don't think about what makes a character charming or likable to other people. Instead, I think of the character as a seed that grows within me.

I can't quite answer what makes Geum-ja special. I think she was a seed that grew into her particular shape of a tree, just like how *Lady Vengeance* itself—the entire story—feels like a tree that grew into the shape it's supposed to be.

As I mentioned earlier, when I first started writing the script, Director Park said he wanted to write something new. So I went into it not adhering to any of the typical philosophies of screenwriting. For instance, most stories start with a protagonist that has a goal, and then they are obstructed by an obstacle. So my first thought was: What if there is no obstacle?

In the movie, we see that Geum-ja quickly achieves everything she was planning. Her initial goal was to capture Teacher Baek [the schoolteacher who used her as an accomplice to kidnap and murder a child] and take revenge on him. That's when I was hit with an obstacle while writing the script: Halfway through the movie, she's already captured Baek and put a gun to his head, so there's nothing left for her to do. Since there were no remaining obstacles for Geum-ja, I had to change the direction, which meant coming up with a new goal. And that's when I came up with the idea that there are four more kids that Baek has killed, and I changed the story so the parents of those kids can also take part in the revenge. Instead of killing Baek to get her own revenge, her new goal becomes avenging the families of the children that Teacher Baek killed.

I think that's what makes *Lady Vengeance* different from other movies: In most stories, there's one goal that the main character is trying to achieve. Even if the goal appears to change halfway through the movie, it's actually what the protagonist has wanted all along—they just end up getting there in a way we don't expect. But for this movie, I wrote the story scene by scene, so the story changes completely when a new goal is introduced. This may be a disappointment for the audience, who are expecting the catharsis of revenge to come from killing Teacher Baek. What they end up getting instead is not the catharsis of revenge, but the salvation of Geum-ja's soul, which she achieves in the process of giving up her initial goal of revenge.

With that change in her goal, there was an additional change, which was the voice of the narrator. Initially, the idea was that I wanted Geum-ja to be introduced as if this were a documentary or news footage. That's why I thought the narrator would be an objective character, played by a very famous voice actor in Korea who often does voiceovers for documentaries. But as the film progresses, this narrator is actually not as objective as she seems, and she actually knows all these secret, personal things about Geum-ja that only Geum-ja would know.

So I asked myself, Whom does the voice of the narrator belong to? And that's when it clicked that it would actually be Geum-ja's daughter, Jenny, who has grown up and is interpreting what her mother's life was like and how Geum-ja's new goal ended up influencing her life. In the end, the film shows that what Geum-ja really wants is not revenge, but understanding and forgiveness from her daughter. By achieving that, she gets the salvation she is seeking.

BLVR: *The Handmaiden* is one of my favorite movies, in part because of the way it deals with truth and deception. Lies continue to be revealed, and there's an inversion of dramatic irony, where the audience thinks they know more than the characters, when in fact the opposite is true—in the end we're outsmarted by the two female protagonists, Sook-hee and Hideko. I don't know if I'm reading into it too much, but to me, the whole movie seems to comment on the nature of storytelling. I'm curious how you thought about the lies and deception as you were writing the film. Do these themes tie into your views on storytelling?

CSK: Yes, I've always been interested in truth and lies, because that's what I work with: I write lies that sometimes have little basis in the world—very well-written, desperate lies that I hope will be transformed into truth in the minds of the audience. *The Handmaiden* is really a movie about storytelling, and in that sense, I really enjoyed writing it and learned a lot about how many layers of story can fit into a single narrative.

Since then, everything I've written, including *Believer*, *Little Women*, and *Decision to Leave*, has included this theme of telling the truth using lies.

BLVR: Another theme or motif I see running through a lot of your work is the idea of the "proxy"—whether that's in the form of a scapegoat, a mistaken identity, a fake, or a substitute. This happens in *Lady Vengeance*—Geum-ja goes to prison in another person's stead; in *Mother* the protagonist, Soo-jin, who kidnaps the abused girl, Hye-na, fills in as her mother; in *Little Women* there's an identity theft; and in *The Handmaiden* the maid Sook-hee takes the place of the noblewoman Hideko at an insane asylum. Is this idea of proxies in your consciousness at all, or does its pervasiveness in your work happen at a subconscious level?

CSK: Maybe it's because I'm a writer and I always feel like I'm partially living the lives of my characters—which I work very hard at—but I feel like I can slip into someone else's identity relatively easily. I don't know if it's an innate ability or something I learned through experience, but I felt something similar when I was raising my kids. I've been a woman for a very long time, but after they were born and as they got older, I felt myself growing into a boy who walks, a boy who sees the ocean for the first time, a boy who learns tae kwon do, a boy who builds with LEGOs, and so on. I'm an adolescent boy sometimes these days. Slipping into different identities is how I understand people, and also how I come to understand my stories and my characters.

IV. THE FORCE THAT MOVES THE STORY

BLVR: I'm curious what makes a female character interesting to you as a writer. When you're creating a new character, what is the first thing you think of? Are there certain flaws or desires that are particularly interesting to you?

CSK: Because I consider every character as a piece of machinery, my first question is always: What makes this machinery move? And that usually translates to: What does the character love the most? What does the character value as much as themselves?

BLVR: When I see these female characters, I can see the ways in which they all possess desire and agency, something female characters in movies don't always have. But the women you write are also complex; they have complex desires. Beyond what you just said, are there other things you think about when you're creating them?

CSK: I don't exactly know the answer, but I can give you an example. When I was working on *Tempest*, I wanted to write a female character that was unlike any other female characters I'd written before. While I was writing *Little Women*, a writer friend of mine had asked me, "Why do you make your characters not lovable until the very end? Why do you keep adding these elements that make them receive hate?" This was a friend I really cherished, so it made me sad to hear that my characters aren't lovable until the very end. With *Tempest*, I took a different approach of writing a character that the audience would be able to easily understand and enjoy.

When I finished the first act of *Tempest*, I had written this very good, straightforward character. But when other people read what I had written, they asked me, "Why isn't she your usual crazy female character?" That's when I realized that people actually enjoy the crazy women I write. After that realization, I continued to write *Tempest*, but now, as the story unfolds, we gradually see how crazy our female protagonist is. So I guess I'm just destined to write crazy women.

BLVR: That actually leads perfectly into my next question: about the motif of the madwoman or "crazy" woman. I noticed that in a lot of your films, like *Lady Vengeance*, *The Handmaiden*, *The Truth Beneath*, and even your Korean [TV] drama *Mother*, there is a very thin line between rationality and irrationality. A woman might be perceived by society as being crazy, but in another context her actions are actually perfectly rational. The inverse of this also shows up, where a man who is mostly perceived by society as being rational is shown to be actually insane. I'm curious if this idea of the "madwoman," or this dichotomy of rationality and irrationality, interests you as you're thinking about these characters.

CSK: I don't think I'm particularly conscious of those things when I'm writing, but there are multiple forces that move a story, right? And of those forces, there's always one that feels like the most ancient and inherent force within a story. When I write stories, I always ask myself, Could this story have happened to people one or two thousand years ago? I want to put the forces or powers that existed a thousand years ago into stories set in a modern context. There are different forces in conflict, and I think within a story, the force that leans toward what is considered irrational in our modern context is the one that's always stronger.

For instance, with the example of *Mother*, running away with a child who has been abused would be illegal in today's system, but I think a thousand years ago, it would have been a perfectly rational decision. So while that action may lean toward the irrational in our modern context, there's a force, a motivation, within that decision that transcends the binary of rational or irrational.

Another example is Seo-rae, the protagonist of *Decision to Leave*. She is from China, but national borders are not important to her. She's a woman who simply follows her instincts, and that's what leads her to Korea. Her journey from China all the way to a small Korean coastal town is almost like an animal, before its death, trying to go back to where it came from.

When I was writing *Decision to Leave*, I tried to categorize the characters as if they were all agricultural products: There are people from the sea and people from the mountains. Seo-rae, even though she's a sea person, was forced to live a painful life in the mountains. That's why she decides that her final destination, her place of death, will be in the sea. She kills anyone in her way, regardless of whether it's legal or not. If her relationship with Haejoon [the male detective and protagonist of *Decision to Leave*, with whom Seo-rae becomes romantically entangled] had worked out, she might have continued to live a life in Korea. But if he had gotten in her way, she would probably have killed him as well.

The forces that move her like this may make her seem like a crazy woman, but she's just following her instinctual logic, and that's what makes her a perfectly rational person—by her own standards.

BLVR: Can you talk a little bit more about what you mean by "the most ancient and inherent force within a story"?

CSK: I may not have felt this way in the past, but these days, when I'm trying to decide why I want to write a certain story, I always look for the pulse of energy or power within the narrative, the force behind it. There are many forces that can move a story. For instance, in a love story, the force could be the character's greed for money, or it could be a relationship within one of the lovers' families. Among these many forces, I try to find the one that's the most powerful, because that is the force that's going to lead the story to its rightful conclusion. So for instance, if we're writing a story based on the power of greed—whether for money or something

MICROINTERVIEW WITH KEVIN YOUNG, PART II

THE BELIEVER: One of your first books to receive widespread acclaim was the often-humorous *Jelly Roll: a blues*. It often seems like humor has an uphill battle when it comes to being recognized as "serious" poetry—so how did you come to bring it into your work?

KEVIN YOUNG: For me there was a moment—probably earlier than that book, but I think it came to its fruition in that book—when I realized poems *could* be funny. Like, you knew they could be different ways, but sometimes poets, starting out, especially—you sit down, and you think, Well, now I'm going to put on my poet's cap and take out my quill and write really serious poems. But to have a kind of *whole* self… Life is absurd and funny *and* serious and sad. The blues helped me understand how you could do all that at once. And for me, what's powerful about the blues is that it's good-time music—it's meant to make you move and dance—but it is also sometimes singing the saddest thing you can ever think of. Losing your home, losing a loved one, losing your dog. But you make a rhyme out of that, or you make something unexpected. And that idea of the unexpected was what also drew me to the blues, and how you could kind of pivot. The blues have that *turn* in it, and I thought that was important, because it's how it feels to be alive. How do you write about love in a time of war? Or how do you write about love in a time of heartbreak? These are *the things*. They're ancient. But I love how the blues talk about them in a modern way, and it really inspired me to try to say it all at once. ★

else—if that greed shapes a person's survival within society, that story immediately becomes one with an ancient force that can transcend both context and time.

BLVR: That's a very insightful explanation. What kind of research do you do in preparation for writing a script, whether it's for a movie or a TV show?

CSK: I actually don't do much research, and I certainly don't do any internet research. My assistant writers do most of that for me, because if I start researching on the internet, it might lead me to start shopping online or watching the news. I really do think a writer's biggest enemy is the internet. So I leave the internet searches to my assistants, and I usually just rely on books when I do my own research.

I have three assistant writers working with me on a new project (I used to work with only one assistant), and we have a daily meeting that we call the four o'clock meeting. This is supposed to be a very simple meeting that isn't supposed to take more than thirty minutes. We don't even have to be in a conference room together—we just each take the meeting from wherever we are and share what we've researched and how we feel about it. But when we all share what we find, it always ends up taking an hour. What's interesting is that my assistant writers usually end up using books for their research as well.

BLVR: What is the role of research in your writing? How do you think about integrating nonfiction or historical facts into your work?

CSK: When I do research, I'm not searching for facts. Rather, I'm on the search for the voice of the character. If I want to make my female protagonist a scientist, I might research botanists or meteorologists. As I learn more about these occupations, I try to see which occupation would make the most sense for the character's worldview.

In *Mother*, the protagonist [of the original Japanese television show that the Korean version is adapted from] was already a scientist that studied birds, but I did feel like that was actually a very fitting occupation for the character. Because when I started to think, Why would someone be fascinated by birds?, that naturally led to the conclusion that the person is fascinated by the idea of freedom. When birds first take flight, they usually leave the nest where their mother was. Her profession wasn't an original idea of mine, but I really felt it was the perfect occupation for the character.

When I reach a certain point where I feel like I know enough, I start writing, and then when I hit a block again, I resume my research. Only after I've written something do I know exactly what I need and whether what I've been researching is correct or applicable. That's when I can actually start researching in a helpful manner.

V. "A SPEED LIMIT FOR WRITING"

BLVR: I want to talk a little more about Korean dramas, because I'm a big fan. After having watched more than

---

MICROINTERVIEW WITH KEVIN YOUNG, PART III

THE BELIEVER: *Book of Hours* took a very different tone and focused on grief. What was the hardest thing about that prolonged meditation on grief?

KEVIN YOUNG: The hardest thing, of course, is missing your loved one. It's a complicated alchemy, because you're trying to capture it, but also not describe it. You have to kind of reenter it and reenact it in a way. And the best poems—whether they're about grief or love or other things—really *enact*, they don't *describe*, and so you reexperience it as a reader. But I think what poems can't do is prepare you. What they can do is accompany you. And that was sort of what they did for me.

I wanted the metaphors and the meaning to come from the experience itself, so I try to not say, *This thing is like something very far off*, but instead, talk about the sound of kids playing in a pool near the terrible hotel you're staying at, which I call the "Worst Western." And you can hear the kids, and how does that relate to how you're feeling? It felt like this echoey, faraway joy—nearby, but so far. And there were other moments like that in the book when I tried to *turn* the experience in a way, or find the myth in it. Like having to give my father's dogs away. It doesn't say this is *like* losing him. It just describes it. ★

one hundred of them, I would say that in general they're very different in both form and content from films and screenplays, especially the ones you've written. When you were asked to write *Mother*, your first TV drama, did you approach it differently than you would a screenplay for a film?

CSK: When I started writing movies [in 2003], it was the golden age of Korean cinema, so I always assumed I would be working in movies forever. But around 2010, that bubble burst, and that was the first time it occurred to me that movies might not be around forever, and that maybe I should start turning to television. Around 2016, I started working on *Mother* at the suggestion of Studio Dragon [one of the biggest and most well-known South Korean drama production companies]. At the time, I had two kids and was busy raising them. I knew I wanted to try my hand at a TV drama, but I wasn't confident, because there weren't many dramas at the time that didn't employ a traditional romance plot, which is a very strong, established structure. I wasn't familiar with the romance grammar of Korean dramas myself, so it was hard for me to imagine myself writing a TV show well. But the idea of remaking an existing Japanese drama—a social and crime drama where a schoolteacher kidnaps an abused child—seemed like a good opportunity. Even so, I remember the advice I received from the producer at the time, that despite *Mother* being about an abused child, it had to have a romance plot. She said that's the general rule in dramas.

I had been thinking about the subject of *Mother*—not the exact story, but the themes—for a really long time, since around 2007 or 2008, when I was pregnant and gave birth to my first child, so I was relatively confident I could start writing it. Once a writer experiences pregnancy and childbirth, it's hard not to be obsessed with the subject for a while. But there were obviously challenges as well: Sixteen episodes felt like too long of a story to tell. As soon as I finished the first four episodes, which took me a little over two years, the show was greenlit, and it was set to be produced [in 2017]. That meant I had strict deadlines, and I basically had to turn in one episode every three weeks.

After I finished writing the sixteenth episode, *Mother* was released the following week; they finished shooting and editing the entire show within that week. That was my first introduction to the difference between making a TV show versus a movie.

BLVR: How was it for you to write on a schedule like that?

CSK: I was so taken aback by that pace of working that I had to tell the producers: "No, I don't think I can work under a schedule like this." Fortunately, they adjusted it for me. I was shocked when they told me that other drama writers usually work on this kind of schedule.

And although I was under pressure to write fast, my own screenwriting process and standards for a good screenplay didn't change, which made me question both myself and screenwriting: How do TV writers write a first draft in three weeks? Just as there is a speed limit for light and sound, there also must be a speed limit for writing that cannot be surpassed—but how fast is fast enough? In the end, I realized I've always been the kind of person who writes what I want, using my own specific process, and no matter how much pressure I put on myself, the results are the same. Regarding the speed at which I wrote *Mother*, I think the episode I wrote the most quickly took about four weeks; most took about five or six weeks, and the one that took me the longest spanned around three months because I revised it so many times. The outcome of that screenplay was similar to the others, but I was mentally stressed because I pushed myself a lot.

Now when I ask myself this question and look back, I realize I'm currently writing at the pace that was demanded of me at the time. Back then, I couldn't believe there was a writer who could write at that pace—one episode every three weeks—but now I'm pretty confident I can keep up with it.

BLVR: There are certain tropes and conventions in Korean dramas. How do you think about storytelling when you are writing for TV?

CSK: Although I've never officially learned a particular philosophy or method of screenwriting, because I've been writing movies for so long, the arc of a two-hour movie has really been instilled in me, which means the stories I have in me are usually that long. Naturally, as I'm writing a story like that, the tension diminishes after two hours.

At some point I realized I was treating each TV episode like it was a movie of its own—the run time of most Korean TV episodes is around seventy minutes. I found myself wanting to write the story completely, as if I were finishing it at the end of each episode, so I started thinking about how my approach to TV writing should be different from film writing. I worked really hard on developing a technique where I would leave something at the end of an episode that would persist into the next.

When I was writing *Little Women*, I had stories of varying sizes. Over the course of the twelve episodes, I was trying to find the best way to harmoniously piece the stories together. Whether a TV show is twelve episodes or sixteen episodes, initially that length of time just felt too large for me, like a story I couldn't quite fit into my pocket. A two-hour movie felt like it would always fit into my hands. I could just kind of play around with it and mold it the way I wanted to. TV shows always felt like a journey without a map. But now, after having worked on three or four of them, I think I'm finally starting to grasp it.

BLVR: I'm curious whether you watch any Korean dramas yourself and if you have any favorites.

CSK: I don't have much time to watch TV dramas, but I am aware of many new and interesting ones that are airing these days. I like the work of Park Hae-young, like *My Liberation Notes*. I also like the drama *Misaeng*. The actors in it are excellent.

BLVR: I've heard of both of those but haven't watched them. I do know they're both considered less conventional dramas—they don't follow the traditional arcs or possess some of the more common clichés. Now that you mention them, I'll definitely watch them. Are there aspects of the Korean drama form that you either like or dislike?

CSK: I have a lot of respect for the tradition of Korean dramas: the traditional way of writing dramas, the way they're made, and the way they've evolved. But I didn't grow up watching dramas, and I didn't learn to write by studying them, so there are a lot of things about them that are very different from my own writing. What I do really like is that the crews for Korean dramas are always very professional, and they're very knowledgeable about their audience.

VI. BIRTHING EVERYTHING FROM MY OWN MIND

BLVR: A few of the films and TV shows you've worked on are adaptations. I'm curious about how you approach adaptation, philosophically speaking. How do you take the kernel of an idea and make it your own? There are adaptations that are obviously more faithful, like *Mother*, perhaps. But then with a show like *Little Women*, you took the general archetypes of the sisters from the original novel only as a point of inspiration and then ran with it in a completely different direction—that show feels wholly original, like an entirely new story.

CSK: When I approach an adaptation, I first ask myself, What do I love the most about the original work? I tell myself I shouldn't lose that thing, and then I forget everything else. For *The Handmaiden*, there were many ideas I initially borrowed from the original work [the novel *Fingersmith* by Sarah Waters], but then I tried to forget them and instead treated them like they were my own ideas. As I progress and continue to work, I can no longer distinguish between the original work and my own original ideas. And I increasingly try to birth everything from my own mind.

There's a short story ["Pierre Menard, Author of the *Quixote*" by Jorge Luis Borges] in which a man tries to write *Don Quixote* by becoming like Cervantes. And by writing that novel, he can pretend he came up with the idea himself, even though he's just copying the novel as it is. I want to approach my adaptations in the same way: Even if I end up writing the same things as the original, I want to treat them like they're my original ideas.

BLVR: Was it your idea to adapt *Little Women*, or did someone come to you and ask you to adapt it?

CSK: It was my idea.

BLVR: That's one of my favorite Korean dramas, so I'm very curious about its creation. So many things happen—like you said earlier, there are so many little stories within the larger arc. When I was watching it, I felt as though I had fallen into a rabbit hole, like Alice in Wonderland. How did that story come to you? How did you develop it?

CSK: When I was working on *The Handmaiden*, the characters were girls between the ages of sixteen and nineteen, so in order to familiarize myself with these kinds of young female characters, I went back to the novels I used to enjoy when I was younger. One of those novels was *Little Women*, but it wasn't as fun as I had remembered, and I didn't enjoy it as much as I once had. I vividly remember how much I loved reading *Little Women* when I was younger. But going back to it as an adult, I instantly felt that the little women were too nice. And that's what led to the idea of writing a story about "little women" who are not nice at all.

Initially, I had thought of a story in which the little women would be even badder than how they turned out to be in the show—they would be more violent and promiscuous. But while I was working on the idea, they turned into the women they ended up being.

BLVR: I'd love to know how you approached the plotting of the show: creating the plot versus creating the characters. Did you have a specific process for figuring out how things happen and how one event leads to another? Or did those actions come out of your development of the characters?

CSK: It's kind of hard to explain. I think most writers don't have the entire twelve-episode story in their heads when they're writing. For me, I initially thought of only the first episode. I created the characters first, and then I tried to think of the plot for that episode.

The first episode introduces the International Blue Orchid Association [a secretive and powerful organization that becomes unveiled as the show progresses] as well as the character of Hwa-young [an accountant who ends up playing an important role in the story], so it contained all the seeds planted for future stories.

At the time I wrote that first episode, though, I didn't know if Hwa-young would end up dead or alive, and I didn't know how evil of a woman Won Sang-ah [a rich politician's wife who turns out to be the main antagonist of the series] would be. But I did know that Hwa-young was In-joo's [one of the three sisters] friend, and regardless of whether she'd be there in spirit or physically with In-joo, I knew Hwa-young was going to follow In-joo on her journey, and Won Sang-ah would turn out to be a big bad villain.

By the time I was on episode three or four, I had already planned the plot up to episode eight. But what would happen after that, I had no idea. And because I had no idea what was going to happen next, I had a really hard time after I finished episode eight. But I just trudged through, episode by episode. I just knew how I wanted the ending to be: It was a story that started with seventy billion won going missing, and I wanted that money to go to the sisters.

BLVR: How did the idea of the Jeongran Society—in English, the International Blue Orchid Association—come about? That idea of a behind-the-scenes, powerful cabal oriented around a magical flower was so fascinating to me.

CSK: The society was inspired by scenes from modern Korean history. I had once read in an article that past presidents brainstormed political strategies in very strange places. So I thought I also wanted a big evil plan being brainstormed in a similarly strange but leisurely environment. And that led to the idea of a particular room in a building. And I asked myself, What would the sign on the door say? I imagined that people inside the room would be playing Go, and next to their game of Go, there would be this orchid plant. So that led to the idea that the sign on the door would say INTERNATIONAL ORCHID ASSOCIATION.

CITIES THAT HAVE BEEN REFERRED TO AS "THE PARIS OF ——"

★ Beirut, Lebanon: The Paris of the Middle East
★ Buenos Aires, Argentina: The Paris of South America
★ Abidjan, Ivory Coast: The Paris of Africa
★ Manila, Philippines: The Paris of Asia
★ Detroit, Michigan: The Paris of the Midwest
★ Kansas City, Missouri: The Paris of the Plains
★ Saint-Pierre, Martinique: The Paris of the West Indies
★ Tianducheng, China: The Paris of the East
★ Tromsø, Norway: The Paris of the North

—*list compiled by Dan Gutenberg*

I also imagined that the members of this community organization would communicate through orchids—I think that idea was inspired by the Sherlock Holmes story "The Five Orange Pips," which I enjoyed when I was younger. When I started researching orchids, I realized they're actually a fascinating plant. They cost a lot of money, and they're treated almost like art pieces. Naturally I started focusing more on the orchids.

VII. TWO OPPOSING PERSPECTIVES

BLVR: I'm curious about your writing process, and if you have any rituals or superstitions you partake in before you sit down to write.

CSK: I don't have any rituals in particular. I wake up every day thinking, OK, I'm just going write a long script today. I imagine people to be shaped like buildings, and the thing that moves people to write is placed inside the innermost corner of the building. In talking with other people, I've realized there are not a lot of people who can just immediately sit down and start writing. I think that in order to write, you have to go through the doors, go through the hallways, go up the staircase, and enter that small, innermost room within yourself. So I try to enter that mental space in my head in order to write every day. And it takes some time to get there.

BLVR: Are there things you absolutely need to write—like a certain genre of music or a completely quiet room?

CSK: I just have to be by myself.

BLVR: I wanted to ask you this question because I'm a mother myself. I know you gave birth while you were working on the movie *Thirst*. Did you feel as though your sensibility or approach to writing changed after you became a mother?

CSK: Yes, completely. I think I'm a completely different person now, compared with when I did not have a kid. The films and TV shows I wrote after I had a child—I don't think I would ever have been able to write them if I didn't have a child. Except for the fact that I don't have enough time to write, I think writing itself has become a lot easier after giving birth, because after having kids, I suddenly had a very clear idea of my priorities in the world. That applies to screenwriting, where I can very quickly identify what's important and what's not important, what's at the foundation of the story and what's just a small detail. I could not do that before having a child.

BLVR: I can see how that would be true. You have worked with the director Park Chan-wook for a very long time now. How has the process of working together evolved? How do you handle conflict or instances in which your ideas clash with one another?

CSK: Before I had kids, we used to work a lot more intimately, throughout the brainstorming and synopsis processes. Now that I have less time, we don't work as closely anymore. These days, I write a full first draft by myself. Then we exchange drafts and comments. But after the first draft, we still maintain our old way of working on one computer together.

Even now, we still occasionally have differences of opinion, which I find fascinating, because I think it means we sometimes have two opposing perspectives, and the tension between these perspectives always ends up in the works themselves. To take the example of *Thirst*, our two main characters, Sang-hyun [a Catholic priest who turns into a vampire] and Tae-ju [the wife of his childhood friend with whom he falls in love], have opposing perspectives. In most movies, opposing perspectives resolve and unify by the end. But in this movie, they are in conflict until the very end. I think the tension between these different perspectives is what makes that film so fascinating, and it's the same in *Decision to Leave*: Seo-rae and Hae-joon have conflicting perspectives, and these perspectives don't get unified through death until the very end; these tensions are what makes our projects so fascinating to watch.

BLVR: One last question: What films, movies, books, or works of art are important touchstones for you as a writer?

CSK: I would say Kafka. There is no better beginning of a story than *One day I woke up, and I realized I was a bug*. I have always wanted to start a story in a way that was as exciting as that. ✶

Translated by Jiwon Lee

THE LAST RESORT

AT BOMBAY BEACH, A HALF-RUINED FORMER VACATION TOWN ON THE EDGE OF THE SALTON SEA, ABSURDIST PHILOSOPHERS, ARTISTS, AND EVERYDAY TOWNSFOLK HAVE UNDERTAKEN A POSTAPOCALYPTIC EXPERIMENT IN RADICAL LIVING

BY **ASH SANDERS**

DISCUSSED: *The Ski Inn; Bombay Beach Estates; Alien Iconography; Walt Whitman; The California Riviera; The Beach Boys; Mullet Island; The Bombay Beach Institute of Particle Physics, Metaphysics, and International Relations; Healthy Opium Tea; Green Jell-O; Volcom Hats; Optimism; Hallucinations; Pub Crawls; Migratory Birds; Full Gonzo; Distributed Consciousness; Theseus*

OPENING ILLUSTRATION BY:
Kristian Hammerstad

It is easy to miss California's biggest environmental disaster. Driving north on Highway 111, you wouldn't expect to find an inland sea. If it's summer, the thermometer in your car could read 115 degrees. But amid the shimmering heat, there are signs of water. All around you, rows of broccoli, lettuce, and alfalfa stretch in every direction. In the fields, farmworkers bend and straighten. The air is sharp with cow dung. A pall of dust hangs over everything.

You are sixty miles north of the Mexican border at Calexico. If you keep going, the landscape will transition from fields to palm trees. You're driving out of poverty and into money, away from one of the poorest counties in California and toward towns with golf courses and named for oases. Palm Springs. Rancho Mirage.

The left turn is easy to miss, the brown sign a seeming anachronism. BOMBAY BEACH. Surely there is no town here, you think, let alone a beach. But if you continue, you'll see hints of life. There are saplings on the side of the road—not much to look at yet but there all the same. In the distance, a squat building hangs on under the punishing sun. THE SKI INN, it says on the '70s-era marquee. LOWEST BAR IN THE WESTERN HEMISPHERE. Indeed, you are 223 feet below sea level here, in a depression known as the Salton Sink.

For now, drive past the bar and look up. In front of you is a giant black-and-white billboard. Four white women in vintage swimsuits smile as they water-ski side by side. Behind them, a sea stretches into vastness. LAST STOP FOR THE BOMBAY BEACH RESORT, the sign says. The vibe is nostalgic, carefree. But where is the water? You turn around and around. On every side of you, dust. Above you, the flat, hard sky. That's when you see the other billboard. This one's more minimalist. Just a few palm trees and some lettering. BOMBAY BEACH, it reads. THE LAST RESORT! You aren't sure if it's a welcome or a warning.

You feel as if you've stepped back in time, into a place people have forgotten. The town isn't large—a little over a half-mile square, its dirt roads named with numbers and letters. But it's big enough to be a lot of things at once. On some streets, you could be forgiven for thinking no one lived here. Old trailer homes sigh on their blocks, their screen doors rusted and hanging. A sign announcing BOMBAY BEACH ESTATES sits next to a huddle of concrete buildings, their doors and windows gone, their abundant graffiti tending toward alien iconography. The scene reads like a developer's erstwhile dream, and a homeowners association's worst nightmare.

But the sense of ruin is not uniform. Here and there, the feeling of absence is replaced by a strange sort of presence. On one street, someone has lined up a series of junked vintage cars to face a movie screen. The cars are empty. The vibe: rapture at the drive-in. Down the road, old TVs have been stacked side by side, their screens painted with abstract shapes. On the roof of a nearby house, there sits, inexplicably, a giant sculpted egg. The scene puts you in mind of Whitman. Does it contradict itself? Very well, then: It contradicts itself. The town contains multitudes.

I first arrived in Bombay Beach several years ago, by accident. Like so many on this route, I had been lured by Salvation Mountain, a giant outsider art installation twenty miles south painted in bright colors and with optimistic thoughts regarding the nature of God's love. On the way back to our motel, a friend suggested we check out the Salton Sea. And that is how we came to be in Bombay Beach at sunset.

The first thing I did was lose my phone. The second thing I did was lose my friends. I was trying to understand why there was a berm around the town, a long earthen dike that blocked the view and gave the place an embattled, medieval feel. I was trying to understand what I was looking at, and how it came to be, and also to wrap my head around the light, which was perfect in a way I can't improve upon with words.

And so I walked. First I passed a large red metal cube hung with glass balls. Then I passed a home painted entirely blue. The Bombay Opera House. But where was the opera? In fact, where was everyone? And where was this so-called sea?

As if in reply, tire steps appeared on the side of the berm. I climbed them. And there it was. In front of me was a hard, flat playa, cracked the way a spoon cracks the glaze on a crème brûlée. The land was the shade of tan that made me want a drink. In the distance, blue in the dust, the sea sat limply, farther away than it ought to have been. I didn't need someone to tell me something was wrong. But a wooden sign did anyway. HELP OUR SEA, it said, a carved pelican perched on top.

The Salton Sea is California's largest lake—and, many say, its greatest environmental blunder. Born of periodic floods from the Colorado River, it is not a lake that is meant to last. For millions of years, the river would breach its banks, fill the Salton Sink, then change its mind and meander back into the Gulf of California. Left without inflows and outflows, the water that remained would evaporate.

That was the rhythm of this place: flood, shrink, repeat. Eventually, humans broke the pattern. Farmers arrived in the early 1900s, when the lake basin was dry. They claimed the fertile floodplain and tried to tame the river. They put bottles in the banks to mark their water claims. They dug canals and levees.

Then came the biblical flood. In 1905, the Colorado River burst through an irrigation cut and raged down its old channel, spilling into the Salton Sink and forming a lake in a geologic instant. It was part natural, part accident, part miracle.

What followed were the fat years. Birds came by the millions. State wildlife authorities brought in fish from the Pacific, which flourished in the salty shallows. Towns sprang up like fever dreams. Celebrities came to see and be seen. Frank Sinatra was there. So were the Beach Boys. And developers had just the name for the place. They called it the California Riviera.

But the new sea was not a riviera. It was, as so much desert water is, a mirage, propped up by runoff from nearby farms and laced with salt and chemicals. If the farmers stopped flooding their fields with Colorado River water, the Salton Sea would die.

And that, as it turned out, is exactly what happened. First came the drought, a parching that started in 2000 and hasn't quit since. Climate change was ravaging the region and devastating the Colorado River, reducing its flow by a fifth in just two decades. Then there were the water wars. Imperial Valley farmers were forced to transfer vast amounts of their water to thirsty California cities. The flow to the lake all but stopped.

The entire Southwest was in a water crisis—and the Salton Sea was collateral damage. No one in power had any interest in restoring a lake in the middle of the desert, especially not one that people thought of, wrongly or rightly, as an accident. And so the sea shrank. Fish died first. Then birds. Toxic dust mushroomed from the lake basin, the air a miasma. The number of asthma cases spiked. Towns emptied. There were cormorant nests made from the bones of other birds out on Mullet Island. Death had come for the sea. Death had come for Bombay Beach.

A struggling town next to a dying sea is not exactly a place you'd expect to encounter a cultural renaissance, counter- or otherwise. But in recent years, a group of artists have moved to the town, parlaying a backdrop of disaster, disinvestment, and despair into an attempt to build a brave new world.

After my first visit to Bombay Beach, I'd often find myself in internet rabbit holes late at night, checking in on the sea and the strange towns around it. Some of it had to do with an impending sense of doom about water. My own hometown of Salt Lake City was surrounded by collapsing waterways: a disappearing inland sea to the west, the imperiled Colorado River to the east. I suppose I was looking to the Salton Sea to get a glimpse of my own future—to see if it was possible to survive next to a dying body of water in a desert that was getting hotter by the year. But it wasn't just the water. It was also the place. I'd seen the town for only an hour or two. And yet I couldn't deny that I had felt something there. It was a sense that, in the midst of disaster, there were people doing exactly what they wanted. It was the sense, I must admit, of freedom.

In one of my late-night rabbit-hole sessions, I found the website for the Bombay Beach Biennale. According to its founders, the Biennale is "a renegade celebration of art, music, and philosophy" on the "edge of Western civilization." It exists to create public art free from the logic of both gallerists and critics—and to bring attention to the crisis at the Salton Sea. From January through April, artists converge on Bombay for "the season," taking advantage of cooler temperatures and cheap rent to create pieces for the Biennale, a multiday party that transforms the town into performance art—or what the founders call "social sculpture." The group's principles are punk rock and to the point. No tickets. No commerce. The Biennale date is spread by word of mouth, and participation is required. There are no spectators at this spectacle.

The idea seemed both preposterous and delightful, a true mix of the high and low: a biennale in a half-abandoned town on the edge of a remote and shrinking lake. It was also an opportunity to scratch a longstanding itch I'd had about this place. Who were these people who had come to this forgotten former resort town at the edge—and the end—of the world? And what kind of new world were they trying to build?

I knew immediately that I had to go. I spoke to someone who spoke to someone who eventually spoke with me. After passing what can only be described as a vibe check, I secured an invite. In the meantime, I was connected to artists who were spending January through April in town, preparing for the festivities.

I called my friend Abigail and pitched her on the trip. For a year and a half, she and I had been rafting the entire Colorado River to better understand the water crisis. I knew she wouldn't want to miss a celebration at water policy ground zero. So I told her to pack—we were going to a party for the sake of the sea. Abigail bought a tent from a guy off Brooklyn Craigslist, who, when he asked where we were going, said he'd been to the Salton Sea to take photographs. "Wild place," he said, and handed us the tent.

We arrived in Bombay Beach and realized we had packed all wrong. Preparations for the festival were underway, and there were RVs and buses everywhere, their generators humming with air conditioning. We were the only ones in a tent. Exhausted, we threw sleeping bags down and tried to sleep. All night, a man raked the gravel in the nearby plaza. Was this performance art or compulsion? We had no idea.

In the morning, the sun rose like an advancing enemy, despite it being April. We ran to the only coffee shop in town—an arts center with a giant fish sculpture in front—and held ice cubes to our brows. This was nothing, people kept saying. Last year, the dust storms were so bad you could barely see.

We were soon added to the town's WhatsApp chat. That's how we got Dulcinée DeGuere's strange request for help. "Is anyone extremely passionate about Jell-O? This may seem like a joke but it is not." Any qualified persons were to report to Zig Zag ASAP. As an ex-Mormon with a proud cultural history of Jell-O making and eating, I felt compelled to oblige. We got directions, and drove across town to provide our services.

Zig Zag was a brightly painted trailer in a plaza across the street from the Bombay Beach Institute of Particle Physics, Metaphysics, and International Relations, the tongue-in-cheek organization in charge around here. A container for the Biennale and other high jinks, the Institute was founded by artists Tao Ruspoli, Stefan Ashkenazy, and Lily Johnson White.

In the plaza, a life-size silver horse sculpture sat gleaming next to several human-sized plaster matchsticks. Across the way, a two-story shipping container with a cutout window presided over the landscape, a jellyfish-like chandelier hanging from its ceiling. As we entered the plaza, two people were busy painting a stage bright red. "This is where the flamenco will be," they kept saying, as if this clarified things.

When we found Dulcinée, she was under the covered porch. As we watched, she pulled items out of Amazon boxes: plastic frogs, a large golden cricket, bags of toy flies, and containers of fake blood. This was for the Surrealist Seder, she explained. She hadn't been able to believe her luck when this year's party fell on the Passover full moon. The whole spirit of Bombay is surrealist, she told me, so they wanted to celebrate it in kind. The frogs and flies represent the biblical plagues, she said, motioning to her loot. The previous night, she'd been hit with an inspiration. She wanted the flies and frogs to be suspended in Jell-O. She showed us a picture from Pinterest, a green, quivering creation of halved hard-boiled eggs faceup in gelatin. "Like this," she said.

The Seder would be on Saturday, Dulcinée clarified. She planned to cover the whole place in red. Red stage, red banners, red cloth in the wind. "And blood on the lintels," I offered. She laughed: "Yes, fake blood on the lintels."

Dulcinée is one of the main organizers of the Biennale. Technically, she's the COO, she told us, but she hates official titles. So she made one up: "I call myself the systems architect," she explained. I asked her what that meant. Well, for starters, she said, we had to understand that we were in a town where a lot of the residents are suspicious of the artists, and a lot of the artists are anarchists. "So my role is to come in and be like, *I'm gonna organize all you motherfuckers.*" In that spirit, Dulcinée had been meeting with townspeople, artists, and the media for months to prepare for the upcoming weekend. The Institute helps fund many of the artists' Biennale creations, but since anyone can be part of the Biennale, she also gives advice about making art in the desert. "I tell people, 'It needs to withstand eighty-mile-an-hour winds. It needs to withstand one-hundred-twenty-degree heat,'" Dulcinée said. She also has to remind people not to build sculptures in random strangers' backyards.

Dulcinée showed us the schedule for this year's party, which she was just about to take to the printer. The entries were so fanciful they'd lost status as information. On opening night, there was a christening of the ship the *Tetanus Tatanka*—no further details. On Friday and Saturday you could choose between a drag show at the Temple to the Scientific Method; a meeting with your inner Wild Woman at the abandoned Bombay Beach Estates; or something called the Ong Ong Healthy Opium Tearoom, also at the Estates. Just then, Tao wandered in. A middle-aged man in a white linen shirt, he had the confidence of a man with old money from the old country—and the impishness of someone who'd been allowed to chase his every whim and curiosity.

Tao was a person whose reputation preceded him. Because he is

Visitors and locals gather for a Surrealist Seder in the town's main square. Photograph by the author.

one of the founders of the event, I'd already heard about him from everyone—and his fingerprints, it seemed, were all over the town. It was Tao who had put the egg on top of the house, just as it was Tao who, directly or indirectly, was responsible for the Bombay Beach Opera House, the Drive-In, and the giant sculptures on the beach.

There's only one way to say this, so I'll say it: Tao was born the son of an Italian prince—and a descendant of the papal nobility. An aristocratic art darling by way of Los Angeles, he was friends with people who wore broad-brimmed felt hats and who ran venues he described, without explanation, as Dadaist hotels. The three of us got to talking, and Tao explained how he first fell in love with Bombay Beach.

In 2007, Tao came to the sea for the first time and was gobsmacked. He loved the ruins, the decay, the general lawlessness. Just then, LA artists were being priced out of their usual havens and venues. Bombay Beach sounded like the perfect replacement—in Tao's mind, it was a blank canvas for trying new things. His then wife was horrified: Why would anyone want to live here? Three days after they divorced, Tao put money down on his first place—a spartan lot with one trailer. Then he started inviting his friends to visit.

Things kicked off in 2015 with a twenty-four-hour happening, where he and his friends Stefan Ashkenazy and Lily Johnson White turned the town into a piece of living sculpture. There was opera in the streets, film screenings at the newly constructed Bombay Beach Drive-In movie theater, and a keynote speech by the philosopher Robert Pippin, who compared the town to the inside of a Fellini film. (I imagined the arias rising in the hot air and mingling with the dust, a ghost song neither past nor future.) From there, the idea grew. A filmmaker and philosopher by training, Tao was interested in places where people were free to make strange art. An absurdist by nature, he wanted a place where philosophy could touch the earth, where jokes and surrealist juxtapositions could prod people into a new mode of living.

If Bombay Beach is an unlikely place to find a gigantic inland sea, it's an even unlikelier place to find an avant-garde art festival. But that's what Tao began to conceive. Venice had its Biennale, he thought. The Swiss had started Art Basel. Why shouldn't the Salton Sea have the Bombay Beach Biennale? The first year, Tao mimicked the Biennale tradition of having country pavilions. As a joke, he planted some herbs in his garden. Their ID tag said ART BASIL.

But for Tao, it wasn't enough to simply throw a party. He wanted a framework, a movement that could contain and direct the energy he was cultivating. He landed on the Bombay Beach Institute of Particle Physics, Metaphysics, and International Relations, painted a trailer home bright blue, started filling the garden with desert plants, metal trees, and old RVs, and brought in an outdoor piano. A small, boxy building was turned into a movie theater with old couches. He called it No Shoes. On the door of his trailer, he stuck a red sticker. DEPARTMENT OF PHILOSOPHY, it said.

Headquarters. Site of future Jell-O-making and general shenanigans.

On the covered porch outside Zig Zag, Tao flopped onto the couch next to Dulcinée and mooned over the schedule. "It's so good!" he said. "Dulce, read them the manifesto!" But Dulcinée didn't want to do that just now. These schedules needed to get to the printer.

Instead, we were given a short rundown of what we needed to know. This year, the Biennale was going to be a bit different from the past. In an effort to respond better to the needs and ideas of the year-round residents, Dulcinée and Tao had stepped back in their role as producers to create a more collaborative event, which would take place every other year, led by the town. "We're calling it Convivium," Tao told me. They'd chosen the name for its many meanings, all of which fit their purpose. "*Convivium* means 'living together,'" Tao said. It could also mean something closer to "conviviality," a sort of banquet or feast. But "what sealed the deal," Tao said, was its biological meaning: "When a certain subset of a species lives in extreme isolation, they start to develop traits specific to that place that separate them from the rest of the members of that species." And that, Tao said, is so Bombay.

Abigail and I wanted to hear more. We asked Tao if he could talk, but he was interrupted by a phone call. He'd be back, he said, but we got the sense he might not be.

In the meantime, we got to work on the Jell-O. I stirred green sugar into hot water in the outdoor DIY kitchen and thought about the plagues visited upon the ancient Egyptians. I updated the plagues for the present situation. Bombay Beach: a pestilence of horseflies, a penitence of floods, a damnation of drought.

When we asked people about the Salton Sea, everyone told us the same things: First, the sea was in serious trouble; and second, if we wanted to understand it, we had to meet Irondad.

Irondad agreed to meet us, and we waited for him at a picnic table outside the Institute. He arrived in a tricked-out Jeep with a vanity license plate that said RONDAD. He shrugged: IRONDAD didn't fit. He was cool in a '90s sort of way, the sort of guy who wore Volcom hats in high school and still wears Volcom hats today. Irondad is an ultra-runner. Every year for the past three years, he has run around the entire perimeter of the sea. It's his contribution to the Biennale, an act of performance art and resistance. From January through March, he trains on the shifting shores of the Salton Sea. Then he races, running for nearly two days straight, measuring and mapping the lake's decline with his own body.

When he started running around the sea four years ago, he told us, it was a ninety-six-mile slog. Now it's ninety-two. In the next twenty years, scientists estimate, the shrinking sea will expose seventy-five square miles of playa. The prognosis: Sooner than later, the Salton Sea will cease to meaningfully exist.

Irondad bought a place nearby just as the sea was starting to tank. But when we asked him why he came to Bombay, he bristled. He didn't want to talk about himself. He wanted to talk about the sea. What he would say is this: Before he found the Salton Sea, he was a nomad, skipping like a stone from place to place. But as soon as he arrived, he felt something. A sense of freedom. It was the first place that ever felt like home. So he stayed. Went all in.

He took up running late in life, in his early forties. "It's never too late to run," he assured us, as if we were considering it. For a few years, he'd run the usual triathlons, races that pushed his body to the limit. But he quickly got bored. "I'd done a lot of endurance races," he said. "But I was asking myself, What good is that doing?"

Then he found Bombay. Like so many artists here, he was nomadic before he arrived. But the second he found this town, he knew it was home. There was something about the freedom here. It was a tough area, lawless, but at least you could do what you liked. He got involved with Tao's crew right away—and started fighting for the sea. He could tell the story better on a tour, he said, so we hopped into Rondad and drove onto the playa.

The main part of the beach was littered with sculptures. A giant swing that had been in the water one year ago sat stranded a hundred yards from the new shore. A yellow door stood in the middle of the playa, leading to nowhere, near a mock bus stop built for a bus that would never come. On the main drag, Irondad pointed out one of his first projects. It was a phone booth. FREE LOVE, it said on the side. On top was a heart and a satellite. In another context it might have come across as cheesy, but Irondad was serious about it. He doesn't believe in a *god* god, he explained, but he's been through enough to believe that there is some sort of cosmic force governing things—a force that can align you with your purpose. He found that here.

I asked him if he had been an artist or activist before he came to Bombay Beach. He said he wasn't. Out in the regular world, he didn't think what he did mattered. But here there was a sense that a person could make something happen, and that there were people you could make things happen with. There aren't a lot of advocates for the Salton Sea, he said, so every voice matters.

He pointed to a spot on the beach. That's where he starts his runs. These days, he said, he sets up a giant inflatable arch that says START and FINISH on either side. Now that his races are more publicized, people come to see him off, he said. He has to give speeches. His face soured.

But the first time Irondad ran around the sea, he didn't announce it. He just suited up and went to the beach. Along the way, he passed his friend Brenda, who asked him what he was doing. "I'm going to run around the sea," he said. She laughed, not sure whether to believe him or not. Another friend followed him down the first stretch on a scooter, waving and honking his horn. Then Irondad was alone, slogging for dozens of hours through punishing heat, mud, and hallucinations.

"You have to understand," Irondad said, "I look crazy on these runs." On his feet he wears snowshoes, so he doesn't sink into the mud. On his face is a gas mask to protect him from the dust. His legs are covered in neoprene sleeves to ward off any infections he might get from the water. He laughed. "I look like I'm in a superhero costume."

Forty hours of running in snowshoes in the mud? Abigail shuddered. She could never. She was being self-effacing, but Irondad took her seriously. "You could, though," he said. Anyone could. "Humans," he said, "are endurance animals."

I asked Irondad why he makes such grueling art. The main thing, he

The artist Sean Guerrero explains his project, the Tetanus Tatanka, *a land-bound ship built of driftwood and car parts. Photograph by the author.*

said, was to inspire people to action. "I want people to think, If one person cared that much to stay up for forty hours to run around this huge lake, maybe I should care too," he said. But he also loves the intimacy of the ordeal—getting to see things that no one else sees. He's seen airplane propellers sticking out of the mud, giant lithium mines with lonely blinking lights in the middle of nowhere. And he also gets to see all the failed attempts that have been made to save this place. There is a restoration site on the south shore of the lake that is so big and bright it looked like a city floating on the water. There are concrete ponds built to mimic wetlands, but they're choked with algae. And there are, of course, the hay bales, dozens and dozens of them arranged on the playa. They're a half-baked attempt to block wind and suppress dust, he told us—but really, they're just ugly. If the Salton Sea were on the edge of Palm Springs, he said, this problem would have been solved by now. But this is a poor area, so no one cares what happens here.

When Irondad is running, he wants just one thing—the same thing he wants when he's not running. For decades, the Salton Sea has been the victim of human hubris, a series of attempts to bend the landscape into a fantasy. It hasn't worked. When the state cut off the agricultural water, one type of intervention went away. Now Irondad hopes people have learned their lesson. "I just hope we don't think our way out of it by further interventions," he said. "I hope that at some point we just internalize that we live within this environment. That we're not masters over this environment."

We headed back to town. The car was quiet until Irondad pointed to a large firepit on the playa. For this year's New Year's Eve party, he said, Tao wanted the theme to be "the End of the World." Irondad countered with "the End of the World as We Know It." Tao agreed, and Irondad designed a giant globe that was suspended over the fire. At exactly midnight on New Year's Eve, the globe dropped into the flames. I asked Irondad why he chose "the End of the World *as We Know It*." Well, he said, he liked the idea of

A sculpture by Judyth Greenburgh, along the fast-receding shoreline of the Salton Sea. Photograph by the author.

the world ending at the beginning of the artist season and starting again at the end.

We'd been trying to reconnect with Tao before the Convivium started. In the end, we came together over logistics. He needed us to move our tent. It was right where the dumpster was set to be delivered. Our conversation about trash receptacles led to an ad hoc tour of the town. Had we seen the tallest ghosts? Tao wondered, referring to an artwork by his friend the artist RJ Paganini. We stood in the sun and squinted at a trio of plaster wraiths. Apparently, the tallest ghost in the world was shorter than six feet. Tao asked if we'd seen the sign on the main drag into town: ATTENTION: NOBODY IN THIS TOWN HAS SEEN THE MOVIE STAR WARS. PLEASE, NO SPOILERS. That was also the work of RJ. We walked across the street to the Institute.

The heat was staggering, coming in waves off the ground like a Wile E. Coyote cartoon. As we spoke, someone was installing a gigantic aboveground pool on some bare dirt near a fence. It was for the whole community to use. "Bombay Beach AC," Tao said.

In the meantime, we sought real AC in the comfort of the Institute trailer. I asked Tao about the Institute's five-dollar name—and how it came to be. He said everything here "is always kind of half joking, a juxtaposition of absurdity and seriousness, playfulness but also depth." He thought it was a fitting vibe for a place like this, which contained so many of its own contradictions. As we spent more time here, he said, we'd see those contradictions. "The Salton Sea is natural and unnatural. It's ugly and beautiful. It's a blank canvas, but it also has a fascinating, rich history." The people are the same way, he said. They're "eccentric, rugged individualists" who are also "keen on being part of a community."

Tao was initially drawn to the idea of making the Salton Sea a haven for philosophy; he was tickled by the idea of seeing something so highfalutin and serious in an environment where you'd least expect it. But the real draw for him was how weird the place was. Nearly everywhere else in America, he said, there's been this flattening. "It's not by accident that you can't express yourself creatively in any of those places or think original thoughts." Tao believes that landscape, in this sense, is destiny.

Tao acknowledged that this place is also fucked up. Without a doubt, this is a climate sacrifice zone. Between the beating heat, the disappearing water, and the general neglect, it could be one of the first places in the United States that will be uninhabitable in the very near future. (As one man I spoke to later described it, the people here will be "cooked alive.")

That was why Tao was launching a new project this year. From now on, his organization would be known as the Bombay Beach Institute for Industrial Espionage and Post-Apocalyptic Studies—a sort of autonomous zone where artists could experiment with different kinds of living in the face of economic and environmental collapse. In a very real way, the world had ended here. What would it look like to build a new one out of the rubble?

Abandoned by the government and forgotten by society, this town could feel pretty bleak. But that was sort of what Tao liked about it. He saw the abandonment as an opportunity. If everyone had given up on Bombay, he reasoned, you could kind of do whatever you wanted here. He recalled walking through town with his friend and Institute cofounder Stefan Ashkenazy a few years before. They both shuddered to think what this place could look like in ten years if people exactly like them succeeded too much. He mentioned the famous KEEP AUSTIN WEIRD bumper sticker. By the time you're making those, he said, it's too late. "I guess I'm sort of optimistic," he admitted, and then paused to decide what he was optimistic about. His friend Mark Wrathall, who was sitting nearby, piped up. Mark is the director of philosophical operations at the Institute, and has known Tao long enough to rib him. "You're optimistic that it will stay bad?" Tao laughed. He guessed so.

I understood why Tao feared the un-weirding of Bombay Beach. In many ways, the Biennale resembles nothing so much as the more famous no-commerce art festival on a playa, Burning Man—which many argue has failed by succeeding too much.

But what about the sea? I wanted to know. What about the residents who live here and can't leave? Wasn't the point of this to save the lake? To reverse collapse? But Tao wasn't so sure. "I don't think that's gonna happen," he said. They tried to save the sea, but the outside world didn't try back. He invoked Stefan again, who once told him, "Somewhere along the way, the idea shifted from communing with nature to commiserating with it."

Late one afternoon, I got a call from Irondad. He was on his annual run around the sea, measuring the extent of the damage. Since I am not an endurance animal, I wasn't there with him. Instead, I'd asked him to call me mid-run with an update. When I spoke to him, he was on hour eighteen of what would ultimately be around forty. He took off his gas mask so I could hear him better. In the background, his feet crunched on the dry playa. Just an hour ago, he said, he'd sunk so deep into the mud that he'd had to crawl across it, spreading himself out like a starfish to distribute his weight. To pass the time, he's been listening to a podcast about the heyday of Versailles—a dive into the vanity and vanitas of a bygone era.

His runs have been getting shorter, distance-wise, he said, but also harder, due to the increasingly bad mud. We chatted for a while, and then I asked him what I really wanted to know: Had he started hallucinating yet? No, he said. That usually didn't happen until hour twenty-four or so. I asked him what illusions come to him when they come. It was strange, he said. He had heard of other runners who encounter guides, magical creatures, or young girls who appear out of nowhere, take a person's hand, and guide them for miles. He didn't have those kinds of hallucinations, he said. "When I hallucinate," he said, "I'll see a tree trunk on the beach, but I'll think it's a sunbather

Two Wild Women dispense advice to the author and her friend. Photograph by Abigail Keel.

lying down. Or I'll see whitecaps and think, Oh, those are boats." He laughed. It was sort of funny because that's what he would have seen if he'd been on this beach fifty or sixty years ago, before all the—before. I knew what he meant. The crazy thing is, he'd never seen those things here in real life. He'd never seen a boat or a sunbather.

"So you're hallucinating the past," I said.

Yeah, he said, he supposed he was.

I'll admit it: I liked Tao. But as the trip went on, I couldn't stop thinking of how he spoke about the town. As a blank canvas. A philosophical experiment. A sort of fait accompli about commiserating with collapse. I wondered how this felt to the residents who lived here year-round, who'd had these philosophies and this party sprung on them. When the artists leave and the sun really gets going, these people don't have the luxury of other options. They've lived here in the fat times and the lean, the floods and the droughts. They would live here regardless of sculptures or manifestos, whether by choice or by fate.

That's why I wanted to talk to Steven Johnson. When Abigail and I found him, he was where he'd told us he'd be: in his yard, surrounded by flatware. It was not even noon, but already it was hot enough to melt a surrealist clock. Steven was sitting in a patch of shade near his front porch, talking to people about fine china. On tables all around him were plates and bowls of various colors and sizes: his weekly antiques sale. Abigail's eyes bugged out. She loves this shit. She considered a quartet of plates shaped like cabbage leaves. I pointed her toward a hunter green pitcher with a John Deere logo on it.

Steven has done this antiques sale for years, between his shifts flipping burgers at the only bar in town, the Ski Inn. He pulled over two stuffed dining chairs to face him and perched on a stool. He was a slim man with glasses and an exasperated expression. He appeared to be in his sixties, but when we asked him how long he had lived here, he said twenty-five years—which is crazy, considering he was only twenty-three. We told him we wanted to know about the town, and the sea. "Oh, well, I don't talk politics," he said mischievously. But before we could talk about the present, we had to talk about the past.

Steven was from LA, but he'd been coming to Bombay with his grandparents since he was a boy. In its early days, Bombay was a blue-collar place that attracted union types. Steven's grandpa was a pipe fitter, he said. His dad was a pipe fitter too. Other towns around the beach were swankier, but Bombay was the wildest. There were five bars here, he told us. Five bars in less than a square mile. "Have you ever heard of a pub crawl?" he asked. In Bombay, the "crawl" part was literal.

Steven had loved this place when he was growing up. There was always something to do. You could go fishing, boating, four-wheeling, whatever.

The Ski Inn, the self-proclaimed "lowest bar in the Western Hemisphere," and the only remaining watering hole in Bombay Beach. Photograph by the author.

And of course there was the light. Steven wasn't trying to be some hippie Sedona person. It was just true. There was something different about the light here, not to mention the wildlife. At one point, he said, you could practically "walk across the lake on the backs of migratory birds."

But then the lake started shrinking, and the people started leaving. In the '80s, in a moment of ironic reversal, the area flooded, wiping out three entire blocks of town. Then Bombay really emptied. All the bars closed except the Ski Inn, followed by both marinas. Now the sea languishes hundreds

46

of yards past the berm, barely a glimmer. Going, going, gone.

Steven stuck around, but recently, things were getting harder. Rents had started to rise. Before the artists started flocking here, you could buy a lot for a few thousand dollars. We opened Zillow. There was a lot nearby with a trailer going for $250,000. Steven took umbrage at this, just as he took umbrage at the artists' attitudes. He was friends with a lot of them, he said. He saved broken dishes for them to use in their artwork. But some of them had an entitled attitude.

He unfolded a copy of the Convivium schedule he had on his lap and began to read in a mocking tone: "'Our work at the Bombay Institute of Particle Physics, Metaphysics, and International Relations'"—that was a great name, he admitted; he loved the name—"'is born out of our return year after year to reimagine society. In a place abandoned by capital and defined by environmental disaster, the Institute has always, always been a staple of our seaside community.'" He paused. "*Our seaside community?*" he said. "What does that say about the people who have been here for forty years?"

This town wasn't abandoned before the artists came. There were already people here—people with minds and opinions and preferences and skills. No one needed to create a community. The residents weren't here for the season; they were here for the duration. They were the ones who would suffer if the sea dried up. If things didn't get fixed here—if the social practices and terraforming and surrealist experiments of the Institute didn't work out—they were the ones who, literally and figuratively, would feel the heat.

It's like the artists have this "bizarre Christ complex," Steven said, and rolled his eyes. But it's both self-congratulatory and self-imposed.

"How's that balsa wood cross you're carrying?" Steven said. "Is it heavy?"

By the time Convivium officially started, I was hot and grumpy. We'd been sleeping in a tent on the gravel in ninety-degree heat, and the sun felt like it had breached the gates of my psyche and entered my physical brain. My skin throbbed. My throat wanted water no matter how many times I refilled my Nalgene bottle. I didn't want to go to the opening party, I told Abigail. I just wanted to sleep. But we went anyway.

The schedule didn't give us much of a sense of what we were heading into. It said, simply, "Christening of the *Tetanus Tatanka*." When we crested the berm, we saw it: a giant ship built out of driftwood and old car parts, with two ragged sails flapping in the desert wind, and its own name misspelled as TETNUS TATANKA in silver-painted letters. There were people gathered around it and people onboard. A woman sat in the bow behind a giant salvaged steering wheel, looking for all the world as if she had a say in where it would go. Everyone was there: LA girls with their cropped bangs and their filler and their vapes; hippies with their unmoisturized beards; people from a nearby techie commune known as Mars, zipping around on their Technicolor Segways. The artist Sean Guerrero climbed into his creation and gave a kind of artist talk. *Tatanka* is the Lakota

---

MICROINTERVIEW WITH KEVIN YOUNG, PART IV

THE BELIEVER: When working on a painful poem like "Book of Hours," do you ever feel like there's a risk of getting lost in your own feelings?

KEVIN YOUNG: I don't. A poem is often a place where you're figuring out how you feel. I don't think it's always like, *Here's how I feel; I want to tell you about it*. That kind of discovery has to happen on the page, and it happens along the way, and I think that is sort of how grief happens. This idea that there are stages that you go through, in order, quickly goes out the window. They're helpful in some way, but I also feel like it's important to know that you start here, you go there, you feel better a little bit, whatever "better" means, and then you feel way worse. The best advice I ever got was to think about tomorrow, and that tomorrow is a different day, and that some days are just terrible. And I think I was used to trying to make every day the best it could be. That can be really dangerous in a way. Instead of just saying, *Hey, that was terrible. It was a horrible day*. There's not a lesson. And poems are a poor payment for the blood and tears. But somewhere, somehow, in the end, they might be comforting. And the last lines of the whole book, and of the poem, are "why not sing," without a question mark. Just like, "why not sing." ★

word for "buffalo," millions of which roamed the West as recently as 150 years ago, before being exterminated by settlers. *Tetanus* is self-explanatory, he said. Mind the rusty nails. The ship was made from wood he'd collected from around this area. In other words, the ship was made from pieces of the past.

After his speech was over, he climbed down. Tao tried repeatedly to crack a bottle of champagne on the hull. When he failed, he popped the cork and poured. Everyone drank out there in the beating sun. Everyone including me.

For the next two days, I went full gonzo. I was both of the party and there for the party. I wore neon parachute pants and a sports bra and carried a bottle of whiskey through the streets. When our tin of edibles melted, Abigail and I took to dipping our fingers in the pink goo and sucking them clean. We went to Café Bosna, a Bosnian coffee shop, in the shell of the Bombay Beach Estates, that stayed open all night. There was a DJ and a box of musical instruments for people who wanted to play along. I wanted to play along, and shook a pair of wooden castanets to the beat. In the abandoned building next to Café Bosna, you could line up to meet your Inner Wild Woman. There were candles on the floor and all manner of dried flowers. Two actual wild women shared one large wedding dress like a pair of conjoined twins. I sat in front of one of them. "What do you long for?" she purred. "What would you be if you could be anything?" In the end she wrote the word *FERAL* on my arm in black paint.

In the Opium room, I was led through curtains to a Moroccan pouf and fed tea from a little ceramic cup while women in robes traced my skin with their long red nails. On our way out, a man invited us to try his mechanical hug machine, then made us a cat sculpture out of bent wire. We went to the Sub Club, a dance spot deep in the playa—the local artists' engineering solution for noise reduction—and danced until things spun. On the beach, an art car that looked like half a dragon and half a bull trawled around, periodically spitting fire from its mouth. A roving gay bar offered Franzia, but I opted for the lemonade stand, where Candi—Bombay Beach's de facto mayor—was slinging something she called Bombay Cyanide. It was a mix of tequila, vodka, wine, Red Bull, and Celsius, she told me. I took one sip and went on the record: I called it "the best drink in the world."

When we got hot, we jumped into Tao's pool, lying on floaties with two dozen other strangers until our body temps went down. Next door to the Institute were tarot readings with a woman named Pharoah. When I arrived for mine, people were using Sharpies to cover Pharoah's trailer with poetry. Other people's messages were bright and breezy. We should eat, they suggested. We should pray. We should love. I realized suddenly that I had forgotten all about the dying sea. I had forgotten that I was in one of the poorest counties in California in a climate and water crisis that would eventually squeeze us all. Perhaps that was partly the point of the party, but I felt guilty nonetheless. I made up for it by writing a line from one of my most depressing favorite poems on Pharoah's wall: "Now that my ladder's gone, / I must lie down where all the ladders start, / In the foul rag and bone shop of the heart." It felt appropriate somehow.

On Saturday night, the Surrealist Seder was seriously delayed. The event was supposed to be invite only, but it was happening in the main square of a small town with lots of people who knew everyone else's business. In the end, a text went out over WhatsApp. Everyone was invited. At dinner, I admired our surrealist Jell-O, which had come out perfectly. A cool wind picked up. The red sheets that Dulcinée had hung billowed and sagged. When the flamenco singer took to the stage, we all went quiet. His voice rose in the hot desert air, plaintive and pleading, as if asking for something impossible. I ate my parsley and thought of the Bible, the plagues and the Exodus. I thought of the longing—collective, archetypal—for the destruction to pass over us.

Halfway through Convivium, I walked into the cool dark of No Shoes for a philosophy lecture on distributed consciousness by an artist named Wanda Orme. As of this writing, I can safely say I still don't know what distributed consciousness is. But, as we huddled there in a small, carpeted room in the impossible heat, the wet chug of a swamp cooler in the background, Wanda said something that made me pay attention: So often, the Salton Sea is referred to only as a disaster. But perhaps there was some value to the devastation. Maybe living next to a dying sea made it harder to live in denial.

In a very real way, Bombay Beach sits at the end of the world, figuratively and physically. It sits at the bottom of a river, at the edge of a sea. It lives at the terminus of all our logic, caught inside everything we've ever done and all that has ever happened. There is also a truth to this place; in other words, a clarity to the tragedy. And maybe that means we're not just stuck here. Maybe it means we're also free to do something new.

Wanda's talk reminded me of a sculpture I saw my first day on the playa, a staunch metal affair made of copper and die-cut lettering. THE ONLY OTHER THING IS NOTHING, it said. I thought about that sign for the rest of Convivium. I thought about it when I got news alerts on my phone from the outside world: men shaved, shackled, and pressed together in a Salvadoran prison. A student protester abducted off the street. Forests opened for logging; the planet sold for parts. I thought about how wide the gap can be between the end of one world and the beginning of a new one, and how, in some places, that gap becomes narrower by virtue of idealism or necessity. And so we sit in that strange lacuna between what we have done and what we must do next. The situation is impossible; there are endless possibilities. The world ends; the world begins again. The feeling is grief. And the feeling is also joy.

The morning we left Convivium, we ate waffles in someone's front yard. They were delicious, but when we went to pay, the man shook his head. They were free. We sat at a plastic table with Tao's mom, Debra Berger; Mark Wrathall; and an artist named Sarah Larsen. Our talk turned, naturally, toward philosophy. When we said goodbye, Sarah reminded us of the tollbooth. The Institute didn't want to charge residents to get into the festival, she explained, so instead, they were charging visitors to leave.

We saw the tollbooth on our way out of town. It was wooden, and the boom gate was the skeleton of a fish—the unofficial mascot of Bombay. There was a sign hanging in the window. STOP, it said. PAY TOLL FOR RE-ENTRY TO THE REAL WORLD. Someone had crossed out REAL and written NIGHTMARE. We stopped and gave a donation to a bored-looking teen, who handed us our reentry pass. "This ticket buys your return to everything you were running from" was printed on it.

As we drove past the Ski Inn, I saw the billboard again. BOMBAY BEACH. THE LAST RESORT! As in: our last chance. As in: our final effort.

Perhaps it was because of all the talking with Tao and Wanda and Mark, but I found myself in a philosophical frame of mind. I thought of Sean Guerrero's driftwood ship, the *Tetanus Tatanka*, made of various pieces of the past. That got me thinking of the ship of Theseus. In Greek mythology, it's said that the people of Athens honored the memory of one of their greatest heroes by preserving his ship for many years. When one board rotted, they replaced it; when the mast listed, they replaced that. The ship hangs on in our collective memory less as an object and more as a philosophical conundrum. If the ship is always changing—always being changed—is it still the same ship?

Suddenly I felt a chill amid the heat. The landscape swerved, became surreal, uncanny. I closed my eyes, and the sea came up to my ankles. I opened them and the sea retreated again. All at once I entered a perpetual present. It is 2025, and there are cormorant nests made of bird bones out on Mullet Island; it is 1965 and the Beach Boys water-ski on a glimmering sea. It is five million years ago and the Colorado River has just gotten going; it is two million years later, and it is pushing over its berm, flooding the Salton Sink. It is hundreds of years ago and the fires of the Cahuilla people dot the edge of a giant lake; it is the turn of the nineteenth century and the first white farmer is planting his stick on the riverbank, saying, "Mine; this water is mine." There are buffalo back east somewhere, their bodies massed and vital on the plains. Then the settlers kill the buffalo and there are none left. The world, as Irondad suggested, is always ending and always beginning, and we are always trapped and always about to break free.

I knew at once that this dream was not supposed to let anyone off the hook—it was not saying that things would be fine, or that we were not responsible for what we'd done or must do. It was more of a desert vision, a mirage induced by heat that made regular objects appear different. The ship of Theseus has long posed a question of persistent identity, of how and when a thing stops being what it once was. But leaving Bombay, I wondered if it could also be a story about how long it takes something to become something else—a new species or a new kind of society. After how many revisions and mistakes, how many repetitions or re-creations of the past? Convivium is a gathering, but it is also a process. Slowly, and in isolation, a group of desert people fumbles its way into a new body, and a new body politic. ✶

Reporting contributed by Abigail Keel

PLACE

THE NUKUS MUSEUM OF ART

by Michael Snyder

FEATURES:
★ Ossuary jars
★ Anti-revolutionary painting
★ Toxic dust
★ Solastalgia

It was a cold, dry night in April, and a crowd had gathered in the center of Nukus, the capital of the Central Asian Republic of Karakalpakstan, to squint through a skein of toxic dust into the illuminated lobby of one of the world's most peculiar cultural institutions: the Nukus Museum of Art.

The dust storm had started earlier that day, staining the sky a sallow, hostile brown as a hard wind blew south across the Kazakh Steppe and over the Aralkum, a desert that used to be a sea. Until the 1960s, the Aral Sea, split between Kazakhstan and Karakalpakstan—a semiautonomous region within Uzbekistan—was the world's fourth-largest inland body of water. Fishing, canning, and beaver-fur industries thrived along its reed-fringed coast, drawing a mixed population of Russians, Kazakhs, Karakalpaks, and Uzbeks to port cities like Moynaq, where they settled in tidy whitewashed houses packed along the shore. By the 1990s, the Aral Sea had shrunk by 90 percent, thanks to Soviet irrigation projects that siphoned water off the Amu Darya river to feed the cotton fields that sprawled across Uzbekistan. As the sea retreated, it left an empty wasteland, frosted in a white rime of agrochemicals and salt that turned the air and soil to poison. Respiratory illnesses proliferated across Karakalpakstan. Temperatures became increasingly extreme, ranging from 10 degrees Fahrenheit in winter to 110 in summer. Water has grown scarce, and arable land has turned to desert.

If Karakalpakstan is known for anything—and in most places, it isn't—it is for this singular man-made cataclysm. If it's known for two things, the other is the Nukus Museum, which grew as the Aral Sea shrank. The museum was founded in 1966 by the Kiev-born artist and collector Igor Savitsky, who first came to Karakalpakstan to record the archaeological finds of the legendary Chorasmian Expedition. As a motley crew of intellectuals, local laborers, and refugees from the Stalinist terror—led by the mustachioed and pith-helmeted ethnographer Sergey Tolstov—dug two-thousand-year-old ruins out of the sand, Savitsky captured their discoveries in voluptuous (if sentimental) pastels, rendering austere mud-brick fortresses in delicate shades of peach and salmon. By the mid-'50s, Savitsky had settled permanently in Nukus as a member of the local branch of the Academy of Sciences of the Republic of Uzbekistan. He spent the next decade collecting textiles, jewelry, and carved wooden trunks that Karakalpak people in hamlets across the region had hidden away in the early years of collectivization; villagers knew him, affectionately, as "the junkman."

Eventually, he approached the first secretary of the Karakalpak Regional Committee of the Communist Party, Kalibek Kamalov, with the idea of opening a museum. Kamalov, a proud Karakalpak, loved the idea. For him, the museum would establish a clear material identity for the Karakalpak people. And though Moscow had long suppressed craft as an entrepreneurial heresy, Savitsky's ethnographic collection, pitched the right way, aligned with the official Soviet ideology known as "the friendship of peoples," which positioned the USSR not as a latter-day Rome but as a multiethnic consortium of nations—a counterweight to the cavalier economic domination of the postwar United States and faltering European colonialism. Think of it as a Soviet "It's a Small World (After All)." (The US and the USSR were never quite as different as they liked to think.)

This proved a useful cover for Savitsky, as he turned his attention to avant-garde painting, which was essentially verboten in Moscow. From 1966 until his death in 1984, he amassed tens of thousands of paintings, coaxing rolled-up canvases from beneath the cots of ailing widows and withdrawing others from the confines of the Zagorsk Monastery in Russia, a kind of gulag for art that was deemed anti-revolutionary. In the process, he conserved an epoch in art history that Soviet authorities aimed to purge from the official record. The avant-garde collection is now justifiably famous. Foreign journalists love to write about it, and in 2024, the Uzbekistan Art and

Illustration by Mizmaru Kawahara

Culture Development Foundation (ACDF) took some of the collection's major works on tour in Florence and Venice—a cultural coup.

But when I arrived in Nukus, I was even more interested in the museum's silver jewelry and quilted robes, and the bands of embroidered cloth used to decorate yurts. I wanted to see the artifacts of a way of life that the Soviet Union had attempted to destroy in the name of its misguided, utopianist faith in technological progress. (Sounds familiar.) What had been lost? What had been saved? What could still be recovered? I was, of course, far from the only person asking these questions. The directors of the museum's archaeology and ethnography departments (Oktyabr Dospanov and Aygul Pirnazarova, respectively) told me that, in recent years, more and more young people—jewelry and clothing designers, as well as college-aged kids studying in the Uzbek capital of Tashkent—have used its collections for inspiration.

That pride is no small thing. In June 2022, shortly after his reelection to a second term in office, the Uzbek president, Shavkat Mirziyoyev—lauded abroad for liberalizing his nation's economy—proposed a series of constitutional reforms that would allow him to remain in power until 2040 (ratified in 2023) and that would strip Karakalpakstan of its nominal autonomy. Mirziyoyev's play to extend his term barely raised eyebrows, but his attack on Karakalpakstan's political status triggered widespread protests in Nukus and brutal reprisals from the state, which shut down internet access, jailed activists, killed several protesters, and wounded many others. Young people led the movement, as young people are wont to do, and within a few days, Mirziyoyev withdrew the proposal, even traveling to Karakalpakstan to present himself as a humble broker of peace. Several activists remain in prison. Savitsky's original argument, meanwhile, seems more urgent than ever: The Karakalpak people exist, they have a language and culture, they have a homeland, and it is here.

And so on that night in April, I joined a crowd of Karakalpak students, foreign architects, regional scientists, and culture workers from across Central Asia to file into the Nukus Museum, where the ACDF was to unveil a significant rehanging of its top floor. The event coincided with the beginning of the tourist season, to the extent that such a thing exists here, and with the end of the Aral Culture Summit, a conference organized by the ACDF about the future of Karakalpakstan and the Aral Sea region. Over the course of the previous two days, agronomists and biologists had spoken of efforts to reforest the Aral seabed with hearty saxaul shrubs and to introduce salt- and drought-resistant crops. Artists had discussed their dreams, fantastical and hopeful and sad, of the sea's return. On the first day of the summit, when foreign speakers graced the stage, the ACDF hosted a gala lunch prepared by a Russian chefs' collective using Karakalpak ingredients; in the evening, a Russian pianist played his own compositions with the National Symphony Orchestra of Uzbekistan, which had been flown in from Tashkent, more than five hundred miles to the east. (The kobyz, a Karakalpak string instrument at imminent risk of disappearing from the region's musical culture, was nowhere to be seen.) The next day, the audience filled with Karakalpaks, sitting rapt as their peers and elders explained all the ways their home could be saved. For lunch, they waited in an interminable line to scoop overcooked lamb and root vegetables from chafing dishes. Throughout the event, young people from Nukus circulated among the invitees, engaged and warm and thrilled to talk about their homeland—its beauty, its tragedy, its possibilities. Fluent in English, almost all of them planned to leave as soon as possible, to study in places where the wind didn't make the air smell like sickness, where there might someday be work and water.

When the doors finally opened at the museum, foreign visitors went in first, locals second. I lingered inside as most of the other foreigners filed out, to catch their planes back to Tashkent. The museum was a revelation. Works by painters whose names I'd never heard of depicted Uzbek grazing lands in improbable shades of pink and blue. There were images of men gathering in poppy-red tearooms, seated cross-legged beneath interpolated portraits of Lenin and startlingly anachronistic megaphones—symbols, like Gabriel's lily, of a new and hopeful annunciation. Between the canvases hung elaborate quilted robes lined with silk ikat, and silver amulets encrusted with roundels of carnelian, cloudy and lustrous as crystallized honey.

As the galleries emptied, the same young people I'd met at the summit hung back. Instead of inspecting the paintings for traces of their own lost landscape, they gathered around a Zoroastrian ossuary jar in the shape of camel, and a long band of wool, framed behind glass, used a century back to decorate a yurt. They gazed up, as stunned and awed as I was, at its narrow surface, covered in delicate abstractions of camels' feet and rams' horns, and of water that had stopped flowing before they were born. ★

MOVE OVER, NEW YORK.
THERE'S A NEW AMERICAN CANON IN TOWN, AND IT STARTS IN CALIFORNIA.

CALIFORNIA REWRITTEN explores the immense literary output of Golden State writers, whose works, editor and California Book Club host John Freeman argues, define a particularly West Coast sensibility and sit at the forefront of a new era of American classics.

> "IN FREEMAN'S HANDS CALIFORNIA IS A LITERARY MECCA"
> —INGRID ROJAS CONTRERAS

JOIN JOHN FREEMAN ON TOUR —

with **HÉCTOR TOBAR**
Skylight | Los Angeles, CA
October 10

with **ELAINE CASTILLO**
Kepler's | Menlo Park, CA
October 21

with **MAXINE HONG KINGSTON**
Commonwealth Club | San Francisco, CA
October 30

with **STEPH CHA**
Bart's Books | Ojai, CA
October 15

at **LITQUAKE**
Verdi Club | San Francisco, CA
October 22

with **DEBORAH MIRANDA**
Portland Literary Arts | Portland, OR
November 3

with **KAREN TEI YAMASHITA**
Bookshop Santa Cruz | Santa Cruz, CA
October 16

at **HEYDAY PRESENTS**
Clio's | Oakland, CA
October 29

heydaybooks.com/california-rewritten

LAURA VAN DEN BERG

[WRITER]

"IT'S NOT AS SIMPLE AS: YOU KILL THE OLD SELF AND YOU JUST MOVE ON. THAT OLD SELF IS GOING TO HAUNT THE SHIT OUT OF YOU ONE DAY."

Laura van den Berg's keys to sleeping well:
Learning how to breathe
Living reasonably
Boxing until you have reached a state of physical exhaustion

The first time I read Laura van den Berg's stories in her debut collection, What the World Will Look Like When All the Water Leaves Us, I was astonished. The stories, teeming with disaster and fantastical creatures—the Loch Ness Monster, Bigfoot, and a Lake Michigan creature known as the mishegenabeg—didn't sound like anything I'd ever read before: The sentences were beguiling, the voice singular. I knew I'd want to follow this writer's work wherever she might want to take it.

I met van den Berg years ago, at a writers' conference in Vermont, and we became friends during a year when I lived in DC; we'd meet to feast on fried oysters and attend readings. She now lives in the Hudson Valley, New York, while I live in San Francisco. We've stayed friends since. Four books later, her work continues to enchant me, and I'm far from alone. Having published two more story collections as well as two novels, she has been awarded a Mildred and Harold Strauss Livings Award from the American Academy of Arts and Letters, a Guggenheim Fellowship, and

Illustration by Kristian Hammerstad

any number of other honors affirming her imaginative genius and originality.

Van den Berg was born in Winter Park, Florida, to a lawyer father and a mother who owned a jewelry and antiques store. When her mother took her to the store as a kid, she kept van den Berg occupied by having her pose in the window displays. In 2005, van den Berg began an MFA program at Emerson College; while there, she studied with, among other professors, Don Lee, who helped her understand the value of shifting "away from writing sentences that sounded lovely and toward sentences that felt alive." She also studied with Margot Livesey, who taught her that "the weird and the surreal are the most impactful when they conjure something meaningful about what it means to be alive on planet Earth." Van den Berg's first story collection came out of her graduate school years.

Her most recent novel, State of Paradise, *is as unforgettable as it is difficult to describe: A ghostwriter of thrillers is living in Florida, and then—what to say? Feral cats roam, a father dies, a belly button shape-shifts, and the ghostwriter is trying to find a voice of her own. I have the evangelical impulse I've always had with van den Berg's books: I want to press it on others, to urge them all to hurry up and read* State of Paradise *so we can discuss it.*

Even better: I was able to talk with van den Berg about the novel, and to ask her some of my most urgent questions. We spoke over the phone about Floridian and metaphorical sinkholes, how to write the most difficult parts of a book, terror, bending time, the rejection of the idea of scarcity, and boxing.
—R. O. Kwon

I. FERAL CATS

THE BELIEVER: *State of Paradise* started with daily meditations you wrote while living in Florida, and at first you didn't realize they were going to turn into a book. Can you say more about that metamorphosis, and how those meditative pieces transformed into a novel?

LAURA VAN DEN BERG: When the pandemic started, I landed in Florida, where my family lives. In addition to the deep strangeness of the early pandemic days, there was the strangeness of being home for an extended period of time with my family, with my mom. It occurred to me that I needed to find a way to document this. Writing the daily meditations was a way to keep me from losing my shit in the early pandemic days.

BLVR: I love this. I'm thinking of what's happening now in the US, how useful it could be to keep a record of the day-to-day changes.

LVDB: Yeah, so I started writing daily meditations on some aspect of the landscape, the weather, the massive feral cat community, the town's quirks, my family, and memories that were surfacing with renewed intensity. I did this for a while, almost a year, and then, when I was maybe six or eight months in, all of a sudden the "I" voice was not quite my voice. It was close to my voice, but it was also not mine. That's the moment when the voice of the protagonist, who's a ghostwriter, started to step forward. I remember that it felt like an atmospheric shift, like the weather in the room changed. That was when I started thinking, Maybe this is evolving into something that departs from my original intention.

BLVR: Do you remember when that shift started, what exactly you were writing?

LVDB: I'd written many meditations on the feral cats that had the run of the place while people were living inside. The cats traveled in packs, and it was unsettling. There was this one house in particular that was kind of derelict. If you paused and looked, you started to see cats everywhere: cats on the roof, cats under the house, cats in the bushes, cats on the porch. I used to joke that if you knocked on the door, ten cats in a trench coat might answer.

I was writing a description of that house when I felt an atmospheric shift. It was minor, at the level of detail. But I started writing things that weren't true. I was slipping away from being faithful to the facts, into this other space where I was capturing a feeling that felt true, but that deviated from lived experience ever so slightly. This didn't make it into the book, but I imagined a confrontation between two cats that both appeared to be ringleaders of their respective packs. Not long after that, I started spontaneously writing passages about ghostwriting, and I had never ghostwritten before. I thought, OK, I'm channeling something.

BLVR: I loved every appearance of the feral cats in this book. And cats, of course, are not especially domesticated even when they live with people. If I look at a cat and then

I look at a tiger, I think, Nothing has changed. You got small and that's it.

LVDB: Yeah. And these were not outdoor cats. They were wild animals.

BLVR: There's an ongoing motif in *State of Paradise* of the varieties of internal wilderness people are trying to escape, and they're not always able to do so. Then there's the external wilderness, like the Floridian sinkholes. That vivid, terrifying image of a snake coiled in a toilet like a massive shit.

MICROINTERVIEW WITH KEVIN YOUNG, PART V

THE BELIEVER: Your new collection, *Night Watch*, takes another tonal shift and has a stark, almost dire atmosphere. You've had that tone in other singular poems, but I don't think you've done it with an entire collection. Would you agree with that? And why do you think that is?

KEVIN YOUNG: It's an interesting question. The last sequence, which is called "Darkling," took the longest. It was a thing I had started and couldn't quite find a form for. And then I was asked to do this MoMA book that was responding to Robert Rauschenberg, who read *The Inferno* and then made these pieces of art. So having that idea, almost like a remove, was helpful at first. But then it was also helpful that it was just Dante, who undergirds everything, and who I read fairly young. And so I worked on the *Inferno* parts, and the Hell parts—of course they're kind of dire. But then, working on the other ones—those ended up being not so dire, but they're not like… Heaven isn't just a moment away. It's a struggle to find it and feel it. I say at one point, "I've come down with a case of Paradise," like that is a thing to aspire to and that then can overtake you. And I kind of put it [*Night Watch*] away. I put it in a drawer. At the back of the book I list all the times I worked on it. And I really pulled it out in quarantine, basically at the start of COVID. I had thought it was too dark, and I pulled it out, and I was like, It feels right on track. ✭

LVDB: One thing about Florida that can be terrifying but also beautiful is the way nature is amplified. You're always aware of the texture of the air, the sky. Florida has violent storms but they can move so quickly. There's always a sense of the landscape and the weather shape-shifting, and there's often the feeling that you're on the edge of something slightly otherworldly.

Even if you live in a high-rise, creatures are still going to get inside. You're aware of the natural world, full of wonder and horror and mystery, and it's pressing on you, pushing against you. Even before I set fiction in Florida, it was difficult for me to imagine writing a story if I didn't already know where it was set. I think that has a lot to do with having grown up in such a forceful landscape.

II. VAMPIRIC YOUNGER SELVES

BLVR: Tell me if I remember this incorrectly, as I couldn't find the quotation, but with your first book, *What the World Will Look Like When All the Water Leaves Us*, did you say you found it fruitful to set fiction in places where you hadn't gone, and that it helped to not research the place? Or did I invent this memory?

LVDB: No, I definitely said that in an interview. Now, though, I would revise what I said. I was really young when I published my first book, and undereducated in a lot of different directions. By the time I wrote my second novel, *The Third Hotel*, which is partly set at a film festival in Havana, I understood I would need to do a phenomenal amount of research. By then I had a much deeper appreciation of the complexities and responsibilities of writing about a place you're not from, a place that's not your place. And even when it is your place, research can be enriching. In his essay "The Autobiography of My Novel," Alexander Chee writes beautifully about researching his home state of Maine. When you're from a place, you can assume you know what there is to know, but when I started looking around and pressing on the particulars, I'd realize I knew the name of a lake, for example, but I didn't know where the name originated from. I learned a lot about where I'm from through research.

So I would go back to my younger self and say, Actually, you should take the research a little more seriously. But also—much like the ghostwriter in *State of Paradise*—when I left Florida, I felt like a person fleeing a burning house. I needed to leave. The whole state felt like a hot stove, and for a long time I was afraid to touch it. My whole family is in Florida, and I love my family, so I would go home, but it would be like a quick holiday visit. I'd be in and out in two or three days. I would have vivid nightmares that the airport would close and I would be stuck in Florida for an indefinite period of time. The anxiety about going back and not being able to leave—I wrestled with it. And so it was the last thing I wanted to write about. It wasn't until I got to a certain place with my own healing that I was open—and not only open but compelled—to set work in Florida. *State of Paradise* is the first book I set entirely in Florida.

BLVR: You've described *State of Paradise* as a hybrid of autofiction and speculative fiction, which I love. You've also said that you wrote some of the most difficult and personal parts on scraps of paper as a way to lower the pressure, which I also love. We've talked in the past about some of the challenges of this kind of writing, and I wonder how you negotiated any anxieties around the ways people can start conflating a novel's narrator with its writer, particularly when there are demographic and experiential overlaps between the two.

LVDB: I was very aware of opening the door to that conflation. There are differences between me and the protagonist of *State of Paradise*. I, for example, have never ghostwritten. But there are a lot of similarities too. She's an independent fictional creation, but the protagonist shares my personal history, more or less. I would call her an author-aligned protagonist. I'm not trying to be elusive here—the history I'm referring to is that, like the protagonist, I spent a long period, months of my adolescence, in an inpatient psychiatric facility. It was a big thing to have happen during a fragile, formative time.

Then I left, moved on, got my GED, went to college, started writing, went to an MFA program, and I didn't talk about that time of my life with anyone. I didn't talk about it at length with my family even. I mean, I disclosed it to my husband at a certain point. I said, "You should probably know this about me." But even with close friends, I didn't, though I wouldn't say it was a secret. My understanding was: That person is dead and gone, and this new person has taken her place. Why would I need to discuss it with anyone or include it in my personal narrative?

BLVR: Yes.

LVDB: But many years later, in my thirties, I was having really intense anxiety attacks. I was going through some rocky depressive episodes, and went into therapy. When, eventually, the full story came out with my therapist, she said that a lot of what I was describing was classic PTSD. I was shocked by that. There was also PTSD resulting from the period of my life that had led my parents to decide it

MICROINTERVIEW WITH KEVIN YOUNG, PART VI

THE BELIEVER: So it's roughly the thirtieth anniversary of your first book. How do you think your work has changed since then?

KEVIN YOUNG: I mean, one wants to be like, *It's only gotten better*. That's the easy answer. I tend to look back and see connections rather than disconnects. Just to take a different writer—looking, for instance, at James Baldwin's early work—you really see moments that then later come true. And you know, for me, in re-reading his work, there's this idea that he keeps returning to about love, and love being what's going to save us, because he's naming the horrors of everyday life, and the state of the nation, and these moments of difficulty and transition. But he's also saying, *This is what can save us*.

I've always been interested in song. Song as a kind of balm. When my good friend Philippe Wamba died, that's the only thing that got me through: listening to music, and listening to Bob Marley specifically, and reggae. And so I ended up writing a poem that uses reggae and Bob Marley as its titles. And I feel like I am still trying to do that in different ways, and music has been really important to me. But I also think the music of the poems changes, and I am sometimes more interested in harmony these days. But then I look back at *Jelly Roll*, and there were moments when I was like, I would like to write something beautiful. I don't know why, but I'd like to be able to write like a song. I love sounds. Who wouldn't want to write "This Must Be the Place" by the Talking Heads? Or Stevie Wonder's "Golden Lady," or any other Stevie Wonder song? ✻

was a good idea for me to be in an inpatient facility in the first place. So it took me a long time to feel like this was something I could write about, and that I wanted to write about. It was actually cathartic. I don't know that I've ever in my life described writing a novel as cathartic, and probably never will again.

What I came to understand is that it's not as simple as: You kill the old self and you just move on. That old self is going to haunt the shit out of you one day. It might be sooner, it might be later, but one day it will. That's exactly what happened to me when I came back home during the pandemic. All the things I had kept myself busy with fell away. I was spending all this time with my family, back in the physical place where a massive unraveling had occurred. And that was the exact moment when that younger self sat up from her coffin like a vampire: *Guess what, bitch? I'm still here.*

BLVR: I hear that. *Hi, remember me?*

LVDB: To write this book felt, in some ways, like integration, like the current and younger selves could shake hands and make their peace with each other. It wasn't something I necessarily wanted to talk about at every book event, but if someone brought it up—and sometimes people had a personal connection to that material, and they wanted to talk about it—I did not feel it was a violation for people to want to have that conversation. And partly because I had been describing *State of Paradise* as a merger of speculative fiction and autofiction, I was conscious of opening the door to those conversations. It didn't feel like people were making assumptions that weren't accurate or that were divorced from reality.

I also realized that, in past books, I had been circling this material. My first novel is dystopian, but part of it is set in an institution. I have a couple of stories in my last collection that deal with suicide. I had been orbiting this abyss for a while, and then it became clear that the next stage for me as an artist and as a human being was to stop circling this black hole in my life and go into it.

III. BENDING TIME AND REALITY

BLVR: There was so much I found moving in this book. One aspect of it that strongly resonated with me is that I keep retelling fictional versions of a massive, endlessly painful loss I lived through when I was seventeen. I keep trying to retell it fictionally, and it keeps being not quite right, not enough, so then I try to retell it again. But most of the memories of what happened are gone. There's so little of it left, as though it also dropped into a sinkhole, this catastrophe that inflected much of the rest of my life. But with each book, I keep searching for the "right," most fictionally truthful version of this story, whether or not that's ever going to be possible. And I wonder if you could talk about this searching urge and how it shaped *State of Paradise*.

LVDB: First of all, that struggle resonates so deeply with me. I think that brings us to the speculative part of the novel, because that's a question that people have asked: *Why not just autofiction? Why the autofiction and the speculative fiction?*

I read about this idea in a *Paris Review* interview with Garth Greenwell: With the most difficult stuff I wrote, I used scraps of paper, receipts, the Notes app on my phone, anything that felt disposable, anonymous. So when I decided I was going to move toward the sinkhole, I told myself, If you decide that you want to get out of the sinkhole, you can do that at any time. You're not going to be stuck in there. You can throw this away. You can delete the note on your phone. You have agency. You can decide how long you want to stay in the sinkhole, if you want to go all the way to the bottom or not. You don't have to get lost in there.

BLVR: This is such a good idea.

LVDB: Ultimately, the most troubling thing for me was not what I could remember. It was what I could *not* remember, starting with the two years leading up to being institutionalized. Or maybe two years is overstating it a little—but certainly the year leading up to the period of time when I was in inpatient treatment, then about a year after. The memories are impressionistic and fragmented. And a total of almost three years is a long time. I remember a few things that happened, but there are a lot of significant gaps and a lot of haze.

And what speculative fiction can do is bend time and bend reality. I felt like I was a character in a speculative world where, with these things that happened, when I would go to touch them, I'd find one sinkhole after another. A little scrap of memory and then the rest would just fall through

ELDERS

by Kyle Carrero Lopez

I ponder how my father's former Jersey cop father
might hear my critiques of police,
if he'd understand I feel how I feel, as many have learned to feel,
and I can still see, in a way, why an Englishless,
poor, dark-skinned Black migrant of his time
might seek power—a snip, crumb, a something—
through uniform

(though, of the Black policeman, Baldwin wrote:
*His entire reason for breathing seemed to be his hope
to offer proof that, though he was Black,
he was not Black like you*,

and there's, too, how my father's father disciplined his clan:
why should it shock, when a brutal man takes brutal work?)

Maybe he'd relate and agree on grounds
that the terrain's changed, just as

an older gent once explains over midday pancakes
in Cherry Grove, Fire Island, sure to state disdain for
the state of things, and how he believed, *in the '90s*,
that to join the force was a force of good

His eyes hum low behind tinted lenses as they lock on mine

Once he says this, and afterward, I wonder when, exactly,
in the '90s he means

If he'd joined AFTER or BEFORE   '91, Rodney King
BEFORE or AFTER   '93, Archie Elliott
AFTER or BEFORE   August '94, Desmond Robinson
AFTER or BEFORE   December '94, Anthony Baez
BEFORE or AFTER   '99, Amadou Diallo

I ponder whether the pre-'90s swayed his career move
If it all, in his '90s mind, might have been isolated mishaps

It was early World Wide Web
(everybody knew less, I guess)

Benefit of the doubt coaxes,
for the moment

He intends to cover this pricy isle brunch,
way outside my threadbare budget

Self-justification goes down smooth
spurting from a man who's been good to you

---

the floor. But speculative fiction is a form that can account really, really well for violations in time, gaps in time, and fragmented or disrupted time.

BLVR: Oh, absolutely.

LVDB: In the past, readers have asked things like *Why do you write these weird books where all these weird things happen?* Before, I thought, I don't really know. Florida, I guess! I made the answer into a joke, but really I didn't know how to account for myself. But I've come to understand my relationship with the speculative genre in a deeper way. It's possible I've always been drawn to these forms where time is heavily distorted, because my own relationship to time was broken at an early age. I may not ever be able to recover or repair what was broken, but I can work in these forms that make space for fractured, troubled timelines.

BLVR: That's so beautiful. I'm reminded of the time when people thought you and I would be enemies because of our different approaches to form and register and style. Do you remember when we were jointly invited to visit a university in Indianapolis, and Kyle Minor told us that his students thought we'd be enemies? They said, *Laura reminds us of*

Black Mirror *and Javier Marías, while R. O. reminds us of Faulkner with clarity. They must be* deadly enemies.

LVDB: That was really funny. The comparisons were very flattering.

BLVR: Speaking of registers, I was struck by the sharp juxtapositions of sorrow and comedy in *State of Paradise*. There were moments when I was having strong back-to-back physical reactions: laughing, gasping, and so on.

LVDB: When my dad died, we had a viewing for him, and I'm lucky to have a wonderful, close, big family. We arrived at the funeral home, all in our somber attire, and we walked into the room. We were going to see my dad and say goodbye. And for some inexplicable reason, Glen Campbell's "Rhinestone Cowboy" was blasting. And I thought that was hilarious. It was so weird. I had done my best to mentally prepare myself to see my dad one last time, but I was not prepared for Glen Campbell. I felt the uncontainable pain crack apart the bureaucracy of death. That howling energy ruptured through to the surface in the form of laughter.

BLVR: Sometimes people are at their funniest when things are saddest, and vice versa. Another question about genre and register: The narrator of *State of Paradise* is ghostwriting plot-forward thrillers. I don't know if you would agree with this, but when I was trying to describe your book to a friend, I said I might call it a kind of existential thriller. Can you talk about thrillers and how the form and vocabulary of that genre might have informed *State of Paradise*?

LVDB: No one has asked me about thrillers, so I love this. When I was in college and living with my grandmother, I took tremendous pleasure in reading the kind of thrillers you would buy at the grocery store. There's a writer named Robin Cook who writes medical thrillers. They're like James Patterson's books, but they're all set in hospitals. I'll never spend the night in the hospital, if I can help it, because of those books. Even though that's not the work I'm aspiring to make, it was fun to be able to incorporate thrillers into the world of *State of Paradise* in some way. I used to really love them.

When I went back to Florida during the pandemic, I thought a lot about how writing grabbed me by the shirt collar and pulled me over to a better place. I was so, so lucky to find language, to find art. I bumbled into a fiction workshop in college, and I read contemporary fiction for the first time, and that transformed me. Eventually, I decided I wanted to write myself. That gave me a focus and direction that changed my life in radical and important ways. What would have happened to me in a sliding-doors version of reality if I hadn't taken that workshop, if I hadn't found writing? I imagined that alternate version as my novel's ghostwriter, as someone who wants to tell her stories in her own language, but doesn't know how. And so she uses her own language to tell other people's stories, and to tell stories that are ridiculous and aren't really saying anything true about what it's like to be alive on planet Earth. Those sections of ghostwriting were very fun to write. I could play around with the unabashedly ludicrous nature of those kinds of plots.

IV. BOXING AS A DEVOTIONAL PROCESS

BLVR: I don't know how they'll hold up, but I just ordered a pile of old Christopher Pike books because I used to love those when I was a little kid, and I want to figure out what made me obsessed. Trying to explain one to a friend, I said, "Someone's walking on top of a wall and the wall gets thinner and thinner and the person falls and gets sliced in half." And the friend said, "What the hell?" But it was terrifying. I've been haunted by it. Speaking of sliding-doors realities, I loved the Alice in Wonderland situation with the narrator's shape-shifting belly button. Can you say more about how that came to you?

LVDB: As you know, half my life is in the world of competitive boxing. And the first time I fought, I put myself in too low of a weight class—that was a mistake I won't make again. I cut so much weight that my belly button popped out. I've always had a standard-issue belly button, and I found the change quite alarming. I would look down in the shower and this part of my body was alien to me. After my fight, when I went back to my normal weight, it popped back in.

Part of what was so unsettling about COVID is that people had such different experiences with it in terms of their symptoms and their recoveries. I wanted to work with that idea of a virus changing a body. I started to imagine the opposite of what happened to my belly button. What if a belly button started to sink inward, deeper and deeper? The narrator even starts using her belly button to store things. I mean, it would be convenient.

BLVR: It would. Sea otters have pouches—they keep their favorite rocks in there. Is there anything you'd like to say here about how boxing has been illuminating for your writing, or how it's perhaps been a counterpart, a companion?

LVDB: The big overlap is that boxing is all about process. If you think of a fight as being akin to publishing a book, it's the moment when you step out of the process and do something in a more public way. I think the fighters who love to fight but don't love being in the process are usually not super successful. I probably love training more than I love fighting. The process, the rhythms of being in the gym, have become devotional.

I taught a course on revision this semester. I'm now in the middle of a giant revision of a new project, and I've been training for a fight. I've been consumed with these twin processes of practice and revision, practice and revision, practice and revision, practice and revision, and they're companionable. And the training supports my writing because I'm forced to live really reasonably. The more rested I am, the more sober I am, the more I have to give to my work. Boxing is probably the single best thing I've done for my mental health. The sport taught me to breathe. I can sleep now.

BLVR: This lifelong insomniac would love to hear more.

LVDB: So controlling your breathing, being really mindful of exhaling and inhaling, that's key to boxing, and we're doing it under tremendous pressure. Amateur fights in particular tend to be fast-paced and chaotic because we have only three rounds. Unlike in a pro fight, which is much longer, we have to get in and get out. So being able to control my breathing under a lot of confusion and pressure—it's helped me with panic and anxiety more than anything else I've tried. I have no doubt it's carried over to writing as well. I train two hours most evenings, and I think being physically exhausted helps with the sleep.

BLVR: That sounds incredible. As you know, I love power-lifting, but I'm not nearly as serious about it as you are about boxing. It's very clear to me that, on the days when I lift, I'm usually better off than on the days I don't.

LVDB: Power-lifting is of course a different sport with a different tempo, but when you're thinking, *Oh my gosh, I'm going to pick up this weight that's bigger than my body*, or, *I'm going to push this weight over my head*—there's something so potent about taking a really deep breath and inhaling and exhaling as you're moving this tremendous weight. It's an elegant metaphor for emotional work: I am moving weight. This weight does not have to stay on my chest, crushing me. I'm going to breathe, and I'm going to move it away. It's empowering. And again there's so much breathing involved.

I want to be chill, you know what I mean? It seems nice, but I have this unfortunate personality: I feel the most alive and connected to the world when I'm in the maw of incredible intensity.

BLVR: Oh, yeah.

LVDB: I suspect you know what I mean.

BLVR: Yes.

LVDB: Sometimes I have a deep envy of people who are like, *I'm just down to hang out for a while.* And I wonder, You don't have the need to feel like you're struggling against some massive weight that could crush you at any moment? And they're like, *No, I'm good. I don't feel that way at all.* What must that be like? Whether it's writing a book or training for a fight, I feel the most alive when I am deep in a thing that's hard and meaningful.

BLVR: Yes, yes, yes, yes. Yes. One of the many reasons I deeply admire your writing is that I feel as though, with each book you've written, I could not have come close to predicting what the next book would be. I also admire the writers whose books can seem to be more similar to one another, but there's so much range in your work. With the novel I'm now working on, I've been grappling with an intense fear that I can't do it, that I'm taking on too much: What if what I'm hoping to do so vastly exceeds my powers that it's not possible for me, not in this lifetime? I wonder if you could talk about these kinds of fears in relation to writing. Or boxing.

LVDB: Yeah, I feel that before each fight. Not that I have so many fights—this upcoming one will be my third official fight. The act of training calms me and grounds me, but in the week leading up to the fight, you don't train as much. You usually take the day before completely off. And that's when those doubtful voices get active: Wait a second. How did this happen? What are you doing? What are you thinking? Why do you think you can do this? With both writing and fighting, it's powerful to hear those intense voices and then still choose to go forward. Whether you finish the book or you don't, whether you win the fight or lose the fight, you can decide: I have these doubts and I will continue to walk forward anyway.

And I feel that with every book. I think: This far outstrips my capacities. How on earth did I think I could take this project on? But I also know, and I suspect you feel the same way, that I wouldn't be as interested in writing a book if I knew every answer going in. And I don't love reading books in which I feel as if the writer knew every answer going in. I recently had the pleasure of hearing Katie Kitamura speak at an event, and she said she feels like readers can tell when a writer is taking a real risk on the page. There is an energy of risk that can transfer from writer to reader and reader to writer, and it's so potent. I want my readers to feel that energetic transfer of risk and leap.

BLVR: Yeah, no, it's true. I do often tell myself, Well, if I were sure I could do this, I'd be terribly bored. So I guess that's the choice: boredom or terror.

LVDB: Boredom or terror, exactly. If I weren't fighting, I would be bored. But I am fighting, so there's a part of me that's terrified. Those are my choices, bored or terrified. And I seem doomed to keep picking "terrified."

V. "WALKING ON PARALLEL PATHS"

BLVR: It's one of my great fears, being bored. I'll end with one last question. I've known you for some years now—I first came to know you through your work and your first book. And you are, as so many people know, such a generous person with your time and with your energy, both as a writer and as a friend. Can you talk about how you think about community and camaraderie, and perhaps especially in this extra fraught time that we're in?

LVDB: Oh, that's such a beautiful question. Particularly last year, when we were both in the book-publication maw, I was so glad to be journeying alongside you.

BLVR: Same here.

LVDB: It feels meaningful to know that I'm walking a path that only I can walk. But there are writers I really admire who are walking on parallel paths. And some of those people are dead, but I'm walking alongside their work. And then there are people like you whom I've known a long time. I can walk parallel to you and to other people I'm in community with, and how beautiful it is that we can turn to each other and high-five.

Those people you can turn to and high-five, those relationships are special. And this can be hard for young writers to hear, because I know it doesn't always feel this way, but I reject scarcity and the feeling that the other writers around you are your competition, and that there's only so much pie. The rejection of the idea of scarcity feels particularly important now because that's one of Trump's false narratives, the lie that there's only so much to go around and so we should protect what's "ours" at all costs.

What we're doing as writers is so much bigger than what can be accounted for by a review or an award or anything like that. It's an energetic transfer, a passing of knowledge and experience from one imagination to another.

And we all struggle with shit. I can think of a million times when I've been disappointed, or when a rejection has hit me particularly hard. And I think talking about it with other people makes us feel less alone. So even when we are touched by the heartbreak of something in our professional lives not going the way we want it to, I could turn to you and high-five you on the path and say, *Hey, this-and-that happened and it really hurt*. And you could say, *Yeah, I know exactly what you mean*. And then we could both keep going. I feel like we can keep going partly because we're able to help each other find the sustenance we need to keep doing our work. I fear this might have been totally incoherent!

BLVR: No, I think people are going to love hearing it. And good luck with your fight. I'll be rooting for you. ✮

SACRIFICE ZONE

A SEMI-REGULAR GUEST COLUMN ABOUT REGULARLY IGNORED PLACES

by Nathaniel Rich

★ IN THIS ISSUE: Forest Denka

You will not find Forest Denka on any map—or any other place. On Google Maps it appears blank, or at least the grayish color Google uses for empty space, called Wild Sand.

Pristine has ever been anything but. The word (from the Latin *pristinus*: "former, ancient, old") has divided lexicographers since its earliest recorded usage. *The Oxford English Dictionary* notes that its original meaning—its pristine meaning—is "relating to the earliest period or state"; "unspoilt by human interference." This much is uncontested. Things get spicy, lexicographically speaking, with *pristine*'s secondary definition: "As good as new... newly made." The metaphorical usage, to describe something that is not original but *seems to appear* original, was, the editors report, "frequently criticized" and "regarded with disfavour by many educated speakers."

Yet the earliest cited usage of the word is, in fact, metaphorical. In 1534

Photographs by the author

The path shadows a polluted drainage canal behind the subdivision, a repository for plastic children's toys, car fenders, and a ceiling fan.

Anne Boleyn wrote to Chief Minister Thomas Cromwell to request that a merchant, convicted for smuggling New Testaments into England, be "restored to his pristine fredome." Since the merchant could not go back in time, he could only be granted the *appearance* of a clean criminal record, and treated as if he had never been convicted.

It took nearly half a millennium, but the debate ended in 1996, when the most exacting of lexicographers, R. W. Burchfield, the don of the *OED* and the leading stickler on the usage of *pristine*, surrendered in the pages of *New Fowler's Modern English Usage*. There could be no lexical distinction, he acknowledged, between a pristine landscape and one that appeared to be pristine.

It feels safe, then, to claim that the most pristine patch of wilderness along the lower Mississippi River is Forest Denka.

You will not find Forest Denka on any map—or any other place. On Google Maps it appears blank, or at least the grayish color Google uses for empty space, called Wild Sand. On Apple Maps it is a smudge of Granny Smith apple, and Louisiana's official state highway map absorbs it into a thick chunk of Shalimar. But Forest Denka is real: 420 acres of pristine wilderness in Reserve, Louisiana, forty minutes upriver from New Orleans.

It is real, but for the last sixty years only a handful of people have been allowed to enter it. In recent years those people have been employees of Denka Performance Elastomer, a subsidiary of Japan's Denka Company Limited, and the operator of a facility that the Environmental Protection Agency has determined emits the deadliest air pollution in the nation. The Denka plant produces a synthetic rubber invented by DuPont in 1931. The compound, originally named "DuPrene," was renamed neoprene; today more a quarter million metric tons of the stuff are sold annually, generating $2.2 billion in revenue. It can be found in the gaskets in your car, your ankle brace, your wet suit, and your beer koozie.

The property on which the facility stands was operated as a rice and sugar plantation since at least 1792. At the height of its operation, the Belle Pointe Plantation enslaved 150 people. Some of these people joined the 1811 German Coast Uprising, which ended with the rebels decapitated, their heads stuck on poles spanning the levee of the Mississippi River for miles. In 1957, DuPont purchased six hundred acres from the plantation's heirs. DuPont soon began producing neoprene and its lethal by-product, chloroprene gas. By 2008 the plant was the only source of the gas in the nation. Two years later the EPA designated it a "likely human carcinogen."

Concerned about the cost of mandated pollution controls, DuPont sold the factory, but not the land, to Denka. A few years later the EPA determined that Reserve had achieved a milestone: the highest cancer rate in Cancer Alley. The residents who live within a mile of the factory, most of whom are Black and poor, have a cancer rate fifty times the national average.

The DuPont property forms a trapezoid, the base running along the Mississippi River levee. The factory, a sprawl of smokestacks and silos and snaking pipes with the footprint of twenty-two Superdomes, occupies the trapezoid's lower-left quadrant. The lower-right quadrant is unoccupied and routinely mowed; the ghostly imprints of the former sugarcane rows are visible in aerial photographs. The upper half of the plot, however, has been left to serve as a buffer zone, abandoned and unsupervised, for more than six decades. During this time a forest has grown.

It is illegal to enter the forest, but then again it has been legal to blast carcinogenic gas into the surrounding neighborhoods for decades, so visitors are free to consult their own moral calculators when considering a tour. There is no obvious point of ingress, but the easiest approach is from the un-surveilled eastern edge of the Belle Pointe subdivision, a suburban neighborhood of modest ranch houses, generous backyards, and heightened rates of cancer and tachycardia. At the edge of the neighborhood, where it abuts the East St. John Preparatory Academy, lies an inconspicuous dirt path.

The path shadows a polluted drainage canal behind the subdivision, a repository for plastic children's toys, car fenders, and a ceiling fan. It continues beside a transmission tower, over a gas pipeline, past the skull of a smallish dog, its teeth frozen in a snarl. It terminates in train tracks, the old Kansas City Southern Line. Built on a steep embankment of crushed granite, the railway marks the northern boundary of Forest Denka.

From the embankment, the forest appears imposing: a dense wall of southern hackberry and black willow, interlaced with vines and crowded with stands of elderberry, giant ragweed, and Japanese wax-leaf. If you walk the tracks a couple hundred yards, however, you reach an area of less-dense brush. Pick your way through the seven-foot stands of ragweed and you can descend into a small clearing. Go on, be brave.

Once within the clearing, you are entirely enclosed by canopy and understory: You cannot see the tracks, the power lines, or most of the sky. At the far end the clearing narrows into a path that meanders deeper into the woods. This trail is about the width of a truck or a mule cart; on an 1892 map of the area, it appears as a country road, with several houses on either side. Although the edge of the forest is dominated by the unstable, fast-growing species common in emergent forests, the interior shows signs of maturation: eighty-foot-high pecan trees, and live oaks nearly as tall, with gnarled limbs trussed in poison ivy. The path is pocked with burrow holes large enough for skunks, raccoons, coyotes. An uninterrupted insect chorus surges, fades back into ambient noise, surges again. Birds are everywhere, or at least their calls: The cardinals and crows are the most garrulous, but from deeper in the woods come the voices of Carolina wrens, white-eyed vireos, tufted titmice, painted buntings, blue-gray gnatcatchers, blue grosbreaks.

After several hundred yards the path ends in a T, joining another long-lost country road that travels laterally across the property and intersects other ghost roads. Someone has kept up the paths—several clear-cut stumps are occasionally visible—but someone has also forgotten about them long enough to allow for their colonization by mushrooms and wildflowers and low plants: balloon vine, hedge parsley, and red-veined bloody dock. The deadly chloroprene gas seems to have had no measurable effect on the forest, apart from barring it from human interest. Joshua Lewis, a professor of river and coastal studies at Tulane University, estimates that Forest Denka sequesters more than 2,000 tons of carbon dioxide each year. It stores more than six million dollars' worth of carbon dioxide. It removes more than 32,500 pounds of additional air pollutants annually. It would be difficult to find healthier air along the lower Mississippi, were it not for the deadly levels of chloroprene.

But in May something entirely unexpected happened: Denka closed the plant. It announced it had ceased neoprene production and would "safely transition… to a mothball status." A press release blamed severe weather, power outages, and the cost of the pollution control equipment mandated during the Biden administration by an EPA advisory and a Justice Department lawsuit. The Trump administration dropped the lawsuit and announced plans to stimulate higher chloroprene emissions, but apparently in vain. What will happen next is unclear. The plant might be sold and recommissioned. It might be retrofitted to produce other toxins. It might be demolished. One thing is certain, however: Eventually, and perhaps very soon, the factory will be abandoned for good, and the maturing forest, unpoliced and unmonitored, abetted by hurricane and flood, will continue to grow, and claim the rest of the land as its own, until the whole plot becomes, once again, pristine. ✶

GAME

THE CRYPTIC CROSSWORD

by Vijay Khurana

FEATURES:
★ Black squares
★ White squares
★ Seeming gibberish

Solving a cryptic is a bit like chewing over a confounding poem. Words that begin as the unlikeliest of associates end up somehow being apt neighbors, relating to one another in a way that makes sense, or at least a *kind of* sense. Good writing can say something without actually saying it, which is also what cryptic clues do: There is meaning in there somewhere, though it's hidden beneath a layer of syntactic legerdemain. OK, so lines of poetry are not codes to be broken, and works of literature are not puzzles with definitive interpretive solutions (a lesson I learned despite the best efforts of an algebraically minded high school English teacher). But crosswords *do* have definitive answers, and finding out what they are can be immensely satisfying to one's sense of linguistic command. Imagine having the power to break down gibberish and reassemble it as sense! Anagrams and synonyms and homophones and abbreviations and even spoonerisms are brought to bear until inspiration strikes, and your pen (solving should be a screen-free activity) fills a column or row of vacant squares. One down: many more to go.

I'm going to assume you're au fait with the kind of crossword printed in, say, *The New York Times*. This is the kind where the clue is generally a "definition," another way of expressing the answer. "One way to make a hole" could be BORING; "Unvarnished" might be DULL; et cetera. There may be some misdirection involved—in a perfect world, "Dodge charger, e.g.?" would be BULLFIGHT—but there's always an equivalence between the entire clue and its answer. In a cryptic, the definition is only half the clue. The other half is wordplay, which is a second means of arriving at the correct answer. It can take many forms, but often it's a second definition, as in "Poet's currency" for POUND. Anagrams are also common, as in "Book van crashed into lepidopterist" for NABOKOV, who, incidentally, loved crosswords and once made one for Véra in the shape of a butterfly. In that example, *crashed* is part of the wordplay because it suggests an anagram: It's a kind of recipe direction to "crash" together the letters of *book* and *van*. Then there's the container clue, all the more devious because it places the answer right under your nose: "Artiste inadvertently shaved Toklas autobiographer."

With a cryptic clue, your job is to work out which bit is the definition and which bit is the wordplay, and find an answer that satisfies both. It isn't necessarily harder than a *New York Times*–style clue, but it is multidimensional where the other type usually isn't. Cryptics demand the closest of readings. Words may be needed for their surface meanings or for their atomic constitution, and different elements will interact differently. Put another way, you need to spot the STEIN in "ArtiSTE INadvertently." If this sounds suspiciously similar to dad-jokery, you're not wrong. Puns tend to play an outsize role in cryptics, a fact that often earns me a raised eyebrow when I gush about these puzzles to People Who Take Literature Very Seriously. But lately, I've begun to defend myself against such superciliary attacks. Never mind the fact that double meanings are everywhere in literature, from Shakespeare to the titles of every single academic paper ever written—wordplay is part of complexity in writing and therefore part of the pleasure we get from reading. Take the Christine Schutt line quoted in a Garielle Lutz essay in this magazine, "The Sentence Is a Lonely Place": "Here is the house at night, lit up tall and tallowy." As Lutz points out, the final word choice is both astounding and perfect. And the joy of that magnetic tension between the adjectives (these words don't belong together, except that they *do*) is a cousin of what a cryptic crossword setter is trying to tease out of their solver. It's no replacement for reading, but sometimes it's nice to look at a line of impossibility and know that resolution and sense are in there somewhere, on the other side of wordplay. ★

Illustration by Mizmaru Kawahara

THE PROCESS
IN WHICH AN ARTIST DISCUSSES MAKING A PARTICULAR WORK
Richard Ayoade, *The Unfinished Harauld Hughes*, 2024

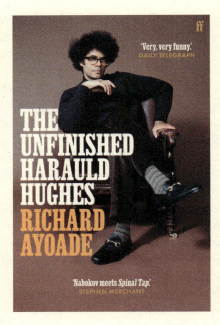

I met Richard Ayoade, the brilliant British author of The Unfinished Harauld Hughes, which is out in paperback this September from Faber, because (possibly through some misunderstanding) he asked me to appear as an actor in his 2013 film, The Double, a contemporary take on the disturbing early novel by Dostoyevsky. Unlike Dostoyevsky, Ayoade became a well-known comedian and character actor before he was thirty. And also unlike Dostoyevsky, he was almost immediately seen to be so charming, so enjoyable, so magnetic and companionable, that he was summoned to be the host of many television programs. Among other programs, Ayoade worked as the host of a humorous weekly travel show and a series about different unfamiliar but clever gadgets, as well as many comical game shows. Behind the scenes, he's also directed music videos and provided voices for cartoons. Before The Double, he directed the delightful and sensitive 2010 film Submarine, featuring Sally Hawkins and Paddy Considine.

I found Ayoade, as a director, to be unfailingly polite, considerate, amusing, and amused. He didn't seem to be agitated by the innumerable surprises and difficulties that inevitably arise in the process of making a film. His demeanor was relaxed, almost languid. But he did turn out to have a steely, determined side, and I did personally find it close to impossible to respond in an adequate manner to his relentless insistence that all of his actors should speak very, very quickly, as this was a key feature of the forceful style of the film. I came to realize only later that this sped-up dialogue actually mirrored the normal pace at which Ayoade's brain functions on a daily basis. And I came to understand that it was this faster-than-normal human brain speed that explained the seemingly impossible fact that while engaged in game shows, gadget shows, cartoons and whatever, Ayoade was at the same time sharpening his skills as a writer. By my count, he now has nine books in print.

The character referred to in the title of Ayoade's latest fiction—the grand and imperious Harauld Hughes—is himself a writer. And of course many writers have invented characters who are writers—but do you know any other writer who has not only invented a character who is a writer but who has then gone on to actually write and publish that imaginary writer's complete works? Richard Ayoade has done that, and if you take out your Kindle and look up Harauld Hughes, Faber will be glad to send you Hughes's collected plays, poems, prose pieces, and screenplays, all in fact written by Richard Ayoade. And you wouldn't call Hughes an unusually prolific author, but before his unfortunate (fictional) death, Hughes did a not inconsiderable amount of writing, representing a perfectly respectable life's work. So inevitably one has to be curious about what Ayoade was up to here. Was this all just a joke? I'm not aware that there's ever been a joke of this length. Are these works parodies? But there are no originals of which they could be parodies, as Hughes never really existed. And they don't in fact resemble the work of any other writer, so they're clearly not parodies. What are they, then? If I had the ability to do so, I would love to summon a great international conference of professors of English literature to try to answer this question. I myself am stumped, because sentence by sentence, line by line, Hughes is a wonderful writer who makes no mistakes, while page by page one does have the impression that Ayoade is being "funny" rather than "serious," except that rather frequently a page will suddenly appear that seems (perhaps almost by mistake?) to be "serious" rather than "funny." Which brings us to the question of the meaning of these concepts or words, "serious" and "funny," which is a question that's both dealt with indirectly in different sections of The Unfinished

Image courtesy of Faber & Faber

Harauld Hughes *and is also a question raised by the book as a whole, a question that Ayoade and I circled around when we talked to each other on the telephone several months ago.*
—Wallace Shawn

WALLACE SHAWN: So in this very hilarious book, *The Unfinished Harauld Hughes*, you, Richard, are the narrator, and you're the central character, in a way. And you seem to be a rather bumbling person whose occupation is that of a "presenter." In the book you're trying to film a documentary about a much greater person, Harauld, who is no longer alive—a playwright and screenwriter who initially fascinates you because when he was alive he looked just like you. Now, to begin with, I'm an American, so I'm not familiar with this word *presenter*. We don't use that word. What is a presenter? Is it just a word for a sort of traveling moderator? Someone who goes to different places or different events and presents them to a television audience? Someone who just appears on a show about a chess tournament in New Zealand and says, *I'm here in New Zealand, and this is—*

RICHARD AYOADE: Yes, well, in this context, where the show is a documentary (although I have heard people use the term *docu-tainment* with a straight face), the presenter is someone who appears and who is in effect saying, *Come this way, look at this…* And so in the book I was asking, Well, what if this rather trivial person who appears on things—myself—is trying to find out about this more profound person? He's wondering, How can I, with my sort of trivial concerns, access this person who seems to be free from them?

WS: And so, in speaking with you for *The Believer*, I believe I'm allowed to ask why you wrote your book the way you did, because in Harauld Hughes you've created a character who looks like you but who takes himself very, very seriously. He's pompous and pretentious. And you make an awful lot of fun of him. He seems to be a sort of alter ego, someone who you might be but who you aren't, and you do mock him quite severely. Now, I myself happen to be a playwright and screenwriter who takes himself very, very seriously, so I took this personally, and I wondered why you mocked your alter ego so severely. It certainly seems to bother you a lot that he has no sense of humor, certainly not about himself. I don't know if I have a sense of humor myself anymore, but I know that when I was a boy I did, and when I was a boy I was what was called the class clown. Actually, we had two class clowns in my class, because Chevy Chase was in my class, and he was also the class clown, but he was much more daring than I was, and in order to be funny he would take the risk of enraging the teachers, which I didn't do. Were you the class clown when you were a boy?

RA: No, I don't think so. Not that there's a contradiction between being a class clown and being studious, but I think I was more studious, and I think I probably was more interested—and there are quite a few funny people I know like this—I think I was more interested in music. In fact, wasn't Chevy Chase quite interested in music? I think he was. Was he a drummer?

WS: Yes, I think at one time he was, and a keyboard player. And in school, when the teacher would play a long phrase on the piano and ask us to sing it back to him, the rest of us could sing the first three notes or whatever, and Chevy could sing the whole phrase.

RA: He's got great rhythm to his speech, brilliant timing. It's strange to me to be talking about humor, because I don't think it's anything I expected to be involved with at all. In so many of the projects I've done, I've felt there was another person in it who was the funny person. Even at school, there were many funny people who I just liked being around and hearing them be funny. At college one of the first people I met was John Oliver—and we wrote sketch comedy together. I felt I was more like someone who wrote material that John Oliver would then deliver, even though we were, I guess, in what we called a double act. I think I was keener for him to do the bulk of the performing. I've always liked making things, and sometimes it's almost more convenient to be in them than to not.

WS: I have to say, there are many pages in your book that are, you know, wonderful pages that you would find in a wonderful novel. You write quite beautifully and insightfully not only about the process of making films but even about human feelings, the love between men and women. Your female characters are marvelously vivid. The relationships are complicated and interesting. And obviously most novelists have a sense of humor—if you think of even Dostoyevsky, or Jane Austen, Muriel Spark, et cetera, et cetera—but, well, they have a kind of commitment to, I don't know what: naturalism? And in your book you stick with a kind of naturalism for maybe two pages, but then you'll introduce something that's so farcical that the naturalistic element is completely disrupted, and you're no longer in the realm of what would be called a novel. It's pure quote, unquote "humor," or I don't know what you want to call it. I mean, is that simply how your mind works? Or...

RA: Well, there are some people, like, say, Ingmar Bergman, where I would say nothing he has ever produced has been funny at all. I know some people say *Smiles of a Summer Night* is witty, but I just... Now, *All These Women*, which was his first color film and was meant to be funny—I remember seeing that and having a thought that I shouldn't have been proud of, which was, I'm funnier than Ingmar Bergman!

WS: I think you are!

RA: As in: He's trying to be funny, and I could definitely be funnier than this. But in interviews and things, he actually is quite funny. When he tells a story about himself, he's self-deprecating and funny. He obviously has access to it, but when he writes—wow, it's really, there's no levity. I suppose I've always liked things that are maybe both. I find it hard not to think about things in, if you want to say, a silly way. I think in Susan Sontag's "Notes on 'Camp,'" at a certain point in defining *camp* she says something like, "Seriousness failed."

WS: Right.

RA: And I think frequently I'll read something great, you know, by Chekhov or Harold Pinter, or I'll see an Ingmar Bergman film, and I'll think, Gosh, if I did this, it'd be ridiculous. I can imagine how a writer—a writer like Harauld Hughes, for example—might write something that aims for seriousness, something he hopes will get a serious reception, but within it there's a failure of some kind. For whatever reason I'm very interested in that. Maybe my impulse is to show the ways that such a writer might fall short of their aspirations, or that their aspirations might be misguided. In relation to my book—and I suppose it's often the case with comedy—comedy is often a bit of a grab bag of things: Here's some farcical stuff, here's some stuff that's maybe a bit more poignant, here's some stuff that's sort of more verbally ambitious, and here's something that's a parody.

WS: Well, this gets into the question of: What is believable? If you watch Arthur Miller's play *Death of a Salesman*, and you see Willy Loman trudging up the steps of his house, you know that that's something that happens in real life, and you can really believe it. You forget you're in an audience watching a play. You're lost in the illusion that you're watching real life. But in your book, you don't seem to want to create that sort of illusion for very long. If it's too naturalistic for too long, you become uncomfortable, and you make sure that some sort of really crazy thing occurs to pull the reader into a totally different realm of existence.

RA: Buster Keaton had a name for some of the things in his films—he called them "impossible gags"—where it'd be, I don't know, someone kicking him, and he falls all the way down a cliff, and then he gets up, and it's a surprise, and it's very, very funny.

WS: And it's great when Buster Keaton does that. But if that suddenly happened to Willy Loman as he climbed the steps to his house... Well, if you were in the audience, it would definitely break the illusion that you were watching a real event, and after that, I don't know—

RA: You'd care less, somehow.

WS: Yes, you might care less. And of course it's clear from your book that you're very drawn to parody, and, wow, you're great at it, which is super fun for the reader. But isn't there a danger with parody that the reader or the audience might care less—might care less about the characters because you're making fun of them?

RA: Well, in parody, there can actually be an intense love for the people you're parodying. In a parody, maybe the idea is that you start off with this slightly cartoonish version of the people, but then—I mean, for example, when I saw the movie *Spinal Tap*, I really ended up caring about the characters; I wanted the band to come back together. But the humor at the start was a way of sweetening the exposition and allowing me to go into a world that was maybe a bit inaccessible. The way into it maybe was through humor—through recognition; it's a gateway—but it didn't seem to stop me from feeling. In many ways maybe it made me feel more for them *because* they were ridiculous. And in fact, frequently I find myself *not* feeling for people in situations that are meant to be "real," because I can tell they're not real. When watching a film, I've never really thought, or not often, Am I watching something made-up, or is this real?

And you know, when I saw Mike Nichols in the film of *The Designated Mourner*, I somehow cared more about him because of how deft his timing was. And also just that face, that grin of his, and the way it seemed he could decide to be funny and then just do it. That somehow made me feel very safe. I felt safe being in his company. And I find that with Dave Chappelle sometimes. There's something about how certain he is that he will be funny that's quite calming. It gives you a sense of security. You go, OK…

WS: Well, they can do this very intimate thing to you, and you know it. You know that they can make you laugh. And for some reason that establishes a bond, and you feel safe with them. Their ability to be funny is of course first and foremost a protection for *them*, but it feels like it's a protection for you, too, for some reason, when you're watching them. I mean, to be sort of basic about it, if you're the comedian, and the audience is laughing, you feel that they're enjoying you. They're liking you, or liking what you do. The comedian is getting a lot more positive reinforcement than someone delivering a serious soliloquy. The person delivering the serious soliloquy isn't sure it's going over well, and that creates a lot of tension.

RA: Yes, I've started to think, Is the urge to be funny some kind of unwillingness to live in tension? You dissipate the tension by saying something funny or presenting a funny image. And something is shared with the audience then. You're saying, *Look at us: We both agree that this is ridiculous. We're seeing it the same way*, and there's an immediate point of connection, whereas if you say something serious, you're thinking, I don't know if we're seeing this the same way, because you just seem to be still. I'm not hearing any sound from you. It's been said that comedians are fundamentally inconsolable people who need constant reassurance.

WS: And of course someone who's being funny is by definition not being overly serious or self-important, so they can't really be mocked. And being mocked is the opposite of being reassured. But of course if you always have to be funny, that can be a restriction, and if you're willing to be mocked, that can give you a certain freedom. So, I mean, I've been mocked. I've been publicly mocked. I suppose I've never gotten over it, in a way, and I'm still upset about it, but it didn't kill me.

For you, though, as a writer, you're funny in part because you have a very keen ear for what's fake or insincere or forced, and you don't want to get anywhere near anything like that. And also I think you have a strong resistance to creating the sort of hermetically sealed, perfectly consistent "realistic" illusion that supposedly "serious" novels or plays usually aspire to.

RA: When I'm watching something, I love the feeling of participating in the thing that's being made in front of me. I enjoy knowing that it's being made and seeing that made-ness, I think. I suppose at some level I'm after an acknowledgment that the people onstage in a play, for example, are making something up. Sometimes I feel that if I don't get that acknowledgment, I'm on red alert. I'm

---

ANATOMICAL EUPHEMISMS IN JAMES JOYCE'S *ULYSSES*

★ Plump mellow yellow smellow melons
★ Plump melonous hemispheres
★ Mellow yellow furrow
★ Manflower
★ Limp father of thousands
★ Languid floating flower
★ Naughty nightstalk
★ Nun rusty from the dew
★ Haw haw horn
★ The milky way
★ That weapon with knobs and lumps and warts all over it
★ Clotted hinderparts
★ Tube

—*list compiled by Chase Bush-McLaughlin*

like, OK, you've really set yourself up for a fall here, because I know you're pretending, and I feel like, Why would you pretend that you're not pretending? Why do you expect me to forget that?

WS: The producer character in your book says that he doesn't like naturalism in theater, because he's always thinking, Why are they pretending we can't see them? He prefers kung fu films. And with parody it's always clear that the actors or the author is not pretending to be invisible at all.

RA: I sometimes wonder whether parody isn't almost like an extreme form of fan fiction, where you like something so much that you want to kind of sit inside it to somehow extend the experience, while acknowledging that you can't do yourself what the people you're parodying can do. When Woody Allen does his Fellini parody, he's saying, *Obviously I'm not Fellini, but I like him so much I just want to sit in Fellini's world a bit. And of course I know that's funny; I know that's a silly thing to do.*

WS: I suppose I feel something related to what you feel, or what the producer in your book feels, because in writing a play, it never feels right to me to begin the play with an empty room and then have characters come into it and talk to each other. That doesn't feel believable to me. My plays have almost always begun with somebody speaking to the audience, acknowledging that they're an audience. Of course I know that that is utterly artificial, because they're reciting a speech, a previously written, memorized speech, but somehow I can believe it.

RA: Yes, when my wife, Lydia, and I saw your play *Evening at the Talk House*, I found that the immediate address relaxed me—well, maybe *relaxed* is the wrong word, but I immediately felt, Oh, I'm in some way being met. And maybe there's something in comedy or with comedians where, more often than not, they're acknowledging the audience, even when they're doing sketches. Maybe that's why people like sketches so much, and they so quickly start laughing, because it's like, Yeah, you're here, we're here, we're all here. There's an acknowledgment of presence.

You know, I've been thinking an awful lot recently about Roy Andersson.

WS: Now, who is this?

RA: Roy Andersson, who did *Songs from the Second Floor.*

WS: I'll be damned. I don't know Roy.

RA: Yes, he's a Swedish filmmaker, and his films are really funny, but there's something in them that goes deeper. The films are largely in tableaux, and there are scenes where very often you're presented with characters who've been in some sort of prior relationship with each other, but through his skill in casting and staging you almost immediately get a sense of where they're at without the normal narrative of *Oh, OK, I saw this person betray that person earlier, so now I can look at this scene in such and such a way.* There's an immediate tension just from people's positioning.

WS: Really.

RA: Within the scene, often there's like a small turn, and it's very—I mean, it's so hard to describe what he does, it's so original. I'd almost say that everything that is said is funny, but there's an incredible vulnerability in it. And I wonder if there's something to be said for work that doesn't push too hard, work that just distills what things are like.

WS: Yes...

RA: And now I'm so flooded by images from his films that I almost can't think.

WS: I'm going to rent these films as quickly as I can.

RA: He presents a number of things that are, in the Buster Keaton sense, "impossible"—an apartment that moves off on railway tracks, a couple flying through the air, a man who is actually cut in half during a magic act, outlandish ritual executions, everyone has this similar gray-white ghoulish pallor, but he keeps a sense of great emotion, of something that is truthful even though it might not be realistic. So maybe Roy is the key!

WS: Did Buster Keaton and Ingmar Bergman have a secret affair and give birth to a son? ✱

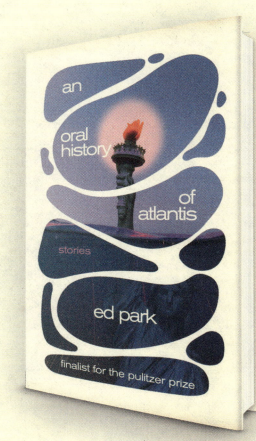

THE HAUNTING OF PENNHURST

CONTRADICTION AND FEAR AT AMERICA'S ONLY PHYSICAL MUSEUM OF DISABILITY

BY **OLIVER EGGER**

DISCUSSED: *Pennhurst State School and Hospital, Paranormal Investigations, Autism, Eugenics, Dr. Henry H. Goddard,* Suffer the Little Children, *Roland Johnson, Demon-Auctioneer, Limerick,* Speaking for Ourselves, *The Pennsylvania Historical and Museum Commission, Nathaniel Guest, The Halderman Verdict, A Moldy Baby Doll, The US Haunt Industry, Randy Bates, Bloody Straitjackets,* Lost in a Desert World, *A Doghouse*

OPENING ILLUSTRATION BY:
Andrea Settimo

PHOTOGRAPHS THROUGHOUT BY:
Anabel DeMartino

I arrived at Pennhurst on an unusually warm fall day. As I walked across the parking lot, the administration building was the first thing to greet me. An impressive redbrick monument of Jacobean revivalism, it towered over the rest of the campus. The midday sun struck its copper cupola like a spotlight. A flight of stairs, sheltered by an intricately carved granite awning, led to thick wooden doors. It was a statement of power, of permanence.

Huddled around it was a series of smaller but similarly designed buildings in various states of disrepair—rootlike cracks crawled across their facades, and plywood was stuffed into the gaping jaws of their window frames. At the center of the campus was a large field, empty except for a metal slide and a swing-less swing set that lay bent and rusted in the freshly cut grass.

The administration building, nine other dilapidated structures, and around 120 acres of land are all that is left of the formerly grand and ever-infamous Pennhurst State School and Hospital. From 1908 until 1987, this Pennsylvania state institution, located in Spring City, less than an hour outside Philadelphia, incarcerated and often abused over ten thousand inmates. Most of those held there were people with intellectual and developmental disabilities, whom the institution initially labeled as "feeble-minded," and, later, "mentally retarded." Today, the remnants of its once-1,400-acre campus have been repurposed into Pennhurst Asylum, a multimillion-dollar Halloween attraction that brings tens of thousands of guests each year to be scared, as advertised, "to the limits of [their] sanity."

For six weeks every fall, over a hundred employees—including performers, makeup artists, costume designers, security guards, and line wranglers—descend on Pennhurst to transform this century-old campus into a professional horror operation. Pennhurst Asylum offers four attractions, but its central feature and namesake is "The Asylum," a haunted walk inside the imposing administration building. Visitors are led through its peeling halls, where the horrors of medical violence quite literally jump out at them. Performers in torn and blood-smeared lab coats, scrubs, and gowns leap out at guests from under operating tables and creep behind them to tickle the backs of their necks. A cacophony of screams fills the building as visitors stumble through the fog-filled dark, where nightmarish scenes—an operating theater in which a rusty blade saws into an exposed brain; a cramped room full of bile-covered patients chained to their beds, howling for their parents—greet them at every turn.

By day, however, Pennhurst Asylum's focus is not on fear, but memorialization. In addition to its attractions, the company owns and operates the Pennhurst Museum, currently America's only physical museum of disability history. Located in Mayflower Hall, a former residential ward adjacent to the administration building, the museum claims to document the same dark history of institutionalization that the attraction's nightly performances caricature as entertainment.

Soon I would get to experience the haunted halls of "The Asylum" for myself, but the beginning of my day at Pennhurst was much less scary: I milled about in a crowd of eighty visitors in sweat-stained T-shirts as we waited for the museum to open and the history tour to begin. Shielding myself from the sun under a swaying, still-green oak, I found it hard to imagine Pennhurst's evening persona. A pair of sisters wearing matching witch hats and black-and-orange-striped leggings played tag in a field. An old couple nursed bottles of lukewarm Dasani in the shade. A family took selfies in front of a dilapidated building.

But there were hints of the horrors to come: a sound check of eerie music floated over from the administration building, and signs warned guests about the dangers of strobe lights. The visitors flipped through books and eyed merch at the pop-up gift shop. One T-shirt featured a simple outline of the administration building and the words PENNHURST STATE school in clean blue block letters, while another depicted a ghostly white face and beneath it the words I SURVIVED PENNHURST ASYLUM scribbled in dripping blood.

Directing the cars in the parking lot was the museum's unlikely director: a twenty-three-year-old recent college graduate named Autumn Werner. With the expertise of a veteran air traffic controller, she answered my questions cheerfully while directing drivers where to park and speaking cryptic instructions into her walkie-talkie.

Autumn grew up nearby and spent her childhood on the Pennhurst property; her father, Jim Werner, was hired there first as a performer (or "haunter") in 2012 and became the operations manager in 2016. Autumn joined the company the year of her father's promotion, when she was just fifteen, as a makeup artist and haunter. Though she now performs only on occasion, she hasn't completely abandoned haunting for history: In addition to managing the museum as the company's history coordinator, she acts as the lead makeup director for the attraction. Later that night, I watched her expertly airbrush leprosy lesions and streaks of blood onto a demented nurse.

While Autumn acknowledges the possible contradictions of running a disability history museum by day while working at a Halloween attraction on the same property by night, she insists that her priority is to honor the lives of those who suffered at Pennhurst. Autumn, like many of the haunters I spoke with, believes it is a sacred place inhabited by the spirits of its former inmates, which she is responsible for protecting. She tells guests on ghost-hunting tours (or, as the company refers to them, "paranormal investigations"), which she runs year-round, that "you have to be nice to our ghosts... If you hear a growl or grunt, it's probably not a demon trying to eat you. It is likely a nonverbal person trying to communicate with you."

Autumn's connection with disability is not superficial: She has Ehlers-Danlos syndrome, a genetic disorder affecting connective tissue that causes chronic pain (and that also allows her to dislocate her joints to contort her arms forward while crawling on all fours—one of her signature moves when she used to haunt). In addition, she is a caregiver for her two younger sisters, who have autism.

For Autumn, this personal connection is important, and she attests that it's also what makes the attraction unique; many of the haunters identify as disabled themselves: Her estimate is 60 to 70 percent. This fact transforms Pennhurst for Autumn. Instead of seeing the attraction as a place that callously perpetuates harmful stereotypes, she sees it as a refuge where disabled people can find work, opportunities, and a close community they likely won't be afforded anywhere else.

Pennhurst was founded in 1908 as the Eastern Pennsylvania Institution for the Feeble-Minded and Epileptic. Even though its current owners call it Pennhurst Asylum, the institution never went by that name; instead, for most of its history it was referred to as a "State School and Hospital" and, in the last few years before its closure, as "Pennhurst Center." Historically, asylums were institutions for people with mental illness who, once they improved, had a pathway back into the community. These "state schools," on the other hand, were essentially prisons, founded on a false eugenicist belief that intellectually and developmentally disabled people had a propensity for violent crimes and therefore should be indefinitely segregated from society and kept from reproducing. (While there is no evidence of sterilization taking place at Pennhurst, dozens of its sister institutions, from California to Virginia, relied on this ideology to justify sterilizing thousands of inmates without their consent.) Pennhurst's 1918 semiannual report to the Pennsylvania legislature included a quote from leading American eugenicist Dr. Henry H. Goddard: "Every feeble-minded person is a potential criminal."

Throughout its history, Pennhurst's "inmates," as the institution officially labeled the people held there, were subjected to unsafe medical experimentation, sexual assault, forced labor, and lifelong incarceration. The campus was chronically overcrowded and understaffed; in 1957, when the institution reached its peak population, there were 3,869 inmates housed in spaces designed for only 2,800. The practices at Pennhurst likely resulted in thousands of preventable deaths.

In the introduction to *Suffer the Little Children*, a 1968 television documentary that brought national attention to the conditions at Pennhurst, CBS correspondent Bill Baldini sums up the horrific treatment: "Zoos spend more on their wild animals than Pennsylvania spends on its… patients at Pennhurst." In 1972, the local Pottstown paper, *The Mercury*, called the institution "the shame of Pennsylvania." (Its infamy lives on: Pennhurst is also the name of a fictional mental hospital in season four of *Stranger Things*.)

The attention brought to Pennhurst's cruelties and the reckoning it inspired ultimately became linchpins for local and national change. One of the key figures in this fight for justice was Roland Johnson, an activist who is sometimes referred to as "the MLK of the disability rights movement." Johnson, who was born with an intellectual disability, was sent to Pennhurst in 1958 at the age of twelve. Over the thirteen years he was incarcerated there, he was subjected to abject racism and abuse by the staff and his fellow inmates alike. For nights on end, he was bullied and raped by higher-functioning older inmates, from which he contracted HIV. He told his parents and the staff—but nothing changed. In his despair, he lashed out and broke the windows in his ward, which led to him being locked in a punishment hall, where he was forced to scrub soiled beds, benches, and walls.

At the perpetually understaffed institution, Johnson was required to act as a ward attendant for lower-functioning patients, feeding, bathing, and changing their diapers and soiled sheets. He was never paid for his labor, but was instead given Pennhurst tokens, which could be used to buy coffee, doughnuts, or other snacks from the canteen.

Johnson was one of the inmates interviewed in *Suffer the Little Children*, and soon after, in 1971, he was released from Pennhurst, at the age of twenty-six. After spending several years shuffling between boardinghouses, and a run-in with the law, Johnson joined Speaking for Ourselves, a Pennsylvania-based self-advocacy organization. A concept that first gained prominence during the disability rights movement in the late 1960s and early 1970s, self-advocacy encouraged intellectually and developmentally disabled people to make their own decisions about their care and lives. At the first Speaking for Ourselves meeting that Johnson attended, in the early '80s, he was so inspired that he rose from his seat and declared, "We have to make some changes!... We're tired of the old system!"

He became a regular presence at the organization and was soon elected the president of its Philadelphia chapter. He gained a reputation for his rousing speeches, which he gave across the state, country, and beyond, inspiring disabled people to become self-advocates. Debbie Robinson, the current executive director of Speaking for Ourselves and a close friend and mentee of Johnson's, said his speeches reminded her of MLK's and Gandhi's: "When Roland speaks, people listen. He pulled us in." Johnson would begin each speech with the same mantra: "Who's in control?," to which the crowd would call out in response, "We are!"

Before his death in 1994, Johnson helped expand Speaking for Ourselves to national prominence, and, with other disabled activists, founded the first national self-advocacy organization, Self Advocates Becoming Empowered. On July 26, 1990, when President George H. W. Bush signed the Americans with Disabilities Act, Johnson was there, on the South Lawn of the White House, as part of a delegation of disability rights advocates.

Johnson's advocacy proved central to Pennhurst's closure in 1987. He and other inmates' testimonies of chronic abuse helped spur the landmark lawsuit *Pennhurst State School and Hospital v. Halderman*, which, in 1984, declared forced institutionalization of persons with disabilities unconstitutional and granted residents of Pennhurst the right to habilitation free from harm. This anticipated not only the closure of Pennhurst but also the nationwide—and ongoing—transition of tens of thousands of the intellectually and developmentally disabled out of state institutions and into local communities, where they could choose to live independently or in group homes.

The Pennhurst Museum is open only on Saturdays and accessible with the purchase of a forty-five-dollar history package ticket. Autumn told me they used to also open it up in the evenings to people who were there for the haunt experience, but a series of incidents, such as guests defecating in the hallways and stealing artifacts, put an end to that. As she explained, "They're here for a scare. They're not here to learn history."

Every history tour is led by a company-trained historian. My tour leader was Joey Vanderloop, a nonbinary person wearing yellow-tinted sunglasses and a shawl adorned with goggling eyeballs. They told me they are likely on the autism spectrum and have a chronic pain disorder.

When I first met Vanderloop, who lives in nearby Spring City, they shifted

A view of the central room in the Quaker Building at the Pennhurst Museum.

back and forth on their feet and nervously laughed as I asked them about their life. But their anxiety evaporated as they shared their passion for the horror genre, which first brought them to Pennhurst as a visitor nearly a decade ago.

After a few visits, they wanted to see behind the mask, literally, and applied and were hired as a haunter for the 2021 season. They soon became enthralled, not only by the horror, but by Pennhurst's history, and for the past three years have served as a tour guide. (They still haunt; later that night I watched them transform under a blood-smeared suit and a steampunk bunny mask. Beneath their mask, which had a microphone inside it that distorted their voice into something describable only as "demon-auctioneer," they oozed self-confidence.)

While Vanderloop said they understand why people might be offended by the attraction, they believe this reaction sometimes comes from a place of ignorance. According to Vanderloop, the haunted attraction has kept the buildings from being razed and turned into condos—and thus enabled the preservation of Pennhurst's memory in the history tours and museum, while also fostering community among the disabled employees.

It was not until they started working at Pennhurst and found themselves around so many other disabled people that they realized there was nothing to be ashamed about in being disabled. The experience led them to seek medical help for the first time in their life.

They also see the act of haunting as a way of "taking the power back," because in a world where people have been taught to be afraid of people with disabilities, inside the attraction the disabled haunter has the upper hand. As Vanderloop said, breaking into a smile, "You're afraid of people like me? All right—scream."

Vanderloop gathered the tour group outside the administration building. "Who here knows what eugenics is?" Vanderloop began, scanning the crowd's faces. Roughly half the people raised their hands. "About average," they said, before launching into a detailed and unsparing explanation of the history of the early twentieth-century American eugenics movement, including Pennhurst's place in it.

Vanderloop appeared small beneath the looming doors of the building. These were the doors that every inmate passed through on their first day at Pennhurst. Most would never leave. As Vanderloop spoke, a sound, somewhere between a hardcore punk guitar solo and a wraith's wail, emerged from inside the building. They didn't skip a beat. "We purposefully put our haunted attraction in this building, in the basement, and in a couple of tunnels surrounding the building because… [those places] never actually housed someone with disabilities." They added, "We did that as a mark of respect to the people living here." (I assume they meant "the people who lived here"—there was a consistent blurring of past and present throughout the tour.)

Vanderloop continued to trace Pennhurst's depraved history as they led us past the administration building and around the exteriors of other buildings, which had once served as residential halls, recreation areas, and cafeterias, and bore large red plaques with their names: LIMERICK, PENNSYLVANIA, and INDUSTRY. While the buildings were quite dilapidated—their porches were overgrown with weeds, and bricks were crumbling away like loose teeth—I knew how rare it was for the buildings to be standing at all. There has been no comprehensive effort to memorialize America's hundreds of former state institutions. The majority have either been converted into jails, apartments, hospitals, or parks, or left abandoned for decades, often without first removing confidential patient records, until they collapse on their own. In 2020, after a lack of funding shuttered the Museum of disABILITY History in Buffalo, New York, Pennhurst gained the depressing distinction of being not just the only museum of a former state institution for the disabled, but also the only physical museum of disability in the United States. (The Museum of disABILITY still operates a virtual museum and recently announced it is reopening in late fall of this year at the Kornreich Institute for Disability Studies at the Viscardi Center on Long Island, in New York.)

As the tour progressed, Vanderloop's voice grew urgent and serious as they told stories of inmates forced to lie in adult-sized cribs day in and day out for years; of mothers who sued the state for custody of their children and failed; and of inmates forced to do hours upon hours of unpaid labor, from caring for other patients to farming under the blistering sun. Vanderloop continually referred to the institution in the first-person plural, as if they themselves were a former inmate: "We had to work very hard" and "We had our factory here," they said, pointing to the ruins of a building on a hill in the distance.

They led us into Quaker Hall, a former ward for low-functioning inmates, which appeared totally untouched since its abandonment. Dusty foam couches and cracked bathtubs lay scattered across the floor, electrical wires hung like ripped guts from the ceiling, and a slash of red graffiti on a stone wall read WE DIE YOU PROFIT. Standing before a large, shattered window, Vanderloop said, "Sixty to 70 percent of our staff identifies as disabled… We are disabled-run and disabled-operated. [Pennhurst] was designed to kill people like us! And right now we're running the place!" A few people clapped. As we exited the building, a crumbled sign on the doorway explained the rules for the company's paranormal investigations: NO CANDLES, DYBBUK BOXES, OR OUIJA BOARDS.

Following the *Halderman* verdict, Pennhurst was shut down in 1987. Three years prior to its closure, the Pennsylvania Historical and Museum Commission (PHMC) deemed the campus eligible for the National Register of Historic Places, a designation that mandates that the state government is responsible for the upkeep of the campus and cannot sell the property without consulting the commission.

While hundreds of acres of the campus were repurposed (for a VA hospital and a country club), the lower section of the property, once known as "the boys' colony," was abandoned for decades, caught in various legal battles and proposals for reuse. Left to the elements and overrun by urban explorers, ghost hunters, and vandals, the buildings, according to Pennhurst preservation advocate Nathaniel Guest, suffered three hundred million dollars' worth of damage. Many were torn down or succumbed to ruin.

In 2008, the state of Pennsylvania, after failing to consult the PHMC, sold over 110 acres of the dilapidated property to real estate developer Richard Chakejian and his associate Tim Smith for two million dollars. After determining that their initial plan to tear down all the buildings for a residential property was unlikely to turn a profit, Chakejian and Smith decided to make use of the buildings and turn Pennhurst into a haunted attraction. (The US haunt industry brings in between three hundred and five hundred million dollars in ticket sales annually, and there are many other prominent haunts at historical asylums, including the Trans-Allegheny Lunatic Asylum in West Virginia and the Brighton Asylum in New Jersey.)

The owners partnered with Randy Bates, who founded the successful Bates Motel and Haunted Hayride in nearby Glen Mills, Pennsylvania, to design and manage Pennhurst Asylum, which opened its doors in the fall of 2010. It was a quick success; the company reportedly had over seventeen thousand visitors and grossed nearly one million dollars in its first season.

In those early years, the attraction's "museum" consisted of a haphazard array of objects placed throughout the queue line in the first few rooms of the administration building. Historical photographs and footage, including the infamous 1968 documentary, were projected on the walls. In the hallways between rooms, monitors played a looped video of an actor dressed as a patient pounding on a window and screaming for help.

In a 2010 blog post about the construction of the attraction, Bates described the design of the museum as the way to intentionally blur the line between where the historical horror ended and the fictional one began.

The haunt itself, which included both a lobotomy operation and a shock therapy room, actively played off Pennhurst's history. The attraction's initial storyline was that Pennhurst had been overtaken by an unhinged brain surgeon (named Dr. Chakejian, after the site's owner), who was conducting grotesque medical experiments that included, according to an archived version of the Pennhurst Asylum website, "psycho surgery… body suspension, light deprivation, and intense drug therapy." Guests were cast in the roles of newly admitted patients being led through each of these unique torments.

Throughout the haunt, actors explicitly mimicked those with disabilities, and historic items from Pennhurst were used as props and scene decoration. In his blog post, Bates describes searching the campus with his crew and finding "a veritable treasure trove of props for our attraction" including surgical lights, operating tables, wheelchairs, medical cabinets, and cups and trays from the former cafeteria. He describes harvesting objects from Pennhurst's former morgue for the morgue-themed room in the attraction: "Stainless steel tables with large drains, stainless steel cabinets, lab equipment and a real, 1930's autopsy table!… I can picture the thousands of customers coming through our attraction knowing that everything in here is REAL. My arms have gooseflesh!"

Despite the attraction's success, by 2014 the company's mortgage went into foreclosure after Smith used the property as collateral to take out a series of risky loans. In 2016, Pennhurst Asylum's property and assets were purchased from the bank by three investors—Derek Strine, Todd Beringer, and Matt Herzog—who bought out the final year of Bates's management contract and fired the remaining leadership team.

The new management, led in part by Jim Werner, has toned down some of the most offensive aspects of the attraction by removing all the historic objects associated with disability from the haunt and mandating sensitivity training for haunters, which instructs them not to mimic those with disabilities. They also moved the museum from the administration building into Mayflower Hall, opening to the public in 2018. During Autumn's time as manager, which began two years later, the museum's artifacts collection expanded from one room to the entire first floor, and staff, such as Vanderloop, were hired and trained to serve as history guides.

After an hour of trekking through the campus, Vanderloop led us into the museum. The cold, damp stone walls of the former residential ward dried the sweat on my forehead. At the end of a mold-stained hallway was a small room bursting with hundreds of objects: patient records, bent wheelchairs, rusted bed frames, photographs of Pennhurst's former baseball teams, helmets, syringes, a wicker stroller with a moldy baby doll inside, bars of pink soap, and a snapshot of Elvis. Some items were in glass cases, while others lay on tables or leaned against walls. Nearly everything was dusted in a thin layer of dirt and flakes of ceiling plaster. There seemed to be no order to the

Autumn Werner (right) putting face makeup on a haunter, who plays the part of "Nurse Betty."

objects' placement. There was no mention of what era in the institution's history each of these objects came from, and no written descriptions of what they were.

Propped against the wall by the entrance was a painting, torn into three strips, that I assumed was done by a former inmate. It depicted a large brown cross with two smaller ones flanking it, rising from rolling turquoise hills. The crosses stood against a sky of total black. The right corner of the image was signed "By Sarah."

Inside one smudged glass display case, I saw dozens of documents recording one woman's entire life, from her admittance when she was a child to her death, inside the institution: her birth certificate, medication reports, letters to her family on her care, illness reports, and a death certificate. I later learned that many of the objects on display, including some inmate records, were left behind after Pennhurst closed and were then gathered by Autumn and her fellow haunters. Other artifacts were purchased by the museum from eBay (confidential records and items from former institutions are frequently resold online as novelty decorations).

Directly adjacent to this room was another space, hardly larger than a closet, which was piled with random items: a brown rusted fan, pastel-colored classroom chairs, typewriters with the keys broken off. It was not clear if this was storage or part of the museum.

Presiding over the scene was a ninety-year-old woman named Bernidine Essick. She leaned up against her walker and wore a PENNHURST ASYLUM 2020 T-shirt with an image of a coughing demon with a head in the shape of a coronavirus. Essick was born in nearby Pottsville, where she lived until her passing earlier this year, a few months after we met. She was a nurse's aide, or what she referred to with a sardonic laugh as a "sanitary engineer," on the second floor of this very building from 1971 to 1987 and had volunteered at the museum for the past six years. (Behind one of the glass cases, I spotted a 1977 "Pennhurst Certificate of Appreciation" made out to Essick.) She was eager to describe to me and the rest of the tour the terrible conditions and mistreatment of inmates at Pennhurst, while simultaneously insisting that she and her fellow employees did their best with the limited resources they had.

Essick was not particularly upset by Pennhurst's second life as a haunted attraction, because it was leading people to learn about the institution's history. What really bothered her was coming back to see the state of the campus after its decades of abandonment. "We had beautiful grounds here, the flowers and everything else, beautiful. And the buildings were pristine, they really were. And [when] I drove [back onto the Pennhurst campus], I thought, Oh my God, it's like jungle city."

The crowd began to shuffle into the museum's second room, an equally dark, dusty, and alabaster-flaked hall that contained re-creations of various areas inside the institution: a residential room, a hospital room, a cafeteria, a barbershop, and a laundry room. In the far corner was a pile of over fifty wheelchairs, restraint chairs, and crutches, all in various stages of being consumed by rust. While this section was more organized than the previous room, there were still no written explanations.

Essick called all the visitors over and we gathered in a semicircle around her. Over the next thirty minutes, she told us a string of graphic stories about "her boys" at Pennhurst: Elmer, John, Louie, Neil, and Joey. Nearly every story was about the inmates being covered in or throwing excrement or vomit.

In one such story, she said, "[Neil] was blind, and I see him feel his way down to bed, and there's two drawers at the bottom. He pulls [open] the drawer and takes something out, but… I can't see what it is, so when he comes out the door… I grab it. Big mistake. It was a solid-packed sock, full of poop. It was slimy, it was wet, it was stinking, and it's in my hand." As she spoke, her rapt audience cringed in disgust and mouthed, "Jesus" and "Wow" to one another. "And we didn't have rubber gloves at Pennhurst!" Essick cried, lifting a trembling hand from her walker and holding it out toward us. Gasps rose from the listeners. I stared at a glass box full of toys: teddy bears, plastic cars, and alphabet blocks—discolored and gray. Shaking their heads, the crowd shuffled out of the museum and into the sudden brightness of the day.

It's not as though the conversion from abandoned historical site to haunted attraction happened without a fight. The Pennhurst Memorial and Preservation Alliance (PMPA), an organization made up of scholars, disabled people, and former employees, was created in 2008, just days after the entire Pennhurst lower campus was sold for two million dollars. Its goal was to preserve the site and build a formal museum.

The PMPA's current president is James Conroy, a scruffy academic who, from 1979 to 1985, led the influential "Pennhurst Longitudinal Study," which followed inmates who had been released from Pennhurst, and found that the vast majority had a better quality of life in comparison with their institutionalized counterparts. Conroy, who continues to study the impacts of deinstitutionalization, believes the attraction is deeply disrespectful: "Would you have a haunted house at Birkenau?" The PMPA led zoning hearings, wrote critical op-eds, protested, and considered potential lawsuits, but for naught. "We couldn't stop it; we failed," he said. To this day, a petition on the PMPA website states that it is "completely opposed to the… haunted attraction at Pennhurst," and instructs its supporters to "boycott this travesty."

However, in recent years, the PMPA's combativeness toward Pennhurst Asylum has begun to lessen. This is because of Nathan Stenberg, a scholar with cerebral palsy, and the current director of disability at John Hopkins, who has researched the disabled haunters at Pennhurst since 2018 and, in 2023, submitted his dissertation on the topic.

In his work and writing, Stenberg straddles the line between the academic standards of traditional memorialization and the spirit embodied by Pennhurst's scrappy community of haunters. He was, until recently, a board member of the PMPA, but he has also worked with Pennhurst Asylum to help it alter some of the most offensive aspects of the attraction, has participated as a haunter himself, and occasionally leads history tours.

Stenberg told me he rejects how the site has become defined through a moral language, whereby typical memorialization efforts led by often able-bodied academics are seen as righteous, while the haunted attraction staffed by disabled haunters is seen as distasteful, if not shameful. Stenberg argues that this narrative erases the disabled people who have found a community at Pennhurst Asylum, receive employment and wages through this job (in 2023, 7.2 percent of disabled Americans were unemployed, nearly double the rate of the nondisabled), and are able to commemorate their history on their own non-normative terms. He is also frustrated by how standard memorialization demarcates institutionalization as a thing of the past, rather than an ongoing experience. (Today, sixteen thousand people with intellectual or developmental disabilities remain in state-operated institutions, a significant number, though a far cry from the nearly two hundred thousand who were warehoused during institutionalization's peak, in the late 1960s.)

Stenberg met Conroy through his research, and in 2020 he took him to the Pennhurst campus, where Conroy was brought to tears while speaking to the disabled haunters. What has followed has been a tense, unofficial alliance between the PMPA and the attraction. The PMPA loaned a series of panels with Pennhurst's timeline to the museum. (These were tucked away in a distant, entirely unlit room. On my tour, no one except me saw them.) It also started a history fellowship to support a haunter-historian. Unsurprisingly, Autumn was the inaugural fellow.

Conroy described the relationship between the two organizations as a double-edged sword, but said his uneasiness is worth it for the chance that some of the attraction's fifty thousand annual guests will leave with knowledge of what Pennhurst truly was. When discussing the disabled haunters, such as Autumn and Vanderloop, Conroy speaks of them in a tone of disbelief. They are "passionate defenders of the sanctity of the place," he said, "even though they go there and act like monsters."

As the last light of day illuminated the somber green of the administration building's cupola, a stream of haunters, security guards, and operations employees poured onto the campus. They entered Limerick Hall, another former residential ward directly mirroring Mayflower Hall on the opposite side of the administration building, to get ready. Chappell Roan's "Pink Pony Club" blared from a speaker as the haunters, of all ages and races, laughed, chatted, and drank Monster Energy drinks and Red Bull while the costume and makeup crew bound them into their bloody straitjackets, fastened their bare-brain caps, and painted oozing sores on their foreheads. When I forgot about the eerie institutional walls towering around me, the scene felt like the backstage before any other production—jitters, snacks, and camaraderie.

Of the over twenty haunters I spoke with, some of them identified as disabled, but it was impossible to verify whether they were in the majority, as Autumn had told me. While most, but not all, of the performers told me they had participated in the supposedly required sensitivity training—which instructs them not to mimic those with disabilities in their performances—few had visited the museum, and most knew little about the history. No one, disabled or not, told me they'd applied for the position with the site's history in mind, but rather because, as one blood-drenched nurse told me, she was "a theater kid in high school," or, as a half scarecrow, half devil shared, because "it was near my house."

However, several disabled haunters did tell me that Pennhurst's history had come to play a large role in how they approached their performances. One such haunter, Bee Hulko, an eighteen-year-old autistic puppeteer (of a massive multi-eyed demon they'd named Lucielle), told me that, like Autumn, they believe the presence of the spirits of past inmates informs their work. Far from recapitulating harm, they said, the act of performing is a way to honor the inmates by showing that disabled people are not the broken and incapable pests that Pennhurst saw them as.

A LIST OF HISTORICAL NAMES FOR (LITERAL) BOOKWORMS

✭ "Worst enemy of the Muses"—Evenus of Paros, poetic fragment, fifth-century BCE
✭ "Ore tineae"—Ovid, *Epistulae ex Ponto*, first century CE
✭ The "stealing guest"—Unknown, Exeter Book Riddle 47, late tenth century CE
✭ The "teeth of the time"—Robert Hooke, *Micrographia*, 1665
✭ "Enemy of books"—William Blades, *Enemies of Books*, 1880
✭ "Puny, rankling reptiles"—John F. M. Dovaston, "The Cure for Bookworms," 1800s

—*list compiled by Jonathan Truong*

"Here I am, bright as day," Hulko said, "ready to go ram a puppet into people's faces and start screaming at them."

The Pennhurst Asylum's operations team itself was divided on how much the attraction plays on the real history of Pennhurst. Autumn, as well as her father, said it no longer exploits medical violence, and claims it is science-fiction-themed. But considering what I saw later that night—patients bound in electroshock therapy chairs with massive plugs stabbed into their exposed brains, mutilated corpses laid out on metal racks in a hospital morgue, and a man in a lab coat sneaking up behind me to ask, "Can I do some little experiments on you?"—I can attest that this is untrue.

Derek Strine, one of Pennhurst's three owners, was more forthright, saying that, for the attraction to be financially successful, it has to engage with themes of medical violence and institutionalization that are of course related to Pennhurst's actual history. (The other two owners, Matt Herzog and Todd Beringer, did not respond to repeated requests for comment.) Strine, a successful real estate investor based in Florida, says that those who complain that the attraction capitalizes on or makes fun of the suffering of disabled people are "not that thoughtful." From his perspective, the critics don't see the attraction as a form of entertainment that simply engages with Pennhurst's history. Instead, they claim that "we [the owners] caused the mistreatment of some of the residents… How can I change what was done [at Pennhurst]?" He added, "It's like saying, *You as a white male enslaved Black people*. My forebears came from Germany and mined slate, so we didn't have any slaves. So that… doesn't stick—I'm sorry."

Costume designer Cosimo Mariano, who has worked at Pennhurst Asylum on and off since its opening in 2010, had a similar response, saying that there is no way the site-specific attraction could or should avoid touching on Pennhurst's dark past. To Mariano, it is an artistic pursuit that shouldn't be censored, and if people find it offensive, they simply shouldn't come. He added, "I don't like square dancing, so I won't go square dancing."

Mariano said the outrage and negative press throughout the years has done nothing but draw bigger crowds. He compared it to Salem, Massachusetts, saying, "The very place Puritans were drowning people to try to keep out witches… ended up with more actual witches per capita probably than anywhere else in the country."

Strine's and Mariano's perspectives, albeit blunt, felt the most honest with regard to what I had seen since arriving. They understood that the attraction draws crowds because of, not in spite of, the real-life atrocities that happened at Pennhurst. And Pennhurst is thereby obliged to give the crowd what they paid for: an experience that captures our collective cultural fear of these abusive institutions and that, in turn, may further stoke prejudiced beliefs about and fear of the disabled people who were incarcerated in them.

Dennis Downey, a former board member of the PMPA and a professor emeritus of history at Millersville University, disagrees with Stenberg's, Autumn's, and the other haunters' claims that this attraction can really be a site of reclamation. "Frankly, it's a commercial operation and makes several million dollars," he said. "Those funds do not go to the survivors, many of whom are still around." None of the three owners openly identify as disabled. (Strine refused to share the attraction's current profits but said that it was profitable. In the 2024 season, haunters made fourteen dollars an hour.)

There is no outward-facing presentation or marketing by the company that emphasizes Pennhurst's history or its disabled staff. There is nothing online recommending that disabled people apply for positions. Nothing even about the accessibility of the attraction. Which, during my visit, required squeezing through tight corridors and climbing up and down multiple flights of stairs in near total darkness.

Alex Green, a lecturer at Harvard Kennedy School and a disability rights advocate, believes that Pennhurst is using the fact that it hires disabled people to "cover the parts of what they're doing that are really reprehensible," he said, adding, "If this were really empowering disabled people, [the horror tours] would not play on so many of the most egregious tropes that have historically led to violence against [them]. Let's not conflate the money with the values."

To Green, the arguments made by the haunters with disabilities and Stenberg felt reminiscent of those made by showmen, carnies, and performers about the benefits of freak shows for the "freaks" themselves. These shows, which operated from the nineteenth into the twentieth century, displayed people with physical ailments to be

Rows of costumes, including dirty straitjackets and bloody gowns, in Limerick Hall's costume room, managed by Cosimo Mariano.

gawked at in traveling exhibitions or in museums. Due to the proliferation of unsightly beggar ordinances, today often known as "ugly laws," which made it illegal for people with a visible disability to be seen in public, these shows became one of the only consistent sources of employment for those with physical disabilities. While now seen as deeply exploitative, the shows were often vehemently defended by the performers themselves. Harvey Boswell, a freak show operator and paraplegic, wrote in the 1950s, "I'm stared at but it doesn't bother me. Nor does it bother the freaks when they are stared at on their way to the bank to deposit… $100, $150, $200, and even $500 per week."

Green also stressed to me that the haunters who are reclaiming this space are unlikely to have experienced institutionalization and harm at Pennhurst when it was operating as a state school. Many of Pennhurst's inmates were nonverbal, had limited to no mobility, and/or required constant care. These disabilities would preclude their working at the attraction, which requires haunters to complete eight-hour-long shifts on their feet in non-accessible and dust-filled hallways. Green believes that a thoughtful memorialization of Pennhurst's history would take into account the perspectives of people with a range of intellectual, developmental, and physical disabilities—but especially those who have historically borne the brunt of the violence of state schools such as Pennhurst.

Local self-advocacy and conventional disability rights organizations that aim to represent that specific subsect of the disabled population, such as the Pennsylvania chapter of the Arc, a national organization founded by parents of people with developmental disabilities, and Speaking for Ourselves, the organization that Roland Johnson ran and brought to national prominence, have continually spoken out against the attraction. Debbie Robinson of Speaking for Ourselves said that if Johnson were alive today, he would organize until the attraction at Pennhurst "would not be happening." As she said, "People's lives was there... He might have had some friends [there]... [The attraction] is not a way to honor the people that lived there. A memorial should be honored."

Frank Orr, a longtime employee of the City of Philadelphia Division of Intellectual disAbility Services, who was an inmate at Pennhurst from 1965 until 1976, told me his wishes are also being disregarded. He is opposed to the attraction because "there were bad things that happened up there." He told me he is most haunted by a memory of watching a fellow inmate—he still remembers the young man's name—drown in a tub. He was part of protests to try and close it. "We tried to fight it," he said. "We lost."

When asked about the people who have said they were offended by the attraction, Autumn agreed that "in honesty, they're kind of right." But she believes it is necessary to fund the museum and the preservation of the increasingly disintegrating buildings at Pennhurst. "A harsh truth we face is [that] if we don't want this leveled," Autumn told me, "we have to do this."

It is true that Autumn and her fellow disabled haunters have been able to create something that almost no university, government, or cultural institution in our nation has been able—or perhaps wanted—to do: a museum of disability. They have saved hundreds of artifacts and records from being stolen or destroyed and many historic buildings from being torn down or left to

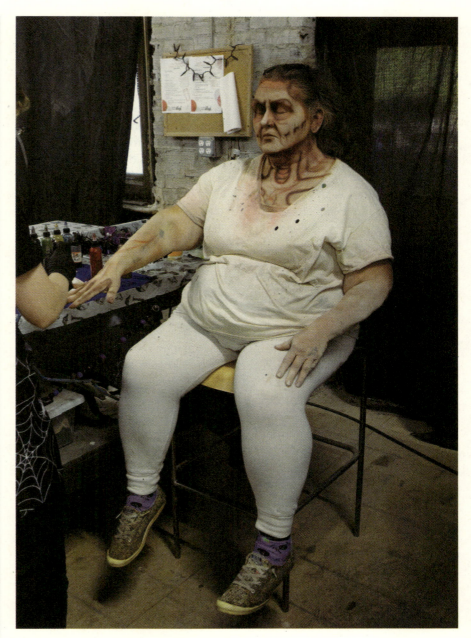

A haunter getting their makeup done before the night's performance.

vandalism, arson, and ruin—the fate of most other state schools. They have told the history of Pennhurst to thousands of guests. The attraction is hard to justify. But it is perhaps even harder to reject.

Despite Autumn's, Vanderloop's, and other haunters' framing of the museum as a way to honor Pennhurst's former inmates, none of their voices or stories are included in the exhibits themselves. And, given the haphazard nature of the displays, what their experiences inside the institution were like is difficult to piece together.

Autumn explained that these gaps are due to the grassroots nature and the limited resources of the museum. However, she hopes over the next few years to improve the space by organizing it more efficiently, weatherproofing the building, restoring artifacts, and, most crucially, finding and centering inmates' voices and experiences. She said she has spoken to and even brought a few former inmates to the museum to get their perspectives and hear their stories. However, it's been a challenge, since most of the people she has gotten in touch with don't feel comfortable reengaging or returning to the site of their trauma. In addition, the number of inmates who are still alive dwindles every year, and among those who are, many don't use speech to communicate.

Still, the omission of these stories felt surprising, given that, in addition to the searing testimonies in *Suffer the Little Children* and the *Halderman* lawsuit, there is a plethora of modern perspectives from Pennhurst inmates readily available, such as a 2023 exhibit called *File/Life: We Remember Stories of Pennhurst* produced by the Temple University Institute on Disabilities, and a series of recorded interviews titled "Pennhurst Lives Remembered," put together by the PMPA. Listening to these stories was the clearest window for me into what life was really like inside Pennhurst.

There's Eleanor Garner, at Pennhurst from 1964 to 1973, recounting a bond she had with one of the "babies"—a term used at Pennhurst for those with the most significant disabilities—that she was tasked with caring for, saying, "She couldn't talk but she understood."

There's Gerry Wheaton, at Pennhurst from 1951 to 1971, describing his work on the Pennhurst farm, and how the farmer did not like him because he named the animals, and how they would "come to me when I called them."

There's Roosevelt Butterfield, at Pennhurst from 1982 to 1984, recalling the moment he saw a staff member push a man in a wheelchair against a wall and crack his skull. He said he had a rag in his back pocket, and went over to wipe "the blood off the kid's hair."

But the most enduring narrative of what life was like inside Pennhurst is the autobiography of its most famous former inmate, Roland Johnson. The book *Lost in a Desert World: An Autobiography* (an oral history transcribed by Karl Williams) is a testament to Johnson's belief in his own capacity and those of other disabled people to speak for themselves.

On the night of my visit, after I emerged from the haunted attraction, I walked past the purple-and-orange-lit garden full of animatronic pumpkin-demons and the mini carnival selling funnel cake, through the gift shop, and, at last, into the parking lot. In my car, I pulled up Johnson's book on my phone. His words, true horror after horror, sprang out at me.

He says, "To tell you the truth, Pennhurst smelled like a doghouse. It just smell like feces. Rats crawling, roaches crawling all over; this was on the low grade wards. Holes in the wall, big holes in the floors. It was awful to see. You would cry to see people living in that kind of filth. Horrible. Feces and pee on the floor, flies coming in the windows."

He says, "I saw a patient got burnt in the hot water in the tub during the day all over his body. The water was hot and they didn't do the temperature. They had the doctors look at him and they sent him over to the dispenser. And they put some salve on him and bandages. It was terrible. And somebody died. I remember they rolled the person out in the hallway and the doctor pronounced them dead."

He says, "They did some tests, psychological evaleration and stuff like that. The doctor keep axing questions. It was so much overwhelming... I was just crying, with tears. I cried that, 'My mommy's gone; my daddy's gone.'"

He says, "I would say I'm a person that was lost and lonely and just in a desert world. And no one to talk to. Just out there in a big institution all by myself. All lonely. That's how I'd 'scribe it. I thought I would be there forever."

He says, "If you had spent your time up there, you wouldn't like it. You wouldn't like it. If you was in my shoe, you would cry."

I looked up as a prison-yard spotlight on top of the administration building swung around the campus. I watched it illuminate the ever-growing crowds gawking at the decrepit buildings, taking pictures of a haunter in a bloody straitjacket, laughing in the crisp air. Out for a fun night—who could blame them? Weren't they allowed to enjoy this? Somewhere between jealous and disgusted, I couldn't look away. I stared and stared, till the swinging light circled around and struck me too. ★

DEBBIE HARRY
[MUSICIAN]

IN CONVERSATION WITH

CHRIS STEIN
[MUSICIAN]

"TO BE AN ARTIST, YOU HAVE TO BE ABLE TO TOUCH AREAS THAT MAYBE YOU DON'T WANT TO TOUCH, OR THAT YOU ARE AFRAID TO TOUCH."

A few pieces of creative advice shared by Debbie Harry:
You can't please everyone all the time
You can never make a big enough fool of yourself
Use the perspective you've earned

As my plans to interview Debbie Harry and Chris Stein of Blondie for The Believer first took shape, billboards sprang up, as if on cue, around Manhattan. Sprawled several stories high was Harry's image, framed in a moody fashion-house ad. A glance up from the sidewalk suddenly felt freighted with the vastness of Blondie's legend: the art and fashion iconography; the timeless hit songs; and the band's enduring influence on countless artists, among them No Doubt, Garbage, the Yeah Yeah Yeahs, and Paramore.

Yet the image of Harry amid the New York City landscape also felt grounding and familiar. In tandem with their early punk peers at CBGB on the Bowery, Blondie achieved wide renown with music that documented and theatricalized countercultural urban life. Just under the surface of the band's tight, shiny pop constructions are vignettes of connection, alienation, and thrills among downtown

Illustrations by Kristian Hammerstad

denizens, variously struggling and striving apart from an indifferent or hostile mainstream.

Harry and Stein founded Blondie in 1974, branching out from the rock-cabaret group the Stilettos, where they first met. The band played small New York clubs with various lineups for years, finally achieving breakthrough success with their chart-topping, critically acclaimed album Parallel Lines in 1978.

Blondie's balance of accessible pop sounds and social subversion is often clinched by Harry's singular powers as a frontperson and stylist. Whether portraying a sex worker who falls for a cop ("X Offender"), an under-the-radar queer missed connection ("Love at the Pier"), or the dueling voices of stalker and victim ("One Way or Another"), she can sound funny and cynical, ethereal, browbeaten, or unhinged—all while maintaining a fine attunement to everyday speech and slang.

Harry's crafting of persona was also a distinctive (and still underexamined) contribution to the feminist energies of punk and new wave. In her persistent multivocality—assuming a range of perspectives and identities through performance—Harry turned sharply away from expectations around the emotional transparency of women in rock that had carried over from the '60s. And although she was conventionally pretty, she was not exactly approachable: A heightened quality to her dress and gender presentation often contrasted with an enigmatic stage presence.

The creative vision of Blondie was further shaped by Harry's partnership with Stein, with whom she wrote several of the band's most memorable songs, including "Dreaming," "Heart of Glass," and "Rapture." Stein's love of film and all manner of pop subcultures became an important influence on the band's lyricism. His and Harry's interest in emerging genre innovators also pushed the band to embrace the disco, reggae, and hip-hop sounds that would gain massive popularity in the decades to come. As a talented photographer, Stein helped define Blondie's stylized look early on, while his images of Harry, the Ramones, Iggy Pop, and many others documented punk's eccentric visual argot, its serious grit and glamour shot through with an anarchic scrappiness.

A new Blondie studio album—their twelfth—is now slated for release in 2026. I spoke to Harry and Stein over Zoom, trading the sweeping scale of the billboard for small squares on an LCD screen. The discussion that ensued was relaxed, gently cantankerous, and roving.

For more than fifty years, Harry and Stein's friendship has sustained itself, built on a shared appreciation of art, music, and each other's points of view. They seem less interested in reviewing their past achievements than in advocating for the things that helped them grow artistically: intellectual curiosity, persistence, and a strong sense of community. As artists who have always been alert to new technologies—from zines to drum machines—they offer a particularly sharp perspective on the potency and pitfalls of digital media.
—Emma Ingrisani

I. "ECCENTRIC AND ENERGIZED AND *CRAZY*"

THE BELIEVER: When did you both start thinking of yourselves as songwriters?

CHRIS STEIN: Well, for me it was kind of out of necessity. We did so many cover songs over the years, and it wasn't something I was averse to, but there was a moment when I knew we needed to get our own material going. When I met Debbie with the Stilettos, they had already been doing original songs.

DEBBIE HARRY: It was the name of the game. We did some club dates where we had to play top-ten hits, recognizable songs, for an audience who were pretty much drunk and there for a simple night out. They weren't downtown, artsy-fartsy people that were looking for an experience. They just wanted to have a good time and hear music they knew.

We were working slightly in that area, to make some money. But most of our focus and energy were on being part of this underground culture. We both understood it very easily—it was really something that we loved and that we knew. And there was already a great history with the Velvet Underground and other groups.

CS: The New York music scene had been pumping for years and years. I mean, fucking Dylan came outta here, somewhat. The Lovin' Spoonful when I was a kid—all that was going on here at the time.

DH: The folk scene in the West Village was very influential, a lot of energy there. Though I don't think either of us was really a big part of it.

CS: I was embedded in it, but I didn't do any performing.

BLVR: There's a book you put out in the '80s called *Making Tracks: The Rise of Blondie*—it's a great document of the band's first few years. At one point Debbie talks about a "non-period of punk": the moment right before punk in the early '70s when the New York Dolls stepped in, and that seemed to be a big shot across the bow for this new movement.

CS: Well, I always say that the first two Rolling Stones albums are completely punk…

DH: That was the crossover from glitter and glam rock.

CS: [The Dolls' impact] was kind of informed by their ragged playing. I don't say that to demean them—they just weren't as tight as Bowie's band. Everybody went to see Bowie's band [the Spiders from Mars] when he was touring around the same period. But the Dolls were much looser.

DH: And their enthusiasm and higher energy, their stance lyrically, and the way they dressed—it wasn't about being a finely tuned machine or a big showbiz thing. It was about being exactly what they were: eccentric and energized and *crazy*, you know?

CS: Equally in there with the musicianship.

BLVR: Earlier today I was looking at a piece by Lorraine O'Grady. She's known mostly as a performance artist, but she also wrote some rock profiles and reviews. She was very interested in the Dolls, and she talks about this feeling during the same period that rock and roll was stagnating. People felt like it wasn't continuing to evolve, and the Dolls were seen as disrupting that by being really ambitious, very theatrical, and also imperfect.[1]

CS: Yeah, bands like the Eagles presented this image of a closed group that you had to be really proficient to get into, and none of us were. We were all enamored of the Stooges and the MC5, and all the stuff that was very raw and struggling.

BLVR: As you were starting to write songs and becoming part of the punk scene in the city, so many of the bands had different sounds and styles. They were complementary, but they were distinct. Did people go off by themselves to compose or come up with new things, or was there collaboration across the scene?

CS: Oh, there was a lot of incestuousness. We used to play Television songs. I don't know if we ever performed a Ramones song at CBGB's—we might have.

DH: I don't know if there was any collaboration in the writing end of it.

NON-SPY-RELATED BESTSELLERS WRITTEN BY FORMER INTELLIGENCE WORKERS

★ *Mastering the Art of French Cooking* (1961) by Julia Child, a former research assistant in the Secret Intelligence Branch of the Office of Strategic Services, a precursor to the CIA
★ *James and the Giant Peach* (1961) by Roald Dahl, a former MI6 agent
★ *The Snow Leopard* (1978) by Peter Matthiessen, a former CIA operative
★ *Chitty Chitty Bang Bang* (1964) by Ian Fleming, a former assistant to the director of the Naval Intelligence Division
★ *The Tragical History of the Life and Death of Doctor Faustus* (1604) by Christopher Marlowe, an alleged courier and agent for the Elizabethan Privy Council
★ *The Razor's Edge* (1944) by William Somerset Maugham, a former MI6 agent
★ *The Little Prince* by Antoine de Saint-Exupéry, a former reconnaissance pilot for the Free French Air Force

—*list compiled by Chase Bush-McLaughlin*

---

1. In "Dealing with the Dolls Mystique" (published in October 1973 in *The Village Voice*), O'Grady was particularly taken with lead singer David Johansen, praising him as "an absolutely fantastic combination of Mick Jagger and Marlene Dietrich."

CS: No.

DH: We all were fans of one another, and so, you know: *paying attention*. I don't know if anybody really wanted to be a dead copy. In a way, the thing that made the scene was that it wasn't a format. There was no format. It wasn't like there was a lot of schooling or trained musicianship. It was about enterprise and feeling, identity.

I think now we find that chops, so to speak, are seen as very, very important: being able to play anything. But the things we could do, and the ways the groups shaped themselves, were at the limits of the players' abilities. And I think that's kind of wonderful. It really creates a sound and an attitude and a zone that you can be in, and it propels itself along.

CS: It's about dealing with your shortcomings, more than this constant striving for some sort of perfection that you have in your head, whatever that might be.

I know what Debbie means about the chops as far as bands go—you gotta be able to shred very precisely at this point. And it also relates to pop music. I really like a lot of modern pop music—there's so much that I am really enamored of—but it does all bounce off itself. She used the word *format*: There are certain formats that everything slips into very easily.

II. INFLUENCE AND OVERLAP

BLVR: In the larger downtown scene—this is even going back to the folk era again—there was also spoken word and poetry and this frantic production of writing and commentary about everything that was going on. I was curious to what extent you imbibed that or found it interesting. Obviously there were people who were overtly associating themselves with a poetry lineage.

CS: Yeah, I saw Patti [Smith] when she was just with Lenny [Kaye].[2] She would come out and do poetry and then bring him out, and it was almost ironic that he was playing guitar too loud and drowning her out. I saw her once, and I thought it was great, but I left going, She should have a band. Why doesn't she have a band? That was before I met Debbie, even.

---

2. Prior to the full formation of the Patti Smith Group, which put out its first single in 1974.

One of my favorite albums of all time, and that I've been listening to since I was a kid, is the soundtrack of *Performance*—the Nic Roeg, Donald Cammell, Jagger movie. There's a track on that from the Last Poets, who totally predate rap music.[3] They came from a kind of slam-poetry situation. So I had been hearing that for fucking ever by the time we ran into rap music.

BLVR: And then the spoken-word, direct-address elements in some of your songs, like "X Offender"—

DH: That was very '60s, really.

CS: You mean the intro thing?

DH: Yeah.

CS: Debbie didn't want to do that initially. I begged to have it done. So we went with it, and it kind of works. But I think she *reads* the lyrics in general. There is a different kind of emphasis from what you heard in popular music at the time. It was a completely different direction that was pulled from B-movies and the fucking newspaper headline.

DH: It was an undercurrent sort of influence—and overlap. There were also a lot of great drag shows that used to come through, and of course those were always layered with [*laughs*] sick, upside-down humor or ironic social conditions. Mixed with some very good music.

CS: We did the *Vain Victory*[4] thing, remember?

DH: Yeah. And I also think that geographically—because it all happened in a relatively small area—that intensified things. Everybody was in everybody's backyard, so to speak.

CS: I know, it was like doing a Zoom call. [*Laughs*] I mean, everything is huge and simultaneous now. People think about

---

3. The Last Poets' self-titled debut album was released in 1970, the same year as *Performance*.

4. The 1975 revival of the play by Jackie Curtis (Warhol superstar, gender-queer performance artist, and playwright). Debbie played the role of Juicy Lucy, and Blondie served as the backing band.

breaking their act on YouTube before they break out at the neighborhood bar. Everybody has this global reach in mind.

DH: In the early days, when we were playing to very small audiences, people who would come regularly had a sense of ownership over whoever they went to see. And some of them actually complained that we were getting too big. There were so many people at the shows that their sense of ownership—their sense of possession—was disturbed.

Along with that, in performance you had to really *own* what you were saying. That fed into why we had to write our own stuff. We were saying something that was very personal, and very local, and perhaps countercultural. A little bit of a fresh perspective. The Talking Heads versus the Ramones and Television: Those are all very personal perspectives. So I think the sense of ownership—by us and by the early audiences—was very parallel, very close.

BLVR: I first came to your music without much of this history and context, and was just responding to the sounds of it, without even seeing an image.

CS: Well, back in the beginning, a lot of people saw the image before they heard the music, because everything was print media at that point. I managed to get a picture of Debbie in *Creem* magazine, and people saw that before they knew anything about the band.

DH: But it didn't have the scope or the scan that exists today. The proportions are totally different. I don't think you can understand the amount of coverage that *Rock Scene* magazine got, compared to—

CS: Anything online. It's like a message in the bottle now. You throw it into the ocean and see if somebody's gonna find it.

III. THE PROJECT

BLVR: I feel like Blondie was sometimes perceived as very fixed and defined, while in so many other ways, the music is so capacious. And even though there was a specific moment you came out of, there's always been the sense of the project as continuing to change and grow.

CS: "Project" is funny to me. "The Project" is great. Yeah, it's ongoing. [*Laughs*] It's just weird now, when we're both this old. There was such a long period when I felt like we were only a cult band, and kind of on the B-list always. I don't know if we've gotten out of that now.

DH: I feel like no. I think we still are.

CS: There's a certain kind of acceptance, at any rate.

DH: We were always looking to the future and to different forms of music for inspiration and enjoyment. So that was a given, and that's something that Chris and I really shared. Sometimes the people around us were not so interested in being inclusive or evolving in that way.

CS: And we were really attracted to obscurity and little niche things, while the mindset now is to go as big as possible. One of the reasons I loved "The Tide Is High"[5] was that I knew nobody fucking knew it. That was part of the equation, I think.

DH: There were a lot of songs that came out as 45s only. They were never on albums, and they were sold in small record stores in small cities, like Newark and Paterson [in New Jersey]. What I'd really like to do is go to John Waters's house and play all his old 45s. Some of the songs he references in *Hairspray* are kind of amazing.

CS: Well, but the Cramps,[6] man—Lux and Ivy were off the hook with that stuff! And they knew every goddamn single that was ever recorded.

A lot of reggae and rap had the first hits only in 45 format. When I first visited London and went to all the reggae stores, there were these little pressings that guys would do—just of [individual] tracks.

BLVR: Debbie, in your memoir, *Face It*, you talk about being exposed to the Method acting approach, but in a musical

---

5. Originally recorded by Jamaican rocksteady group the Paragons and released as a 45 single and B-side by the noted Kingston, Jamaica–based label Treasure Isle in 1967. Blondie covered "The Tide Is High" on their 1980 album, *Autoamerican*.

6. The influential rock band, formed by romantic partners and avid record collectors Lux Interior and Poison Ivy in 1976.

context: rehearsing songs over and over again in order to reach a certain emotional pitch and projection. I was wondering whether that experience factored into your sense of performance in Blondie.

DH: I was fortunate to learn about the Method. The famous actors who used it are all terrific. And I think that maybe nowadays it's considered normal, or just the way acting's done.

As far as the guts of it all, it's obvious to me when I watch vocal contests on TV. There's such perfection, such insane technique—almost operatic, some of these singers—and yet it's not: *Who are they? Who is that person?* Technique can be like an insurance policy. But sometimes flying by the seat of your pants, without insurance or without a parachute, is what really makes you good. It really makes you better.

To be an artist, you have to be able to touch areas that maybe you don't want to touch, or that you are afraid to touch. And I can't honestly say that I get there every single time. When you're doing multiple gigs in a row, you don't always achieve those moments that you really want to achieve.

The dragging in of technique for me was never about singing well and being melismatic and all that. It was about being in the fucking moment and delivering the thing, almost to the point that it's scary and you're threatening somebody. And the threat was not always a threat of danger.

CS: You know, we grew up with Alan Vega and James [Chance][7] having fights with people in the audience. It was very confrontational.

DH: Yeah, but also, as one of the few girls around, being emotionally confrontational at that time. Singing "I'm gonna get you, get you, get you,"[8] the reaction was: *Well, what is she gonna do? Is it good or is it bad?*

In most cases I'm threatening myself by putting my shit out there for somebody to step on, or step in. That's what performance is all about. And I'm certainly not the only one to say that.

CS: Interesting.

---

7. Of the bands Suicide and the Contortions, respectively.

8. From the chorus of "One Way or Another."

DH: Chris might say it. [*Laughs*] We tune in and give in to the embarrassing moments. Sometimes the embarrassing moments are the best.

CS: Debbie has this line I really like: "You can never make a big enough fool of yourself." Which I think is great. And then I see these things about Taylor Swift having a runny nose onstage, and it's like this huge fucking deal.

IV. WAKE UP, SHITHEADS

BLVR: I'd love to talk about your upcoming album.

CS: We have a new album. There is a track I've been wanting to do for forty years that we actually recorded. It's OK. It's kind of raw.

DH: I think it's a very interesting group of songs. In truth, it's what we've always done: presenting our take on a bunch of different flavors. We have a sort of punky pop song that Glen Matlock[9] contributed.

You can't please everybody all the time, but I think the longer we play, the better we get at it, because it does require musicianship as well as some perspective. We're fortunate that we've been given so much perspective, and we're goddamn fucking fools if we don't use it. That's as political as I'm going to get. But, you know: Wake up, shitheads. Let's go.

CS: Well, you know what they say—they've got their heads so far up their asses, how are we gonna be able to shove them into the guillotine? [*Laughing*]

DH: We haven't really got a name yet, but our working title was "Ignore the Explosion."

CS: Which is a song line. I like that. I would stick with that.

DH: And we're going to do some kind of dedication to our drummer, who recently passed.[10] That's about as much as we can say right now. Hope you like it. ★

---

9. Songwriter, bassist, and original member of the Sex Pistols.

10. Clem Burke, who joined Blondie in 1975.

THE LABYRINTH

ONE BIDOON FATHER'S ALL-CONSUMING AND OCCASIONALLY ILLEGAL EFFORTS
TO ASSEMBLE THE PERFECT PERSONAL LIBRARY

by Mona Kareem

When it came to books, my father had absolutely no shame. On his first day at the ten-day Kuwait International Book Fair, he'd pile stacks of books at a publisher's booth and ask him to keep the books under the table because he feared they'd sell out before his salary hit his bank account. The publishers happily agreed, as they knew he was a serious buyer. But sometimes they fell too easily into his trap. When one of them went to use the bathroom and left his booth unattended, the monster would go into the booth and swiftly grab the bags of books from under the table, before proceeding on his daily tour. When I anxiously protested this scheme, he rehearsed the various scenarios with me: "If someone stops me, I say that it's my bag, and I left it there because it's heavy. If the seller himself catches me, I play nice and demand to know where he was: I was trying to find him to pay him his money." With the kidnapped books in hand, my father would make runs to the parking lot to place them in the car trunk, before returning to search for new victims.

The book purchases, too, weren't always innocent. Sometimes they acted as covers for hidden thefts. "I'd say I gave them a good deal: paid for five books, and took two extra," he'd explain to me, a "fair repricing method." He'd remind me that we did not "steal"; we simply "took" books that we loved, and would read. Sometimes he'd take my cousin Youssef with him, or one of my siblings. I didn't mind covering for my father; everyone found me adorable, especially when I discussed books with them. Dad would gesture to me to distract the booksellers as he dropped the jewels into his bag. He'd then join in the conversation, waving a book: "Ustaz, how much for this one? What? Three dinars is a lot. Where is my discount?" He'd heckle them, joke with them, engage them in twenty-minute-long conversations. My theft skills were mostly limited to distracting sellers, though

93

Illustration by Kristian Hammerstad

sometimes we reversed roles, if we had already negotiated what books we needed from a given publisher.

But at no point was I to become as good a thief as my father, or as my cousin Youssef, who has since made a life out of bookselling. One time, my father and cousin declared that they'd be stealing a ten-volume encyclopedia: Jawad Ali's *Tārīkh al-'Arab qabla al-Islām* (History of the Arabs before Islam). I stood in my place, terrified, too speechless to talk them out of it, too short for their sight line, lost in between them. They discussed the steps quickly, filled with excitement. I protested their plan, saying I couldn't come along, and they agreed that I should stay behind. My body couldn't move an inch, but my head was turning left and right, scanning the surrounding area, as if I'd have dared to warn them if someone appeared. My cousin grabbed seven volumes in one fat hug and walked toward the door, aiming for the parking lot, while my father slipped the remaining volumes into his bag. They walked to the end of the aisle as my father chanted gibberish words after my cousin, in hysterical thrill and laughter, then continued on his tour of the fair.

My father's bookish interests would come to define much of my childhood and adolescence. As a young person, I took his intensity to be that of a passionate reader and collector, but as an adult, I began to connect it to his past. Spurred by my own experience of loss and separation after moving to the US, I started to unpack the many stories he told of his books, those dead and alive.

1.

The local bookstores were a different story. They were a red line for his thefts for reasons he didn't disclose. It could have been because he was a favorite customer. They took care of him, admired him, always tried to get him the books he needed. They appreciated his thorough scanning of their shelves, how he emerged from the dust with decades-old books that had been recklessly shoved to the back to make space for new ones.

Almost every Friday, we'd get up early, while my siblings were still asleep. My mother made breakfast, and the three of us would enjoy some rare moments of quiet, eating eggs, scrambled with tomatoes and onions, with sides of feta cheese, olives, and pita bread. If one of the little devils got up early, we'd send him to get fresh bread, or chapati. When we finished our breakfast, leaving my mother to clean up after us, my father and I would get into his 1987 gray Chevrolet Caprice, which my siblings and I had named the Titanic, a car always on the verge of breaking down.

On these trips, I'd sometimes have a list of titles written down, books that my father didn't have that I had come across in my reading. I was in pursuit of "comprehensive knowledge," as my father taught me to be. "You can never be a good writer if you don't read all sorts of books. A poet who only reads poetry can't go far." He'd then proceed, quoting Gramsci: "A comprehensive knowledge is essential for the organic intellectual," though I wasn't sure if Gramsci ever did write such a statement. Something my father was certain to do was to name-drop. In the same sentence, he'd open with one name, link up to another halfway through, then close out with a third. Usually they were Western writers and thinkers; he was a big fan of the Enlightenment. He called them his "universal tribe," his glasses lingering on the tip of his long nose. I soon came to realize that even when my father had a brilliant idea of his own, he preferred to credit it to one of his favorite great whites.

When the Titanic arrived in Hawally, one of the main urban areas where Arab immigrants are concentrated, we'd go first to al-Orouba bookstore. (In the '80s, the demographics of Kuwait consisted of a majority of South Asian and Arab migrants, a 40 percent citizen population, and an undisclosed percentage of stateless Arabs, or Bidoon, which included my own family. After the Gulf War, these percentages didn't shift much, but certain groups, such as Palestinians, Iraqis, and Bidoon, were painted as coconspirators in the occupation and targeted with various forms of forced displacement.) Al-Orouba was a small shop established by a professor of Arabic literature at Kuwait University. We'd get to the bookstore before the owner himself was there for his daily check-up visit, perhaps because he went to Friday prayers and my father never did. Located on a narrow street covered in potholes, where it was always a struggle to find parking, the store had a wide glass front that offered a good view of its interior. Once you entered the L-shaped shop, the checkout counter was on your left and the magazine section on your right. The ceilings were at least ten feet high, every inch leading up to them stacked with books. Beyond the front section, the rest of the shop was organized around two aisles and a storage room at the back. The bookseller, Mr. Adel, was an Egyptian man of my father's age. He had a white beard and a quiet manner. He was always happy to see us, especially since most people entered the store by mistake. He'd patiently clarify to those lost souls that "it's a bookstore, as in we sell books, not notebooks," before directing them to the stationery shop next door. At the time, it was an insult for any bookstore to carry notebooks and pens, a bad look that could scare away serious customers like my father. But in the late 2000s, al-Orouba devoted its entire front section to notebooks and pens, in an attempt at survival.

Before we delved into the shelves for the next hour or two, Mr. Adel would voluntarily provide us with updates on his inventory. I took these updates seriously. He'd point with his index finger, and in his calm voice say, "We just received those titles from Cairo, and over there are the ones from Beirut. Outside, there are a few new issues of the usual periodicals." Sometimes my father would have a follow-up question about a book he had requested, even though he knew very well how long it took to order and receive one. "End of the month, inshallah," Mr. Adel would respond.

My father and I had two approaches to book shopping. Sometimes we began in the same section, and while shopping we brought each other's attention to certain titles, exchanged opinions on whether a book was worth buying, which translation was better, what publishers to avoid because they were too commercial and therefore less rigorous. This was the slow approach. Other times we each began in a different section, and at some point met in the middle. I'd go to my father for feedback, or to impress him with a book I had captured. My father taught me not to leave a single bookshelf unturned, at least the ones within my physical reach. Even the books hidden behind other books must be checked, because on rare occasions, the ones in the back were the special titles, out of circulation, not glossy or new enough to attract customers—but to us, they were treasures. My father loved dead books, though he didn't necessarily care for first editions or nice covers. He cared for "good translations, good writers." He was naturally a comparatist, and he owned all Arabic translations of Cervantes, Dante, T. S. Eliot, Whitman, Gabriel García Márquez, and would indulge in long explanations of which translators had failed and which had done a good job, without having read the originals. He was obsessed with translation traitors: His monolingualism was a source of anxiety, and he wanted the translation to be faithful, to be a mirror, because why would anyone dare interfere when translating the greats! After an hour or two at a given bookstore, we'd have completed our search, proud of our picks, tired and dehydrated, our lungs agitated by the dust. We'd conclude the trip with a private meeting in a corner of the shop, as far as possible from the bookseller and his customers, calculating the overall cost, estimating the probability of a discount, and assessing if there were books to leave on hold until our next visit.

Although al-Orouba was not the only bookstore in town, it was our favorite—reliable, focused on literature and philosophy, with a small inventory of regional magazines and periodicals. Some weeks, my father might find himself energetic enough to suggest that we visit other bookstores. We might go to Qurtas, in the old city, which enjoyed a bigger space, modern and brightly lit, with a traditional faux mud facade. The books at Qurtas were more expensive, focused on history and politics. Although I published my debut with Qurtas, the publisher never offered me an author's discount, perhaps because they were too broke to be generous! There was also al-Rubayan's disappointing bookstore, which we visited to kill time or to check on its owner, Mr. Yahya al-Rubayan. Once a vibrant place that functioned as a press, a bookstore, and a gathering space (or so I was told by my father), the al-Rubayan's I knew felt more like a haunted and suffocated place. Mr. Yahya seemed to have given up on his shop, often complaining that people didn't read books anymore. The inventory didn't change, as he rarely bothered to acquire new books. As he aged, so did his curatorial taste, which seemed traditional and out-of-touch. My only enjoyable visit to al-Rubayan's was when Mr. Yahya declared bankruptcy in 2007, opening to the public the store's massive storage basements, where books were sold for the equivalent of one dollar each. The basement contained many books printed in Iraq prior to the Gulf War, after which they could not be showcased, due to an official ban on anything Iraqi in Kuwait—whether it was a book printed in Iraq, a cassette tape of

Iraqi singers, or even a TV show whose closing credits included the name of an Iraqi actress! But following the execution of Saddam Hussein in 2006, the Kuwaiti state relaxed, and Iraqi books and songs were no longer prohibited materials to be exchanged in secret. A fourth bookstore, one we rarely visited, was That al-Salasil, where a Palestinian bookseller once managed to provide us with a copy of Abdelrahman Munif's *Cities of Salt*, which was banned for its criticism of the oil state and satirizing of the Arab Gulf's ruling families. Today, That al-Salasil and al-Rubayan's continue to operate, but Qurtas and al-Orouba had to close. That al-Salasil switched to a commercial model that relies on selling popular books, while al-Rubayan's was saved by a special presidential grant after declaring bankruptcy. In 2012, a year after I left Kuwait, I found out that a fire had erupted at al-Orouba, devouring thousands of its dusty books in the span of hours.

2.

Between the 1992 Gulf War and the 2011 Arab uprisings, most of the books sold in Kuwait came either from Egypt or Lebanon. Arabic writers aspired to have their books printed in one of these countries because of certain advantages. Egyptian publishers emphasized low production costs to keep prices affordable, a legacy of the 1960s socialist era. Lebanese publishers, on the contrary, favored high quality and fine design while also enjoying an easier distribution network through the port of Beirut. These factors played a role in establishing Cairo and Beirut as the centers of Arabic culture, because unlike elsewhere in the Arabic-speaking world, publishing has not been limited to state institutions. In Kuwait, the National Council for Culture, Arts, and Letters stands as the largest publisher. The council, established in 1973, has translated and printed thousands of plays, magazine issues, and scholarly and scientific books, which are sold for stabilized prices across the Middle East and North Africa. Yet for unknown reasons, the council never bothered to print books by local writers. Although it was occasionally criticized for this, the council's bureaucrats didn't care to explain the exclusion. Utilizing oil revenues to subsidize books, they aim to represent the state of Kuwait abroad as a charitable patron. It was also thanks to oil wealth that the council was able to resume production after the Gulf War. For independent presses and bookstores, however, nothing was the same: The small country that had once been committed to the socialist aspirations of Arab nationalism became overnight a chauvinistic place suspicious of anything progressive and regional. Intellectuals who found refuge in Kuwait, working, publishing, and organizing, were no longer welcomed. Leftist politicians had to either declare their loyalty to the regime or withdraw from domestic politics. The publishing scene that was initiated and fostered by progressive forces, local and regional, was made futile. A press like al-Rubayan's, which takes credit for publishing many of the old guards of Kuwaiti literature, became a lifeless place. They rarely published new titles or hosted book launches or panels. Qurtas also relied on the bookstore model to support its operations before closing its doors in 2011.

The post–Gulf War era, during which Kuwait became patriotic, xenophobic, and conservative, is the context I grew up in as a young reader and writer. Practically, this meant that the literary scene was austere, marginalized, and small, yet intimate and comradely. Readers, writers, cultural journalists, booksellers, and publishers knew one another personally, yearning for one another's company and intellectual exchange. My father and I attended almost every event organized by the council, despite our critical opinions of the outdated conceptions, aesthetics, and general taste of its curators. We found in these events an opportunity to gather in public spaces, even if it entailed listening to an old generation of writers whom we referred as "the dinosaurs of literature." We were reconciled to the fact that we were attending these programs as haters, so we could gather after to drink tea, exchange snarky remarks, and bond over our alienation. At times, this pushed us to come up with alternatives, like when my father co-organized a weekly Tuesday Cultural Salon, where local authors gathered to share works in progress and new releases, or to present on a random topic of interest—say, Buddhism or post-structuralism. Sometimes the salon organizers would persuade a guest speaker who was visiting Kuwait at the invitation of the council to join the salon for an impromptu reading. Wherever the events were happening, whether they were official or clandestine, books were key; they were the center of our social life. My father and his friends who attended the salon developed a communal practice of using copy and fax machines to exchange texts, including entire books, and especially poetry collections. An Egyptian, Syrian, or Lebanese friend would return from his annual visit to the homeland with books he deemed worthy and graciously make copies of them, using workplace machines, to share with the rest of the group. I remember reading the poems of Fouad Haddad and Ahmed Fouad Negm in fax copies that an Egyptian poet sent to my father over the span of a week, as they discussed or recited them to each other on the phone.

3.

My father considered himself a better patron of books than many of the publishers and salespeople he encountered: "Books want someone to read them, not someone who keeps boxing and unboxing them—they get tired, you know." If you were to pull any of the books off his shelves, you'd notice that they were all in good condition. He'd never bend or stretch the cover to make his reading experience easier. Books that were printed in Egypt were known for their poor production quality (rough paper, manual stitching, gluing), as well as for their painted covers, and my father took pleasure in their maintenance. A novel by Sonallah Ibrahim, for example, was guaranteed to become a pile of loose papers by the time you finished reading it, as the dried glue crumbled page after page. My father, with his years of experience, managed to find the right method to deal with such crises. He'd first lay the book down, however disembodied, arranging its organs for a new incarnation. He'd use a long ruler to line up the pages, making sure the parts of the book were in perfect alignment, before applying the glue on the right side of the pile of pages and cover. With a tiny paintbrush, he'd spread the glue evenly, controlling any accidental spills that might turn catastrophic. He'd then close the book, as if embracing it between his palms, shutting his eyes for a brief moment, taking a deep breath in, and exhaling out. Finally, he'd place a heavy glass ashtray on top of the book to seal the union of paper.

But to my father, being a good patron of books was not just a physical experience. Sure, he never allowed me to annotate or underline books while reading, and certainly not with a pen (a fact that shaped my reading behavior: I continue to use pencils only). "Mistreating books," as he described it, was a crime he punished me for by temporarily revoking my access to his library. He had the tiniest handwriting, and made the utmost effort to avoid marginalia, except for a little star, an arrow, or one word, if necessary. He argued that his methodology not only "paid respect" to books; it allowed him to re-read any book in a new way, with no prior annotations to distract from or limit a unique reading. He kept sticky notes and A4 paper close to him while reading, in case inspiration struck. Mostly, he wrote down titles referenced by the author, so he could go searching for the cited works in the future.

Although books weren't necessarily the most affordable passion, my father believed they were made for people of his social class. "Books give you salvation," he'd casually philosophize. "They are for the wretched of the earth." And when I asked, "So have you found salvation yet?," he'd pause, exhaling out of his large nostrils, swallowing as if a word were stuck in his throat, before answering: "All the knowledge in the world couldn't afford me a blink of rest!" This association with salvation was also why my father believed that rich people did not, and could not, read. If they were wealthy, then they must be happy. If they were happy, why would they read? Whenever we ran into someone rich at a bookstore or a book fair—meaning someone who could afford to buy books without checking the price tag or haggling with the bookseller—my father would begin to grumble. He'd express pity for the books bought by that rich customer, for they'd not be read, and chances were they'd not get to see new places and new owners, because rich people would never have to sell their books to make the rent. My father would direct my attention to a rich customer and say: "Look at this, this is tragic, they don't *deserve* this book. Who's gonna read that book now? Certainly not this man. Tragic!"

My father was always late on rent. We had to move to a new apartment every other year. He'd miss two or three months of rent, and it became easier to find a new home than to pay what was owed. For each relocation, he'd divide the family into two groups: one to pack the entire house, and the other to pack the books. (I was always in the latter group, despite its physical demands.) He intentionally had no system for packing the books, so when we arrived at the new apartment, he'd have an excuse to come up with a new ordering system—"Let's organize them by genre this time"—which also meant by author and by size. What was an exhausting process for the family—the lack of stability, the repeated loss of neighborhood friends, and the memories associated with each home—was to my father an exciting opportunity to indulge once again in his books.

When it was time for Kuwait's annual book fair, which took place in November, he was certain to miss paying the rent. (In his head, the house rent was always liable to become a personal loan, when needed.) There were years when he went out of control and also borrowed money from friends to be able to afford his purchases. He justified it by saying the book fair happened only once a year, a singular occasion when all the publishers of the Arab world brought their hottest and latest releases. If he didn't buy what he needed, they'd either run out of copies or sell them to local bookstores, who'd then resell them for double the price. These were horrifying scenarios to my father—it didn't make sense to miss out on the special season, only to buy later at a higher price.

4.

At the age of sixteen, my father had had to drop out of high school to support his family, after my grandfather was laid off. He had eight siblings—one sister was already married, and everyone else was too young to help. Though he wasn't good at playing big brother, he helped his siblings have futures that he couldn't have himself: They earned their high school diplomas and found decent jobs. He funded their marriages, including that of one brother who failed at his first marriage and had to remarry. My siblings and I often said that my father could have become a doctor or a professor, had his life taken a different turn. That was until the day we opened his suitcase of official papers and read his school reports, which revealed some scandalously low scores. He had failed his classes repeatedly but somehow managed to get passing grades by the end of every school year. Growing up in the '70s, my father lived through Kuwait's so-called golden era, when the country was pluralistic and hungry for development and culture. As a stateless man, he had access to public education, employment, and health care, but not to housing or voting rights. To my postwar generation, whether stateless or migrant, even these basic rights sounded fictional. We grew up in a segregated society where we weren't allowed to live with or attend schools with Kuwaiti citizens, and had no access to public higher education, health care, employment, or housing.

Two experiences influenced my father in his formative years. The first was the fact that my grandfather bought books for him, usually of the premodern Arabic canon. I'm not sure whether my grandfather was aware of which books he was buying, considering that he was an illiterate man. When his friends visited for afternoon tea, my grandfather would send my father to buy the daily newspaper, then order him to read the headlines to the guests, all of whom were illiterate, too. Sometimes a story would spark their interest, in which case my father would have to read the full story to them. This early practice influenced how my father read newspapers and magazines: He'd start by reading all the headlines first, marking stories of interest, before returning to read them in full.

The second was also Mr. Sami, a Palestinian teacher in his thirties, who founded his school's newspaper, or what they called the "school's wall newspaper" because its few copies were pinned to various boards around the school, requiring readers to read them while standing. Mr. Sami organized my father and other classmates into a team, assigning topics for stories, and guiding them through the writing and editing processes. For Mr. Sami, there was a value in politicizing these young men and in helping them find a connection to literacy that went beyond education and professionalization. He was the one to introduce my father to modern Arabic poetry and to give him a sense of how to go about choosing books to read.

After dropping out of high school, my father started reading, writing, and attending events, including plays and concerts. He'd walk into a newspaper office and ask to meet the literary editor, with a typed-up short story or a poem of his in hand. He proudly recalled an encounter when the Egyptian writer and translator Abdel Rahman Badawi, at the time serving as a professor at Kuwait University, told him to "soak your poem in that cup of tea and drink it." There were also the editors who threw his work into the trash after he left their offices, and, alternatively, the ones who called him "promising" and published his work. He was proud of his failures and successes alike. He wasn't a usual man; he loved to challenge the norms, to trespass into spaces not meant for someone of his class. As a young boy, when his readings were still limited to celebrity magazines and the literary sections of daily newspapers, my father built a small wooden booth in their backyard and charged kids money to enter it; they'd browse the latest magazine issues, and stare at pictures of celebrities, which he collaged onto the walls. He promised his cousin, "If you wink at Samira Tawfik, she will wink back at you." His customers, often unsatisfied, would demand a refund—but my father honored no such requests, blaming his customers for their lack of imagination.

In the '70s, every school in Kuwait had a library, updated regularly with periodicals and new releases. One of the memorable aftermath scenes of the Gulf War was of the library books in ruins. Instead of reorganizing the destroyed libraries, some people decided it was easier to dispose of the books so as to speed up the cleaning process. My father and his friends drove around trying to salvage the books, often arriving too late to the scene. They heard stories of personal libraries abandoned, especially by Palestinians who were forced out or banned from reentering Kuwait. Landlords searched for book buyers, sometimes giving the books away for free so they could get rid of them and lease the abandoned apartments to new tenants. My father felt remorse at having failed to save all these libraries.

The stories of libraries lost during and after the war only amplified the personal loss he experienced. By the time I was born, in December 1987, my father owned a private collection of at least five hundred books, which he would later have to sell during the war. The country was occupied for seven months, and no one had jobs to cover their basic needs. Somehow my father managed to find a man to buy his books, so he could afford groceries and baby formula. Over the following decades, we heard the story of his sold library countless times, and each time, new details emerged, while others retreated. He'd sometimes begin the thread of the story from that moment of desperation, painting a picture of the war, how late in the timeline of events the sale took place, how many times he had resisted the idea until all other means were exhausted, the phone call he made to the buyer who had owned a bookstore before the war, and how the latter had paid a visit to my father's study and with a quick glance realized its quality. The buyer sent a couple of men to box and transfer all the books, while my father tried to salvage a few in the final minutes, to steal his books from their future owner before the men carried them away. It all happened too quickly and easily: The speed and ease seemed most disturbing to his grief. He had hoped for some difficulty in locating the buyer, some resistance that would delay the sale just long enough for the war to end.

Sometimes the story would be retold, against our objections and eye-rolling, because the narrative was triggered by an encounter. If he came across a certain book that he had a fond memory of buying for his first collection, he'd use it as the entry point to the same old story. He'd explain where he'd first encountered the book, its plot, its price or first-edition cover, how a friend had tried to borrow it from him but he'd refused, because "lending a book is foolish, but more foolish is returning a book." In his usual hyperbolic manner, my father was an excellent unreliable narrator. All his stories about that sale gave the impression that his books were forever lost, not only from his own library but from the entirety of the Arabic language. We were meant to conclude from this story what a great father he was, the sacrifices he made for us. Instead, we responded to his story with subtle mockery, especially in the presence of the many books he had compiled since that sale. We were more interested in the buyer than we were in the seller, how that buyer had a strange faith that books would outlast the war.

5.

By the time I migrated in 2011 to the United States, my father's library contained at least two thousand books. He kept an Excel spreadsheet of all the titles, containing the number of pages, edition, issue year, size (S, M, L), as well as the author, the translator, and the country and name of the publisher. My father took pleasure in this data-entry process; he savored it for days, skimming through the pages before entering the biographical information of a book into Excel, which always lagged for a few seconds before finally opening. He had nicknames for the spreadsheet: For a few years it was Sisyphus's Rock, and later he renamed it the Labyrinth. Although I was an essential part of assembling that second library, there were certain aspects of it I was excluded from—the data entry, for example, the placement of the books

SAI'S CLOSET
(IN EXTENDED TRIANGLE POSE CHEST AERIAL)
by Soham Patel

Sorting through more remembered days when I found my gender some joyous ones: Was born a daughter yet there's a picture of me at about age three circa the early 1980s in which I have on a blue collared button up jumpsuit with a yellow necktie dyed in an orange floral print. I don't remember but am told I wanted to wear that tie every day and if I couldn't I'd throw myself on the floor in tantrum. I've also seen a picture of my second cousin at age three wearing a white and red dress just a few days before his first haircut but that was just for laughs kali haswanu matteh I'm told.

When they had to run some errands before moving from Bowling Green to DC, Jen and Evan for the first time left their firstborn alone at home with Jenny and me when he was maybe six months. We brought him a onesie welcome to this world gift with a unicorn printed on it and I have a hoodie to match, it's electric blue. Jen yelled in, "Teach him everything you know!" as she walked out the door. We started by telling baby Henry about how Prince played every instrument in all his songs and about the Love Symbol he invented and I can't remember what after that but Hank didn't cry the whole time while hanging out with just us.

The first Operation Sappho I went to was upstairs at Donny's Place that leather bar shut down now in Pittsburgh but I never went into the basement. I love that tan blazer I'd wear it for sport those days I sported so much I wore it out. Caldwell has photos from those Sappho dance parties some mounted at the Warhol I wish I still had my Gutter Glitter show clothes oh I miss those bright femme shiny short mod go-go frocks how they'd show off my swole from the miles of bicycle commutes warrior one-two-threes 11:11 kaan pakad squats and leg day work.

---

exclusively detained in his room, the administrative decisions about how to organize them. In my final years in Kuwait, however, my friendship with my father, which was entirely fostered by and oriented toward books, evolved into a trust he shared with no one else. I was exempted from the common wisdom of the two fools (the book lender and the book returner), and he began to store some books in my bedroom (mostly because my mother wouldn't allow his books to "occupy" more of the house), and to trust me to exile some books, like when I convinced him that "no one reads Hanna Mina anymore," leading to the sale of seventeen volumes of the Syrian novelist's complete fiction.

Just as we were getting settled into this more egalitarian ownership of the library that we had curated together, stolen together, and for which he had sometimes paid, the time of my departure arrived. I was accepted into a graduate program in New York, and my lifetime dream of leaving the boring city of Kuwait was finally coming true. I took only one book with me, just for the flight, and it was Borges's *Seven Nights*. I was excited to build my first library—really my second, but the first that was my own. I often found myself acquiring books that my father and I already had, as if subconsciously attempting to rebuild what I had left behind before building anew.

Whenever my father found someone traveling to the US, he asked me if there were any books I needed. I turned down his offers, explaining that I could find all the books I needed in America, and that I no longer needed the Arabic translations; in fact, I had to focus on reading in English. I was more interested in the Arabic books he had, books we usually took for granted, unlike the translations that made up our joint passion. With every traveler, he sent books he knew I liked, despite my objections, until at some point he decided to resolve my resistance by explaining: "Whom would I leave this library to when I die? You're gone, and I don't trust anyone here to take care of it. I think we should try and salvage as many as we can in the meantime." ✶

JAMILA WOODS

[MUSICIAN, POET]

"I THINK MUSIC HAS A HEALING ABILITY TO BRING US FROM THE SPACE OF WHAT WE KNOW TO WHAT WE DON'T KNOW."

A few of the people Jamila Woods has named songs after:
Nikki Giovanni
Eartha Kitt
Octavia E. Butler
Jean-Michel Basquiat

Jamila Woods is a polymath: a multi-hyphenate artist, a teacher, a student, a singer, and your favorite poet's favorite musician. Born and raised in Chicago, Jamila has released three critically acclaimed solo studio albums: Heavn (2017), Legacy! Legacy! (2019), and Water Made Us (2023). Tracking Woods's journey as both a human and an artist, each record builds upon and explodes the previous offering, a new intervention into the sonic landscape. Jamila has said, "I think of songs as physical spaces," and if we know that Woods is a poet and that the word stanza means "room" in Italian, then we can think of each of her records as a different kind of public-private space that she's inviting the listener into. Her music is at once a rallying cry for the collective, a home for recollection and re-collecting oneself, and a grounding space to connect with land and history.

Woods's writing and performances are keystones in the architectures of both the literary and music worlds. Often, Woods includes performances of poems on

Illustration by Kristian Hammerstad

her albums and in her live shows, blurring the lines between song and poem while inviting us to consider the porousness of the boundary between different forms of art practice and expression; in this way, she insists that the container is meant to serve the vision. Doreen St. Félix writes in her review of Heavn, "It makes you wish all singers were poets." And it's true—with each listen to a Jamila Woods song, layers of meaning slough off to reveal new, subtle profundities at the level of the lyric, as Woods's voice bobs and weaves and braids through the instrumentation.

I first met Jamila Woods at the National Poetry Slam in Boston in 2011. We were competitors in a semifinals bout. I was on the San Francisco City Slam team, and she was a member of the Providence Poetry Slam team, and I remember to this day the feeling when she got onstage and performed, in the voice of a pigeon, "Pigeon Man," a poem that is somehow simultaneously hysterical, estranging, and critical of the systems that produce gendered violence. My first thought was: We're definitely losing; and my second thought was: I've never heard a poem that does this before. (To this day, I teach that poem regularly when considering voice, persona, and the imagination.)

Later that year she came through the Bay Area with her "adventure soul" duo, Milo & Otis, to perform at a reading series, "The New Sh!t Show," that I ran in the basement of an antiques store in San Francisco. Below the surface of the world, in a packed and smoky basement filled with drunks waiting to hear poems, over a lone bass, Woods's voice pierced the scrim of our collective misanthropy. As she sang ("It ain't worth it. / I'll kiss your fists. / You'll get through this. / Just have faith, sis") all of us rose, planted our feet on the good ground, and let the music move through us with our arms lifted toward the heaven of the low ceiling. It was one of the most moving performances I've seen to this day. (This was the song "The Joy" by Milo & Otis, which you should listen to while reading this interview.)

If Jamila was a dynamic and transformative artist and performer fifteen years ago, the arc of her creative life and impact has expanded exponentially. Outside of her three tremendous solo studio albums, she also constantly makes genre-defining and -defying work as an artist deeply rooted in her communities, collaborating with justice-oriented organizations on creative projects while also teaching younger generations of artists new ways of being authentic in a mediated and surface-oriented world. As a longtime fan and friend and first-time interviewer, I was lucky enough to have a little chat with Jamila about where she's at in her creative life following the release of her third studio album, Water Made Us. In the following conversation I press her on when her long-awaited book of poems is going to come out and gab about the necessary quiet spaces between art-making.

—*Sam Sax*

I. UNCERTAINTY AND SURPRISE

THE BELIEVER: How are your year and your creative life after the release of your last record?

JAMILA WOODS: I'm having a slow, hibernating winter. I'm not going outside much, but I have so many things I want to learn and do this year. So it's a lot of visioning and realizing that I can do only one thing at a time; I can't do everything at once. By visioning, I mean literally sitting around daydreaming and envisioning what I want my life to look like. I should maybe use another word, because I'm one of those people who can't really see pictures in my mind too well. It's more about imagining how I want to feel, and then asking myself: What has to be in place in order for me to wake up and feel this way more of the time?

BLVR: What are you finding through this process?

JW: I really want to learn sound healing. I start training with a teacher next week. I also want to have a poetry book at long last, so I'm working on that while taking some workshops. I recently finished my last album for my record deal, so I no longer have this built-in structure to my creative work. Now I'm kind of like, Whoa, what could my work grow into?, and just asking that question to the sky.

BLVR: You finished your third record in your deal with your label, Jagjaguwar. Do you already feel the impetus to make another record, or are you thinking about a different form?

JW: Having a record deal is a great thing—it was very supportive because I know I work well with structure. But I also don't work well under a lot of pressure. Even though my label didn't pressure me, it was almost like being in school, like: I gotta turn in a project. My brain just kind of goes into this *Oh no, people are waiting for me* mode, and I'm really excited to not have that feeling anymore. I will want to work with a label again in the future, but for now I want to be in this interstitial space and not have anyone waiting on me to do anything. Just mentally, spiritually, it feels good. I like being in an exploratory phase of just making things and seeing how I feel about them.

While making *Water Made Us*, I had a long period of wandering. It was stressful because I was like, Why is this taking so long? But I realized I had to let myself surrender to the time that the process takes. So, yeah, I'm excited to just play and get into a space of: There's no purpose to this. I'm just doing this to see what comes out.

BLVR: It makes a lot of sense that this period of exploration follows *Water Made Us*, because to me that record is so rooted in ecology and thinking about the replenishments of both body and the earth as necessary processes. Do you feel as though what you're doing now is an extension of that record?

JW: I love how you used the word *ecology*, because it's so perfect to think about the process of creation as relational and cyclical: Sometimes it's raining; sometimes the clouds are just above us and the water is evaporating. You can't see what's happening, but *something's* happening. I love thinking about that. This whole year feels very uncertain. So, yes, I think it does make sense for this period to come after *Water Made Us*. I've also been more into human design.

BLVR: What's that?

JW: It's kind of a combination of astrology, I Ching, Ayurveda—all these different forms of knowing. One idea is that every person has a specific emotion that signals that they're "aligned," and a different emotion that's a sign that they're out of alignment. For me, when I'm aligned, it's a *surprise*. I love the relationship between uncertainty and surprise. I tend to be a person that likes to have a plan and see what's coming—but if I always know what's gonna happen, I can't have moments of surprise.

For me, human design is like an app running in the back of my mind that I check on every once in a while. As I'm noticing and tracking my emotions, I keep an eye out for those feelings that are signs of alignment or not. When I feel disappointment (my sign that I'm not aligned), I try to do something grounding and get out of my own head. There's also advice on how each person should approach making decisions. I'm supposed to think about things for a whole moon cycle in order to see how I feel about something through various moods over a month. It's not realistic for every little decision, but I try to take that time for bigger decisions for sure. And it's been affirming to embrace that approach as someone who used to feel a lot of stress and overthinking around making decisions.

II. SPACE IS THE PLACE

BLVR: I was curious about your connection to place. I think of you both musically and lyrically as connected to a lot of Chicago art traditions. What is your relationship to place—both in your music and in your life? I'm specifically thinking of that line from your song "Way Up": "Just 'cause I'm born here don't mean I'm from here."

JW: Place feels really important to me, specifically Chicago and the community I have here. Growing up, I had a distinct feeling of out-of-placeness in my predominantly white neighborhood and school environments, and also in my predominantly Black church environment. Inside, my home was vibrant and loving, but outside I felt like I was always trying to adjust something about myself to fit in. When I was writing "Way Up," I was getting into Afrofuturism, and it blew my mind, the idea that if I could just imagine I was from somewhere else—like in the Sun Ra film *Space Is the Place*—all of a sudden the relevance of all the bullshit would be decreased. Knowing that my Blackness is this vast other universe gives me an alternative source to draw my sense of self and value from. It's like going to school and feeling invisible, but knowing that when I get home everybody will think I'm funny and laugh at my jokes.

The same thing happened when I started writing poetry as a teenager. It was like, I'm at school; nobody thinks I'm cute. Then I'd go to an open mic and everyone would listen to my poem and show me so much love. The artistic community in Chicago became my other universe; it made me feel like I mattered and like my voice mattered. Chicago is still this grounding force for me.

When I started working on my third album in Los Angeles around 2022, I found some really beautiful friends and collaborators there. It was also disorienting at first, because a lot of music-business things in LA operate with more of a focus on industry. I was used to a more grassroots approach, because for better or for worse, Chicago doesn't really have a huge infrastructure. My Chicago creative community gives me an energy that I carry with me wherever I go. It's a very diasporic feeling, that drawing my sense of myself from somewhere else helps me navigate new spaces.

BLVR: When did you first start making poems?

JW: I first started writing poetry in high school. There was an after-school program in Chicago where you got paid to be an "apprentice artist" and learn from creative mentors. Through that program I discovered open mics and youth poetry slams and I got hooked. I think having the experience early on of getting paid to create art and seeing teachers who wrote poetry for a living was really impactful for me. Writing music also started for me in high school. I was very into Imogen Heap, and I had just gotten my first laptop. She made a lot of her music by layering her vocals on her recording software, so I started doing the same thing.

BLVR: If a movie was made about your life, is there a section you feel would make for the most dynamic film?

JW: Ooh, that's a good question. I've been thinking a lot about this moment in my childhood when I went to this Black summer arts camp. The program was very cool, but for me it was traumatic. There was a singing teacher who made everyone go around in a circle, stand up, and sing a song. I was getting more and more nervous, and then it got to my turn, and suddenly all the songs in the universe escaped my brain. I could not think of a song. I had been wanting to sing something like the *Full House* theme song. It just escaped. Eventually, the teacher was like, "Just sing 'Row, Row, Row Your Boat.'" And I did that, and I was crying, and yeah, it was just so embarrassing.

I've been thinking a lot about my voice, post-pandemic. There was no singing live for a year and a half, and then all of a sudden it was like, *We're opening back up*, and I was going on tour. So I had all these shows, and then I had all these issues come up with my voice, a condition called muscle tension dysphonia, or MTD, where you're overworking and straining your vocal cords but not producing much sound. I was doing all this doctor-recommended stuff: vocal speech therapy, daily exercises, and larynx massages. Then at a certain point I felt like there was a spiritual layer to this condition, and it had to do with how I had learned to temper my self-expression when I was younger: always wanting to say the cool thing, or being nervous in a situation and not wanting to express myself, code-switching, et cetera. If I was directing the movie of my life, I would want to trace how I learned to express myself, including moments like that camp moment, and also moments in poetry spaces that allowed me more freedom and agency.

MICROINTERVIEW WITH KEVIN YOUNG, PART VII

THE BELIEVER: Your work has tended to focus on the Black experience, the legacy of the Civil War, and other topics relating to race. What do you think of this current moment we're in, where there's so much debate about DEI and so forth?

KEVIN YOUNG: What's interesting is the ways the poets have been writing about all this. I edited this anthology of African American poetry. It came out in 2020. I finished the introduction on Juneteenth in 2020, and this was in the midst of the George Floyd protests and the pandemic. And I was pulling out this book of poetry and trying to sort of say, *How can one write about now?*, and also to say, *Oh, maybe I have, in writing about Hell and Paradise*. Or Purgatory, which it felt like in some ways. And what struck me in editing that anthology is that the poets in that book—over hundreds of years of African American writing—were always writing about these things. They had the desire to witness and say, *This is what I know*. So the moment is both new and also not. And it's really important to keep that in mind, and to turn to poetry as a way to remind us of both things—of the urgency, but also of the legacy. ✲

BLVR: Wow, I would love to see this movie. What was dealing with MTD like?

JW: I first developed MTD in 2022. Since I started singing professionally, I always had a certain anxiety about my voice—it would feel really high stakes whenever I got sick and lost my voice, like, Will I lose out on this gig or have to cancel a show? The MTD showed me that this anxiety was manifesting in a physical way. After spending years inside, I now felt all this pressure to perform, and that pressure was making my body physically tense up. Although it was scary at the time, it was really helpful to realize what was going on so I could start to shift how I relate to my voice and how I metabolize stress and anxiety.

III. SONGS AS WORLDS

BLVR: What first brought you to music? Were you drawn to its healing potential?

JW: I was raised in a household where my mom and my dad were both healers from different modalities. My dad is a physician and trained other doctors in a hospital. My mom also went to medical school, but her passion is alternative medicine and learning from Eastern and African healing traditions. Growing up, I saw this balance between science, or what can be studied, and what doesn't make any fucking sense. My mom's just like, "Yeah, I helped this person cure their claustrophobia. We did hypnosis and found there was someone in their lineage who was buried alive. And now they are able to drive their car again." I'm like, "What? That's so cool!"

I think music has a healing ability to bring us from the space of what we know to what we don't know. It's wild to me to think there are so many ways we could be healing our bodies or restoring people who have committed harm within our communities. There are Indigenous healing practices and restorative justice practices that have been around for centuries, and we've lost them. They've been violently taken away from us. I'm fascinated by the process of recovering and honoring ancestral, intuitive ways of knowing in my work, making them feel present, and seeing how useful they can be in healing and sustaining ourselves.

BLVR: I'm curious how you think of collaboration in the context of healing or as an extension of healing, and about what role music has in transforming community, especially when you're partnering with a social justice or climate justice organization.

JW: I made a song called "Teach Me" in partnership with a Chicago organization called the Social Justice Portal Project. Barbara Ransby, who runs the Portal Project, is a legend—she's an incredible historian and activist who has taught me a lot through how she moves in the world. She asked me to choose from a list of social justice themes and write a song inspired by what I learned. I saw "climate justice" and was intrigued because I had heard of climate change but never the framing of climate justice, which considers how environmental issues intersect with race, class, gender, and colonialism. I was really inspired by the work of Vandana Shiva, an environmental activist who writes a lot about transforming the way humans relate to the land. She encourages us to shift away from having an extractive relationship with

---

MICROINTERVIEW WITH KEVIN YOUNG, PART VIII

THE BELIEVER: Right now there are a lot of political and technological challenges for writers and literature and publishers and the media in general. How do you think the future looks in that regard?

KEVIN YOUNG: I try not to predict, even though poems can be prescient. There will always be poets, and we need them more than ever. The real danger is some of what I talked about in *Bunk*. There are the falsehoods and all this stuff, some of which is part of the fabric of our fabulist history. But I also think there's a way in which what I call the Age of Euphemism—and I'm not sure if that's even a strong enough word—is really a risk. Like this idea that words aren't what they say, and we're just fine with that. Poets *labor* over a word. Sometimes people say, *You're really good at language*. You feel terrible at language if you're a poet; you're just like, *I can't get it right*. But that desire to get it right is so important, and so much a part of thinking through history, thinking through the present, but also thinking about the future. And all those things are tied up in poetry. ★

the land to a more reciprocal relationship. The lyrics of the song are reflecting on this shift. Writing this song also opened up a collaboration with Slow Factory, an environmental and social justice organization. I think about songs as worlds. When thinking about collaborating with organizations, I ask myself, Who can build out the world of this song with me?

I feel like music offers a *softening*—that was the word that came to mind, or maybe *opening*. It brings us back into our bodies. Singing always brings me into my body. And when I'm really tapped into listening to someone, it grounds me in a way. So even during my shows I'm very intentional. If I have something to say, I want to guide the audience into a space of openness to be able to receive it—especially if it's something that's spicy or something that people might not be receptive to right off the bat.

IV. MUSIC AT THE END OF THE WORLD

BLVR: Expanding on this idea of collaboration, your new album, *Water Made Us*, seems to be in deep conversation with Toni Morrison's essay "The Site of Memory." And on your album *Legacy! Legacy!*, each song is named after a different artist who shaped you, which I see as a conversation with the people who've shaped your thinking and the traditions from which your creative work springs. I am curious how you think about the concepts of inheritance, citation, and collaboration. How do you think about your relationship with other people across time?

JW: You're asking me about the idea of citation. I feel like citation is an act of love, an honoring of the ingredients that make up my ideas and of the wisdom that's been passed down to me. I think that comes from my poetry education, where we'd write *after* poems; it was always celebrated, to name where your influences are coming from. The relationship between myself and those names in the album is interesting, because the idea wasn't to represent that person fully with the song. The idea was more to honor how multifaceted James Baldwin or Nikki Giovanni is by saying, I can't possibly represent that in a song, but I'm gonna take the part that's reflected in me in this moment and make a song about that.

It's kind of like using their ideas and their work as a lens through which to talk about myself, you know? To talk about my own relationships, about compromise, through the lens of, say, Eartha [Kitt]. I think the concept of legacy helped me because I didn't have to care about making a better album than *Heavn*. I only had to care about making a song that was worthy of being called "Giovanni" and that did justice to what Nikki Giovanni means to me.

BLVR: Yeah, that song's so beautiful. Has it taken on a different resonance for you after she passed?

JW: I feel like she's just always so present for me. I am very grateful I got to meet her in 2022 when she received the Poetry Foundation award in Chicago. Yeah, if anything, it just makes me want to go read the poems of hers that I haven't read.

I feel grounded in the fact that I'm a unique expression of life, so whenever I'm interpreting, sampling, or building on what someone else has done, I know I'm doing it from my unique point of view. And still I can be doing that in my corner, and someone in a totally different place can create something that feels akin to what I've made, because we're pulling from the same sources or have had similar experiences. So it's this simultaneous holding of my own uniqueness and knowing that many people are cut from similar cloth. I like to exist in between those two thoughts.

BLVR: Speaking of another person named on that record, I was just re-listening to the song "Octavia" on *Legacy! Legacy!* and was curious about your relationship to Octavia Butler.

JW: I'm just so in awe of her. She was so prescient, so psychic. She studied the natural world. I really just appreciate her wisdom and her clarity.

I remember being at the Huntington Botanical Gardens in Pasadena, where her papers are and where she spent a lot of time. I was seeing certain plants and could recognize them in her work—like, This is the alien tentacle in the *Xenogenesis* series. I could see where she saw stories in the world around her.

BLVR: I love the idea you mentioned earlier of music as a means of softening or opening people up to other worlds or other ways of being in the world, and also as a means of honoring the work that people are doing. What do you think the role of art is at the end of the world?

JW: Whenever I see the word *apocalypse*, I always think of Franny [Choi]'s poem "The World Keeps Ending, and the World Goes On," and the knowledge that my ancestors have also experienced this apocalyptic and despairing feeling. That brings me some solace and also becomes the impetus to do justice to their work.

When I was putting together the *Water Made Us* tour in February 2024, I wanted to create an opportunity for people to ground themselves and get in touch with their emotions. At a certain point in the show I wanted to say, *Hey, this is what I'm feeling. Can we feel this together for a moment?* So in terms of making art at the end of the world, I always think about the utility of things I make, which comes from going to church with my grandma when I was little. It was just so clear that all the music in the Black church has a utility to it. This music is so you'll know when we're passing around the [offering] plate. This music is to inspire you to put money in it. This music is to help you transition from being in this prayer space to sending you back out into the world. This music is for the people who are getting up and shaking their bodies, shaking off whatever pain they're in. It just felt like there was such a use to the music. So I think there's always this element of thinking, What is this for? when it comes to my work.

V. AN ENDING AND A BEGINNING

BLVR: My partner, Micheal, had a question about how prayer shows up in your music, particularly incantation—taking a phrase and imbuing it with more power through repetition.

JW: I love that. I was just thinking about a quote I read when I was making the album. Jessica Dore, a social worker and author, was saying how every time you say a prayer, it's like you're invoking all the intention and power of every single person who's ever said that prayer. So because of that I started singing "The Lord's Prayer" song, which I learned in church, as part of my morning ritual. I don't take everything with me from my church experience, but I definitely take the vessel of the prayer and what it meant to the people before me. What I aspire to do with a song is to have it be a vessel in that way, so people can connect with not only what I intended when I wrote it, but what they intend for themselves.

I feel like my song "Holy" does that. I don't think every single song does that, but I love thinking about prayer as an act of devotion and how prayer also teaches you to devote yourself to your relationship to other people.

BLVR: Beautiful. This leads me to my last question. How do you think about the writing life versus the musician life? How do you think about genre and what the right vessel is for a project? Also, I know there are so many of us waiting for that first book of Jamila Woods poems to come out, so what's going on with that?

JW: A lot of times people want to know about the difference between a song and a poem, or what the relationship is between the two. I don't always know the line between a song and a poem, but regarding the writer life versus the musician life: The two lives do feel distinct. My musician life is inherently collaborative in a way that's more structured—there are people I like to create with and a team that supports me. I've been living that life for a long time in a public way, whereas, even though I've been doing poetry for a long time, I feel like a poetry baby in a way, because I haven't published a full-length book and I've never done my own poetry tour. I still feel like, Do I know how to do this?

But it's also kind of nice to feel that way, because I don't put so much pressure on myself. So right now I'm trying, by osmosis, to feel that way about my music too. What if I am doing this for the first time? How can that energy help invigorate the process? I do want to blend more of my poetry with my music, and music into my poetry, so the page feels musical. I want interludes in my poetry books too. What would that be like?

Right now we're in a nine-year cycle in numerology—we're not quite at the end, but we're not quite starting a new cycle either. We're in this interstitial year. That is exactly how I feel: I'm still going to do some shows this year that are centered around my album *Water Made Us*. But I'm also about to close out the chapter of my three albums and see what could come next. So yeah, it feels like a good time to be a baby. ✶

MOSTLY EVERYTHING
THE ART OF TUCKER NICHOLS

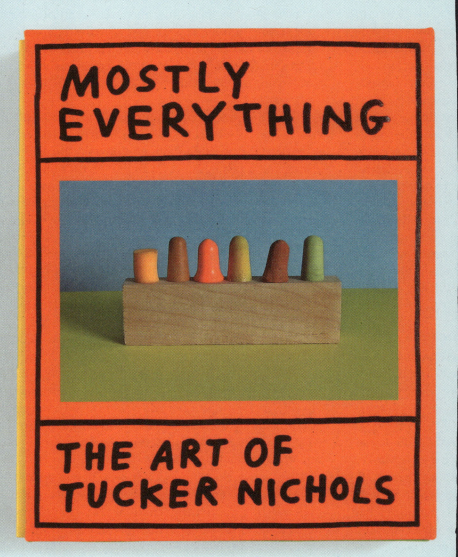

The first career-spanning book from Bay Area artist Tucker Nichols

Mostly Everything: The Art of Tucker Nichols attempts to capture, in one extravagant volume, decades of the artist's varied work, from drawings with words, drawings without words, paintings, and sculpture, to large- and medium-scale public works, editorial illustrations, picture books, doodles, notes, charts, lists, and more.

Bound in a luxurious, hard-to-describe double-hardcover book, with two spines and two overlapping cover boards, and clocking in at over 300 full-color pages, *Mostly Everything: The Art of Tucker Nichols* contains a lifetime of making that can't quite be contained.

OUT NOW FROM McSWEENEY'S

THE WAY BACK

A ROTATING GUEST COLUMN OF WRITERLY REMEMBRANCES.
IN THIS ISSUE: THE FIRESIDE ON LINCOLN AVENUE

by Peter Orner

A family of seven around a table in a packed Chicago restaurant. The meal's over. The plates have been cleared. All that remains: the white tablecloth, scattered silverware, half-empty glasses, what looks like a breadbasket. The Fireside on Lincoln Avenue in, I believe, 1946 or '47.

From left to right: my great-grandfather Sam Orner, a South Side real estate developer and/or slumlord, depending on whom you ask. I never knew him. He died in the mid-'60s. His right leg is crossed over his left, exposing a bit of pale ankle. Silk socks, newly shined shoes. That perfectly round Orner head. In a past life we were all bowling balls. Glasses, hard little eyes. He's not smiling. Sam is a man who believed that to smile was to demonstrate not only weakness but stupidity. Not a scowl, more like a scoff. As if to say to the photographer who's been employed to move from table to table to commemorate whatever festive occasion this is: *Egg people to smile? This is what you do for a living?*

Next to Sam is his wife, Anna, my great-grandmother. She's wearing a giant flowered hat. Maybe it's Easter brunch? We're Jews but that wouldn't have stopped us from going out for Easter brunch, if that's what people did. No kidding, like she's got a small patch of garden on her head. Daylilies? Her, I knew. We called her Grandmother Orner and after Sam's death she moved into a residential hotel in Hyde Park called the Flamingo. She lived there for twenty-eight years. A big pink place on the lake between 55th and 56th. My grandfather used to take my brother and me for visits. It was like having an audience with a dying pope who never died. We'd be ushered, separately, into the bedchamber. She'd ask questions without looking us in the eye. She'd be gazing out the window at the iron-gray lake.

"How's your schoolwork?"
"It's good, Grandmother Orner."
"Progress in arithmetic?"
"I'm so-so in math."
"Grammar?"
"I'm better at making things up."
"And how's your slut of a mother?"

This would have been in the early '80s, around the time of my parents' trench warfare divorce.

"She's well, Grandmother Orner."

"Good, good."

And she'd swallow a dry swallow. That will be all. Dismissed.

In the photograph, she's leaning away from her husband. Something almost organic about it, like she's a tree angling away for more sunlight. She is smiling a little, a faint, restrained smile of pride. Not in the hearty family gathered around her but in herself. *Look at me here at the Fireside in this glorious hat. Have you ever seen such a hat?*

Next to her, her son my grandfather Cyrus, just two years home from the South Pacific. We called him Papa. A Navy man. Young, virile, tough. Not yet completely bald. He's in the insurance business and things are going well. Founded his own company. Finally out from under the boot of his father. The war liberated him, made a man of him. Trouble would come later. Something to do with not retaining adequate cash reserves caught the attention of regulators. Murmurs of fraud. Embezzlement? The state's attorney began to sniff around. No charges against my grandfather were ever filed, but it was enough to ruin his reputation and eventually the company went bust. But that's all in the future. Right now he isn't even forty and he's poised to conquer LaSalle Street.

Illustration by Mizmaru Kawahara

THE LETTER
by Gabrielle Bates

A man wrote me a letter from prison that included very specific details about my life. When he told me he was my grandfather, I knew it was impossible, but I still believed him. He apologized on behalf of himself and my mother. You seem to have done well, he said. Despite. That touched me. Holding the letter, I walked outside and stood under the red tree. I "remembered" the murder then. The philanderer in the trunk. *Not my father*, I reassured myself. *Not him in there, on fire.* But I shivered regardless. Thoughts of blazing heat always make me cold. I "remembered" the car's windows, open just a millimeter, and the hatchback's seams, smoke like a hundred black cats flattening under a gate, escaping. I saw that expansion of the most rainless clouds. Letter folded in my hand, I walked the direction I usually walked, up the big hill to the power lines. One can hear the power there. At least I think that's what one hears. If I focused, I could feel my hand touching the paper, then the words touching each other, then the textured place where scar tissue meets fur on a grown horse, one abandoned young with a bridle strapped to her face (later saved through surgery and fed the most delicious apples).

This brunch has been interminable. He can hardly sit still. And now what? Some fop with a camera? *Go ahead and take it already, will you?*

Next to Papa, my father. In a little jacket and miniature bow tie, he stares directly at the camera across death and years. He's dead. They're all dead. They haven't even digested their food. It's three o'clock on a forgotten Sunday afternoon in the late '40s. My father is ten, maybe eleven. His hair is combed upward into a wisp of a wave. He's a cute kid and it's freaky how much he looks like his grandson, a person he didn't live to meet. My father, whom I never loved and spent much of my life avoiding. Whom I've portrayed in fiction as a small, angry, ineffectual ogre. He once asked me to stop writing about him. He said, "Enough already. You've made your point."

Have I? And what point was it?

He sits beside his mother. Lorraine. We called her Nonie. It's Italian. We're not Italian. She picked it up somewhere and ordained herself. *Call me Nonie.* Before she met my grandfather she was a show girl. From thirteen to eighteen, she danced on stages across Chicago. The Selwyn, the Illinois, McVickers, the Edgewater Beach Playhouse… I've got a stack of her publicity photos. My grandmother, scantily clad, her body contorted into shapes I didn't think were humanly possible. On this day, misery is so entrenched in her deep-set eyes it seems irreversible, which it turned out to be. The story has always been that while Cy was off cavorting on a beach in the Solomon Islands, she was landlocked in Chicago with two "difficult" squalling kids. She resented it for the rest of her life. *I gave up the dancing and the adulation for this?* It didn't help that Papa never stopped talking about the war and how much of a party it was. Nonie taught exercise and dance into her mid-eighties but always said teaching wasn't performing. She lived long enough to bury the daughter who sits beside her.

My aunt Rachel. At seven or eight, she's the only one at the table who's having mercy on the photographer. "Big smile," he'd said, and so she's giving him one. Pigtails and her favorite dress. Of them all, her life was the shortest and hardest. Mental illness everyone in the family pretended she didn't have. Except my father. The two of them, brother and sister, hated each other with a mysterious, ancient, Balkan-like hatred that seemed to predate even their births.

He'd say, "As a kid she was crazy, and now? She says there are spooks in her walls."

And it was true: She did believe the CIA had bugged her apartment.

Nonie said the tiny noises were just the neighbors. Or termites?

The cancer couldn't be pretended away. Cruelty upon cruelty.

For our birthdays, Aunt Rachel would always buy us stuffed animals from Granny Good Fox on Wells.

And last, with her chair already pulled a little away from the table, Nonie's mother, Grandma Spinner. I'm not sure I've ever known her first name. She's clutching a big handbag and looks about to stand up and make a quick exit. *I got to get away from these people.* Her long face, no hint of roundness. What's more tenuous than being related by marriage? She, too, has a hat. A simple white hat, and, though it's wide as a sombrero, it does seem a kind of tacit protest against the flamboyance of her rival's flowered monstrosity. Her own husband has been dead so long she can no longer even conjure his face. A cobbler who died at thirty. Was it pneumonia? She can't remember. Anyway, all she wants now is out. The Orners, being from Hungary, always considered themselves a cut above, a little more western, a little less shtetl, than the Russian Spinners.

She's lost a daughter to these haughties. But what can she do? Marriage is marriage.

Nobody in this picture is touching anybody else. And that's it right there. My inheritance of distance. We've always held ourselves apart, even from one another. Not on my mother's side, but her relatives are all from Massachusetts and I'm not from Massachusetts. I'm from Chicago, and, better or worse, I'm from these people. If I could, I'd split in a Checker cab with Grandma Spinner, her white hat and kind, horsey face. There's a laugh somewhere in her tight lips, as if she's in on a joke only she knows. Nobody she's just had brunch with is in on it. Orners are like that. Sealed in our separateness. No joke would have penetrated, at least not one made by a Spinner.

When Grandma Spinner flees, I'll remain at the table.

And when I run out of stories, which feels like every day lately, I turn back to these faces staring out of an old photograph thumbtacked to the wall. My screwed-up bloodline. My beloved dead. Without them, what would I ever have to say? Sam, Grandmother Orner, Papa, Dad, Nonie, Aunt Rachel. To tell is to mourn. It's also to resurrect. And I'll tell again how Nonie used to dance on stages across Chicago. McVickers, the Selwyn, the Illinois… How in a way her life ended when she stopped performing at eighteen to get hitched.

Or did it? Do I read her expression wrong? Is it more resignation than misery? How many years did she have left as a show girl?

I'll try again to understand why my father despised his sister and vice versa.

Or did they? Was their hatred at least partly an act?

Was Sam a slumlord?

Papa an uncaught fraudster?

All the hours I spend asking unanswerable questions.

And at the Flamingo, Grandmother Orner, still somehow alive, still breathing, longs for the lake beyond the window. ✶

GUNS THAT APPEAR IN CHEKHOV'S PLAYS

✶ Heavy revolver on the desk of the late General Voynitsev (*Platonov*, 1878)

✶ Borkin's hunting rifle (*Ivanov*, 1887)

✶ Revolver on the table beside herring and cucumber pickles (*Ivanov*, 1887)

✶ Rifles, pistols hung on the walls in Ivanov's study (*Ivanov*, 1887)

✶ Gun of unspecified type in Ivanov's pocket (*Ivanov*, 1887)

✶ Smith & Wesson revolvers, triple action, with an extractor and central sights, owned by Popova's late husband (*The Bear*, 1888)

✶ Gun gifted to the "Wood Demon" by Orlovsky (*The Wood Demon*, 1889)

✶ French revolver—not an "honest English one"—heard offstage as Voynitsky kills himself (*The Wood Demon*, 1889)

✶ Konstantin's hunting rifle, used to shoot a seagull (*The Seagull*, 1896)

✶ Vanya's revolver, used to fire upon the Professor (*Uncle Vanya*, 1897)

✶ Yepikhodov's loaded pistol, never fired (*The Cherry Orchard*, 1904)

✶ Carlotta's hunting rifle, slung over her shoulder as she appears in male military uniform (*The Cherry Orchard*, 1904)

—list compiled by Tess Wayland

A REVIEW OF

ON THE CALCULATION OF VOLUME (BOOK III)

BY SOLVEJ BALLE, TRANSLATED BY SOPHIA HERSI SMITH AND JENNIFER RUSSELL

When my husband asked about the book I was reading for this review, I told him it followed a woman who was stuck in November 18. Her husband, I said, was not. She woke up every morning and explained to him that she had lived this day before, until she couldn't bear to go on explaining, and she left. "So," he asked, "he's also lived November 18 before, but she remembers, and he doesn't?" That was, I supposed, correct. "Then," he said, "he's the one who's stuck."

This is a conversation that could well be found in Solvej Balle's septology *On the Calculation of Volume*, which is ultimately about time, in all its guises—time as change and repetition, as history and memory, as materiality and disappearances.

In the third volume of the series, Tara Selter is still caught in the same November day. But where the first two volumes trace Tara's growing loneliness as the year she has been sharing with loved ones disintegrates into one endless solitary autumn, the third finds her in the company of three fellow denizens of her day. Here, Balle considers what it looks like to build shared understanding with others in the wake of catastrophe. The four new companions compare their experiences and debate the nature of time: Is it a container? Or is it a train? Is it layered, like tectonic plates, or more like the edges of a garden where things "merge together or overshadow each other as they grow"?

Throughout the novel, Balle manages to destabilize even the reader's sense of time. Tara's careful notes have so far served as the series's time-keeping system, her numbered journal entries tracking her days. In this book, however, we learn that her count may be off. Henry D., the first companion Tara meets, has also been keeping a tally, and he has a different total. Their counts are off by only a day, yes, but when Tara first slipped through the "fault in time," she thought that it, too, seemed like "a minor variation, an error in a sequence of numbers…

Publisher: *New Directions* **Page count:** *144* **Price:** *$15.95* **Key quote:** *"We're a strange bunch inside a container of time. If time is a container, that is, says Henry. He thinks it's more like a train, and we are all seated in the same compartment. As if we are on a journey."* **Shelve next to:** *Vigdis Hjorth, Franz Kafka, Karl Ove Knausgaard, Yoko Tawada* **Unscientifically calculated reading time:** *One mid-November day under a medlar tree*

a problem that can be solved," as she put it in the first book.

Balle has proved remarkably adept at filling both her characters' "container of time" (as Tara likes to think of it) and her readers'. Her novel of repetition reveals not a deadening monotony but rather the remarkable richness of each moment. Her spare, attentive prose demonstrates the way careful attention can transform seemingly familiar silences into a lushly textured masterwork of sound. She also excels at a subtle form of suspense: Her novels are carefully plotted even as, by their very terms, a kind of nothing continues to happen.

Not long after getting stuck in the eighteenth of November, Tara notices that the food she buys from the grocery store sometimes fails to return to the shelves when the day resets overnight, and she becomes concerned that she is a "monster" who is "eating up" her world. But it is Ralf and Olga, two of Tara's new companions, who are the ones to insist that their material impact should be the group's first priority. As Ralf says, "If we wake up one day and there are no more eighteenths of November, isn't it our responsibility to ensure that the day we leave behind is the best of all possible eighteenths of November?" The questions Balle raises—of what we owe one another, how we come to agree on what constitutes reality, and what happens when our shared vision of the world cannot hold—have an uncanny ability to feel both timely and timeless.

Ralf is intent on initiating a new project, aimed at stopping as many "injuries, fires, accidents, deaths, tragedies and disasters which occur on the eighteenth" as possible. Toward the book's close, the rest of the group has gotten on board. Inherent to this quest, of course, is the sense that by trying to repair the damage in this day, they could put time back on its usual path from one day to the next. This hope goes mostly unstated. "We couldn't talk about hope without talking about longing," Tara explains, "and no one wanted to talk about longing today."

—*Meghan Racklin*

Illustration by Pete Gamlen

A REVIEW OF

FRONT STREET: RESISTANCE AND REBIRTH IN THE TENT CITIES OF TECHLANDIA

BY BRIAN BARTH

If you've visited the wealthy towns of Silicon Valley, you've probably seen people living on nearby streets, sleeping in tents, in vehicles, or on the sidewalks. You might have offered them money, looked away, or crossed the street. How did so many people, you might have wondered, end up homeless in the shadow of the tech heartland? That is the question journalist Brian Barth set out to answer when he moved to the area at the start of the COVID epidemic. He imagined a book that would introduce readers to characters and investigate solutions—not a journey that would change the trajectory of his life. But that is what happened.

Yes, we meet memorable characters in *Front Street*, but we also follow Barth's personal reckoning as he considers a society—and specifically an affluent state—that leaves so many behind. The book begins as Barth is experiencing the worst year of his life, precipitated by a divorce and then a move to rural North Carolina, where he lived, literally and figuratively, on Solitude Lane. From there, he plans a trip to the Bay Area, and moves into an upscale apartment in Cupertino, the Santa Clara County home to both Apple Inc.'s headquarters and to a large tent city known as Wolfe Camp.

Barth has only to step outside his apartment to meet the camp leader, Kent, wearing an unbuttoned dress shirt and "harlequinesque" mask, who grew up a few blocks away in a well-off family, but has since been through divorces, drug habits, and a prison stint. He relies, like many of the encampment's residents, on dumpster diving, which earns him about three thousand dollars a month. So why doesn't he use that money to rent a place to live? For starters, it's not enough to cover living expenses in Silicon Valley. But the truth, Kent says, is that "here, I'm with people. It doesn't excite me to be alone. There's great depression in that."

Barth gets to know the residents in a way he didn't expect to. There are arguments, messes, mental health crises in the camps, but also ordinary life events, celebrations, and deep friendships. Early on, he reminds himself not to judge, or to follow the path of the "poverty media" that offers a one-dimensional view of the homeless. But he faces a common journalistic dilemma: Can he take notes but also offer support?

The deeper Barth delves into the lives of his subjects, the more involved he becomes in their struggles. At one camp, he puts down his camera to help residents move their belongings, after witnessing days of emotional turmoil as their sleeping spaces were torn apart, their possessions discarded during repeated sweeps. At Oakland's Wood Street Commons, which has a flea market, bike repair shop, and café, he joins the protest of an impending sweep.

There is, Barth learns, no single reason why people are unhoused, and no easy fix. In California, where 30 percent of the nation's homeless live, governors and mayors have been declaring new strategies for at least twenty years, with little success. At the Crash Zone, in a dusty area near the San Jose airport, Barth meets Lisa "Tiny" Gray-Garcia, a well-known Bay Area activist and cofounder of *POOR* magazine, who believes that the unhoused should be empowered to develop solutions. Tiny is not waiting for the government or nonprofits, and she has little patience for journalists. "We don't give a fuck about telling our story over and over again," she tells Barth. "What for? So that you can sell more books?"

And Barth listens. His book offers no top-down solutions or tidy endings. At times his discussion of how to counter the ills of capitalism can seem overly idealistic and his criticism of nonprofits somewhat misplaced. We may have outsourced our responsibilities to a homeless industrial complex, but would we need to do that if our government offered basic services?

Politics aside, you don't have to agree with Barth to keep turning the pages. He provides a deeply moving account of people "doing Front Street," facing the world from where they are. Despite the escalating wave of sweeps, they have what often escapes their housed neighbors: community. Barth ends up remarrying, settling in the Bay Area, and dedicating himself to a more spiritual life—but he is forever changed.

—*Katherine Seligman*

Publisher: *Astra House* **Page count:** *304* **Price:** *$29.00* **Key quote:** *"'Doing Front Street' means not hiding in the bushes. It means owning who you are, facing the world on the other side of the poverty veil."* **Shelve next to:** *Matthew Desmond, Kevin Fagan, Sarah Jones* **Unscientifically calculated reading time:** *Amtrak ride from San Francisco to Portland, Oregon*

Illustration by Pete Gamlen

A REVIEW OF
THE BOOK OF HOMES
BY ANDREA BAJANI, TRANSLATED BY ELIZABETH HARRIS

Andrea Bajani's most recent novel, translated from the Italian by Elizabeth Harris, takes as its structure a list of seventy-eight "homes" (repeats allowed), each the title and premise of a brief chapter. The book flits between years, between Rome and Turin, between our protagonist's childhood and his middle age. Throughout Bajani's pages, architecture proves paramount. Photos of digitized floor plans float between passages. The prose looms delightfully over rooms and walls in close detail (by comparison, Bajani rarely describes a human face). But home, the book contends, is not always a place with walls. Here are some of the "homes" to which Bajani devotes a chapter: a bank account, a wedding ring, a white Fiat Panda, a soccer field whose white boundary lines have long ago faded from sight.

The book opens. On the first page of the first chapter—titled "Underground Home, 1976"—our narrator informs us that he'll be referring to our protagonist, henceforth, as "I." A vertiginous grammar ensues ("I begins to crawl") and follows us across the novel ("I understands that metamorphoses exist, that the universe can capsize at any moment"). In a book obsessed with the uncertain line between public and private life, Bajani's decision to strand his reader on the median strip between the first and third person is no accident. Here lies one of Bajani's chief gifts: His writing performs, not merely details, its preoccupations. All of Bajani's characters in *The Book of Homes* are nearly nameless—they don generic titles like "Mother," "Little Girl," "Virgin Girl," and "Prisoner." Of course, the book must come to terms with the frailty of these names. In one passage, "I" admits a startling fact: "his father is also a son."

The Book of Homes depicts a man in the throes of a more or less ordinary life, complete with a batch of private devastations: cancer, adultery, the pandemic, all manner of familial strife. Meanwhile, history lurks at the novel's borders. As a child, our protagonist watches footage of a "prisoner"—the kidnapped Italian prime minister Aldo Moro, we assume, although the book, true to style, never names him. One of the book's "homes" is the Red Renault 4 where police discovered Moro's bullet-riddled body, a car whose color our protagonist will never forget, a color he feels "like a twinge in his hip, a kind of national pain." And yet this is not a novel about Italian political turbulence, about the Years of Lead. It is a novel to which history is peripheral. It is also a novel fascinated with peripheries, their express power. History abuts the novel, thus determining its edges.

One character in this book won my heart most of all: a turtle who lives in our protagonist's backyard (referred to, aptly, as Turtle). Turtle is our protagonist's first love. In childhood, "I" craves a diet of lettuce, and his movements become "turtle-induced," a quiet homage to his reptilian friend. But Bajani's turtle is not simply a companion: By equal measure, she is a survivor. She survives—outliving housing arrangements, humans, and other, more imperious-seeming animals—precisely because she carries a "home" on her back. A home, like all homes, that both protects and ensnares her: "her carapace is her incarcerator," Bajani writes. "Turtle's home is also her tomb," he writes elsewhere.

The book closes. I feel as if, in some ways, the novel has held me at arm's length, or even tried to escape me. Bajani is a genius, a first-rate inspector of domestic minutiae and the muted catastrophe of familial life. He has written a wondrous and laudable book, full of containments and escapes. It's only fitting, then, that the book itself seemed to desire detachment from me, its reader. Perhaps I am to Bajani what his novel's "Sister" is to his protagonist: "the limb he has to leave behind in the trap, to save himself."

—*Ricardo Frasso Jaramillo*

> **Publisher:** *Deep Vellum* **Page count:** *267* **Price:** *$17.95* **Key quote:** *"Paris is easy to imagine. It's already in our heads, so takes little effort. Firsthand knowledge isn't necessary. The stereotype, the frozen imagination, will do. All it takes is a little microwaving in the brain."* **Shelve next to:** *Tessa Hadley, Guadalupe Nettel, Kirmen Uribe* **Unscientifically calculated reading time:** *The time it takes to reorganize your most chaotic closet*

Illustration by Pete Gamlen

A REVIEW OF
THE AUTOBIOGRAPHY OF H. LAN THAO LAM
BY LANA LIN

In 1933, Gertrude Stein published *The Autobiography of Alice B. Toklas*, a modernist reshaping of the memoir form, written from the perspective of her life partner. Cast from this mold comes Lana Lin's latest publication, the curious and incisive *The Autobiography of H. Lan Thao Lam*. Lin's book brings to mind a flushed cheek: It is warm and self-conscious, a personal history infused with social criticism. The author and her titular subject—two domestic partners for a quarter century—are both artists, experimental filmmakers, and educators living in New York. Together they make up Lin + Lam, a multidisciplinary research collective birthed from a shared standpoint on feminism, national identity, and postcoloniality. Like Stein, Lin writes from Lam's point of view, frequently about herself. She takes on the role of an "autobiographer-detective" tasked with untangling and plaiting their experiences, which are sweeping in scope.

For Lin, these include a "lonely and sterile" childhood in Naperville, Illinois, potholed by bigoted classmates; a move to New York City ahead of 9/11; Fulbright-funded excursions to verdant Taipei and a ramshackle "resort" in Malaysia with Lam; a breast cancer diagnosis and treatment midway through her doctorate. For Lam, these include a childhood in Mỹ Tho during the Tet Offensive, accentuated by accounts of shrapnel by their bassinet; refugee camps and makeshift tin houses before their emigration to Mississauga, Ontario; burgeoning genderqueer expression, partly impelled by Lin's mastectomy and chemical menopause ("those outward female attributes, removed").

Lin, foremost a celebrated filmmaker, uses the uncanny in cinema—from E.T.'s wrinkly exterior to Jordan Peele's doppelgängers in *Us*—as cultural yardsticks to catapult readers into the world of today. Lin's own filmmaking practice (which she writes conspicuously little about here) is also somewhat supernatural, thematizing migration and collective memory through avant-garde images. Cultural criticism thus seems a natural landing strip between Lin's and Lam's more vulnerable histories.

Publisher: *New York Review Books* **Page count:** 224 **Price:** $18.00 **Key quote:** *"How to wade through the contradictions of suspecting that the very thing that makes you distinctive within a homogeneous environment is what makes you invisible?"* **Shelve next to:** *Eula Biss, Jamaica Kincaid, Jackie Wang* **Unscientifically calculated reading time:** *A round-trip voyage from a bustling city to the suburbs and back, ideally via train*

Lin describes her own and Lam's pasts with a focus on the sensory: the smell of hot rubber in the sun; the flavors of white almond Jell-O, sapodilla, and mangosteen; or the tactility of thumbing through slim volumes of Chinese morality tales, in which "selflessness" and "servitude" are the preeminent virtues. Lin explores the idea of selflessness by way of form: She gives up her immediate perspective in service of a shared narrative. I think of my analog experiences growing up in Mississauga, where I, too, crashed my bike while riding at full tilt, smoked out traces of my present self as a teenager, and returned to be biopsied in my early twenties. I conflate myself with both Lin and Lam; and the author, in turn, conflates the two of them through a language of fusion.

Lam is Lin's "human prosthetic" as the narrator confesses to taking pleasure in being "fused together... seeing each other *in* ourselves." Such wording recalls Becca Rothfeld's interpretation of the "interhuman" and the erotic potential of being rewritten, completely and constantly, by another person: "This cycle of me changing you, the changed you changing me, the changed me changing the changed you, and so on," as Rothfeld puts it. Lin invokes Eve Kosofsky Sedgwick—to whom the author devoted a chapter of her dissertation, and, by chance, later shared an oncologist with—for her capacious definition of the term *we* and the pluralities it invites.

The spaciousness to invent (and deconstruct) the self is Lin's most compelling quality as a writer and filmmaker. In the short film *Unidentified Vietnam No. 18*, an addendum to Lin + Lam's first shared project concerning the historiography of 1960s propaganda films, a ghostly figure fades in and out of a mausoleum-like hallway, obscuring itself at will; Lin does the same with this wondrous little text, peregrinating across continents, anatomies, and identities as both herself and her lover, as stalwart narrator and evasive subject. She resolves at the finish, "I am I, Lan Thao Lam, and I am Not-I, Lana Lin," or, *I am the you that is in me.* —*Saffron Maeve*

Illustration by Pete Gamlen

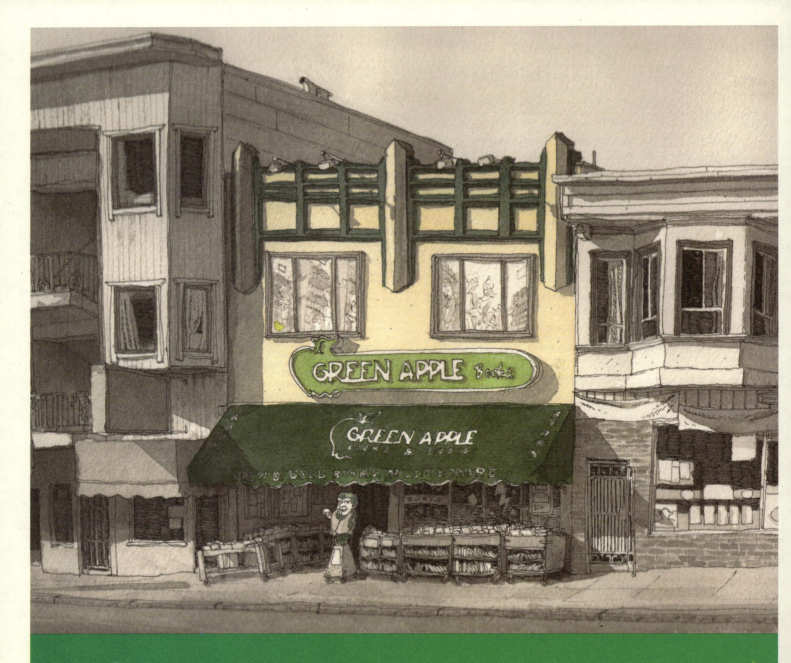

A trio of independent bookstores in San Francisco.

Hosting author events, most of them free, at our Books on the Park location 2–3 times a week.

GREEN APPLE BOOKS
506 Clement Street (Since 1967)

BROWSER BOOKS
2195 Fillmore Street (Since 1976)

BOOKS ON THE PARK
1231 Ninth Avenue (Since 2014)

greenapplebooks.com

COVER TO COVER

SURVEYING THE COVERS OF GREAT BOOKS AS THEY CHANGE ACROSS TIME AND COUNTRY.
IN THIS ISSUE: *THE CRYING OF LOT 49* BY THOMAS PYNCHON

Compiled by Chase Bush-McLaughlin

IRAN
Cheshmeh
2019

CROATIA
Ceres
1998

JAPAN
Chikuma Shobō
2010

BRAZIL
Companhia das Letras
1993

EGYPT
Dar al-Tanweer
2017

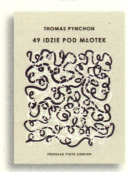

POLAND
ArtRage
2010

ITALY
Einaudi
2005

GREECE
Ýpsilon/Vivlía
1986

UNITED STATES
J.B. Lippincott
1966

TAIWAN
Chingwin Publishing
2014

LITHUANIA
Lietuvos rašytojų sąjungos leidykla
2005

GERMANY
Rowohlt
1986

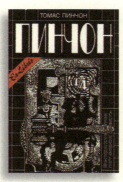

RUSSIA
Simpozium
2000

SERBIA
Svetovi
1992

SPAIN
Tusquets
1994

An indisputably enjoyable section of **GAMES & PUZZLES**

THE PUZZLE OF INCREDIBLY WIDE AND DEEP KNOWLEDGE

IF YOU COMPLETE THIS PUZZLE, YOU ARE A GENERALIST OF BROAD SKILL AND GREAT RENOWN

by Ada Nicolle; edited by Benjamin Tausig

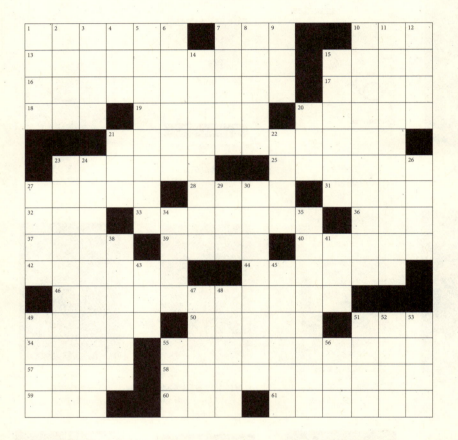

ACROSS

1. Fellow travelers
7. Decorates for Halloween?
10. Yukon manufacturer
13. Sports Resort gaming attachment
15. Part of FOMO
16. Becomes cringe, say, as an old post
17. Empire in the 1747 novel "Letters from a Peruvian Woman"
18. "Let's GET it!"
19. Give a boost
20. Reflective piece
21. "Murder, She Wrote" genre
23. Yanny or ___ (viral 2010s auditory illusion)
25. B-to-B stretch, say
27. Attendee of the King Abdulaziz Camel Festival
28. Handmade-goods outlet created in Brooklyn in 2005
31. Skeleton requirement
32. Beer originally called "Best Select," for short
33. Source of meals on wheels?
36. Muscle worked by dips, informally
37. ___ kid (tech-obsessed toddler, in slang)
39. State with a namesake raptor
40. Depiction of a far-off land?
42. Stick with Scotch, say
44. Bad, in Newspeak
46. Ask why things can't be different, e.g.
49. Doesn't let settle
50. Turn away
51. Verb that's a homophone of 53-Down
54. Resusci ___ (model used in CPR training)
55. 48 hours from now, poetically
57. Carnaval de Québec, e.g.
58. Soft spot for babies?
59. Dramatic TV drama settings
60. Assigned reading during a Shakespeare unit, say
61. Possible recipient of a hand-me-down dress, casually

DOWN

1. Scoreboard side
2. La ___ (Spanish football level)
3. Doesn't take responsibility, say
4. Networking event attendees, potentially
5. Intoxicated
6. Stay out?
7. Play idly, as a guitar
8. Like some OJ
9. Drone spot
10. Army officer associated with chicken
11. Used a pin to unlock something, maybe?
12. Bananas, so to speak
14. License that allows for adaptation of work, as long as the resulting product maintains the same license
15. Certain deli counter purchases
20. "... you don't need me to list them all"
21. Meadow mouthful
22. Nondairy milk source
23. One with whom you might share a flask
24. Quantitative measure of coolness
26. Removal of a typo, e.g.
27. Condemn what you just said, in a way
29. Something to wash down a scone
30. "You've heard of Bach, Beethoven and Brahms? Well, from now on it's going to be ___, Schumann and Schroeder!" (Charlie Brown quip in a 1952 "Peanuts" strip)
34. Viv, to Will
35. It's totally tubular!
38. Ruling
41. Word to condemn what you just said
43. Signs off on
45. New ___ (possibly terrifying paradigm shift)
47. Mass destruction
48. One might require a planner
49. Secure site in a hotel
51. Blue text?
52. Jus ___ (birthright citizenship)
53. Plural noun that's a homophone of 51-Across
55. "Diary ___ Wimpy Kid"
56. 2018 sitcom starring comedian Howery

(answers on page 124)

JACKET CAPTCHA
CAN YOU IDENTIFY THESE NINE BOOK COVERS?

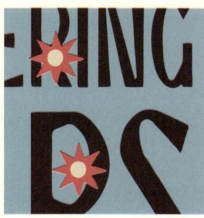

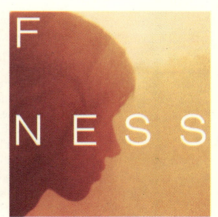

COPYEDITING THE CLASSICS

10 ERRORS HAVE BEEN INERTED INTO THIS PASSAGE. CAN YOU FIND THEM?

by Caitlin Van Dusen

TARZAN OF THE APES (1912)
by EDGAR RICE BURROUGHS

Darkness had now fallen, and an early moon was sending its faint light to cast strange, grotesque shadows among the dense foliage of the forest.

Here and there the brilliant rays penetrated to earth, but for the most part they served only to accentuate the Stygian blackness of the jungle's depths.

Like some huge phantom, Kala swung noiselessly from tree to tree; now running nimbly along a great branch, now swinging through space at the end of another, only to grasp that of a further tree in her rapid progress towards the scene of the tragedy her knowledge of jungle life told her was being enacted a short distance before her.

The cries of the gorilla proclaimed that it was in mortal combat with some other denizen of the fierce wood. Suddenly, these cries ceased, and the silence of death reined throughout the jungle.

Kala could not understand, for the voice of Bolgani had at last been raised in the agony of suffering and death, but no sound had come to her by which she possibly could determine the nature of his antagonist.

That her little Tarzan could destroy a great bull gorilla, she knew to be improbable, and so, as she neared the spot from which the sounds of the struggle had come, she moved more warily and at last slowly and with extreme caution she traversed over the lowest branches, peering eagerly into the blackness for a sign of the combatants.

Presently she came upon them, lying in a little open space full under the brilliant light of the moon—little Tarzan's torn and bloody form, and beside it a great bull gorilla, stone dead….

Tenderly she bore him back through the inky jungle to where the tribe laid, and for many days and nights she sat guard beside him, bringing him food and water, and brushing the flies and other insects from his cruel wounds.

Of medicine or surgery the poor thing knew nothing. She could but lick the wounds, and thus she tenderly kept them cleansed, that healing nature might the more quickly do her work.

(answers on page 124)

Follow The Chicago Manual of Style, *17th edition. Please ignore unusual spellings, hyphenations, and capitalizations, and the that/which distinction. All are characteristic of the author's style and time.*

120

CLASSIFIEDS

Believer Classifieds cost $2 per word. They can be placed by emailing classifieds@thebeliever.net. All submissions subject to editorial approval. No results guaranteed.

NEW & RECOMMENDED

DO YOU DREAM OF CLOUDS? Do you live in a cataclysmic time? Do you want to know how Kurt Vonnegut's brother made snow and caused floods? *Nightshining*. "A riveting exposé" —Jonathan Lethem. "Kabat has next-level powers of discernment and shimmering prose." —Paul Chaat Smith. https://milkweed.org/book/nightshining

PUBLICATIONS

CAMSHAFT 10 IS AVAILABLE at camshaft.ink. A North Coast zine stepping up to hardcover. This is a limited edition collection of short stories and poems in horror and science fiction. You'll laugh, you'll shudder, and have much to ponder after reading this beautifully hard bound book.

PAPER AIRPLANE is the grown-up version of the magazines you loved as a kid—fun, fascinating, and uncynical writing, games, comics, photos, art, and activities. No ads. No A.I. PaperAirplane.pub.

LISTEN UP

MARSIFICATION: A tale of planetary grief, a concept album in 16 vignettes, is an audio artwork that invites you to float in the zero gravity of astrocolonial dreams and the nightmares that fuel them. Listen at www.marsification.com or your music streaming platform of choice.

FREE MUSIC—Longtime reader of *The Believer* (20+) has finally made an album of songs that he is happy with and he hopes to share them with likeminded readers: Existential lyrics and mellow music, with a few upbeat indiepop songs. PAWL: Mystic—> pawl.bandcamp.com

HELP WANTED

DO YOU KNOW what's good in Nebraska? Please txt: 647-462-7992.

FELICITATIONS

HAPPY RETIREMENT, BOB! Us folks in accounting chipped in and got you a little something. We asked Bev what you might like, and she said a new set of golf clubs, but, frankly, that was a little outside our budget, so we got you the next best thing—a subscription to *The Believer*. Happy reading!—Your friends at TechnoCorp

WELCOME TO THE 30+ CLUB—Santiago, your new member packet will be arriving in the mail. In the meantime, you'll see that the Merlin Bird ID app has been installed on your phone, and a 500-count bottle of ibuprofen has been placed in your medicine cabinet. Oh, and don't worry—that grunting sound you now make every time you get up or sit down is perfectly normal. Enjoy your 4th decade!

APOLOGIES

TO EVERYONE AT THE JW MARRIOTT BALLROOM LAST NIGHT, I would like to say that I am deeply sorry. By the time the father-daughter dance came along, I was a few too many gin and tonics deep. Still, that's no excuse for grabbing the microphone out of the DJ's hand and regaling the crowd with what, in the clarity of sobriety, I now realize was a very wedding-inappropriate story of the groom's college days. This incident was made all the more unfortunate by the fact that, on my way back from the bathroom, I had inadvertently wandered into the wrong ballroom, and was not delivering my speech to the wedding party, but instead to a room full of horrified strangers. Though, in my defense, to a blurry-eyed drunk, a quinceañera dress does look an awful lot like a wedding dress. Happy 15th birthday, Josefina! And once again, my sincerest apologies.

MISSED CONNECTIONS

A MAN AFTER MY OWN TART—You were the tall, muscular, bearded man at the community bake sale who brought the rhubarb custard tarts. But you left in a hurry before I had a chance to introduce myself. A mysterious virtuoso baker? Color me intrigued. There were so many questions I was dying to ask you. For starters, did you blind bake the crust? How long did you refrigerate the dough? Why did you score the rhubarb at an angle? Please find me at the next bake sale. I simply must have that recipe!

WHAT'S YOUR SIGN? At the march last month, we were both holding signs that said "THIS IS A SIGN OF THE TIMES." Clearly, great minds think alike. And if that's not a sign, then I don't know what is. See you at the next one, handsome.

SEEING DOUBLE: You were the Pedro Pascal look-alikes at the Pedro Pascal look-alike contest I organized at the park. Which, in theory, was a great way to meet men who look like Pedro Pascal. Sadly, I never caught any of your real names and thus have no other way to contact you. Shall we try again a week from Saturday?

SERVICES

TEXT YOUR ADDRESS, I'll mail a postcard. 917-412-6791. Brian McMullen.

PSYCHIC SERVICES—Do you wish to know what the future has in store for you? Wonder no more, for I, Malachi the Magnificent, am here for all of your fortune telling needs. Cross my palm with silver and I will reveal all you wish to know. There is no need to contact me directly. If you require my services, I shall find you.

CHECKING IN

HI SWEETIE, it's your mom. We haven't talked in a while, so I thought I'd try you here. Just writing to say hi. Give me a call when you get a chance. Xo

Illustrations by Tomi Um

NOTES ON OUR CONTRIBUTORS

Robbie Arnott is a Tasmanian novelist. He's been shortlisted for the Dylan Thomas Prize, twice-shortlisted for the Miles Franklin Literary Award, and has twice won the Age Book of the Year. He lives in Hobart with his wife and children.

Gabrielle Bates's book *Judas Goat* was named one of the 2023 "Books We Love" by NPR, and one of the top four poetry collections of 2024 by *Electric Lit*, and was a finalist for the Washington State Book Award in Poetry. Originally from Alabama, she is currently based in Seattle, where she works for Open Books: A Poem Emporium, cohosts the podcast *The Poet Salon*, and serves occasionally as a visiting faculty member at the University of Washington Rome Center and the Tin House Workshop. You can find her poems in *The New Yorker*, *Ploughshares*, and elsewhere. gabriellebat.es

Heather Christle is a poet and writer whose most recent books are *Paper Crown* and *In the Rhododendrons: A Memoir with Appearances by Virginia Woolf*. She teaches in the Creative Writing Program at Emory University.

Steven Duong is the author of the debut poetry collection *At the End of the World There Is a Pond*. His writing has appeared in *The American Poetry Review*, *The Best American Short Stories 2024*, *Guernica*, and *The Drift*, among other publications. A creative writing fellow at Emory University and an editor of short fiction at *Joyland* magazine, he lives in Atlanta.

Oliver Egger is a writer and editor based in New Haven, Connecticut. His writing can be found in *The Boston Globe*, *The Brooklyn Rail*, *The Florida Review*, and elsewhere. He received the 2025–2026 Rosalynn Carter Fellowship for Mental Health Journalism. For more information check out his website, oliveregger.com.

Art, culture, and science writer **Nick Hilden** produces the Writers Talking Writers interview series at *Publishers Weekly*, and his work has appeared in *The Washington Post*, *Al Jazeera*, *Rolling Stone*, *Vanity Fair*, *Esquire*, and many other places. He edited the English translation of an upcoming book by Nobel Peace Prize laureate Narges Mohammadi and serves in a number of ad hoc editorial capacities.

Emma Ingrisani's writing has also appeared in *Full Stop*, *Post-Trash*, and *The Creative Independent*.

Ricardo Frasso Jaramillo is a writer of poetry and nonfiction. His work can be found in *The New York Times*, *McSweeney's Quarterly Concern*, *Zyzzyva*, and *The Yale Review*, among other venues. At present, Ricardo is pursuing a PhD in creative writing and literature at the University of Southern California. He is at work on a poetry collection and a historical nonfiction book.

Mona Kareem is the author of four poetry collections, including *I Will Not Fold These Maps*. She teaches Arabic and comparative literature at Washington University in St. Louis, Missouri.

Vijay Khurana's debut novel, *The Passenger Seat*, was shortlisted for the Novel Prize. He lives in Berlin, where he also works as a translator from the German.

R. O. Kwon is the author of the bestselling novels *Exhibit*, a *New York Times* Editors' Choice; and *The Incendiaries*, a finalist for the National Book Critics Circle John Leonard Prize and the *Los Angeles Times* Art Seidenbaum Award. With Garth Greenwell, Kwon coedited *Kink*, which was also a bestseller and a *New York Times* Notable Book of 2021. Kwon's books have been translated into seven languages and have been named best books of the year by over forty publications. Kwon's writing has appeared in *The New York Times*, *The New Yorker*, *Vanity Fair*, and elsewhere. Born in Seoul, South Korea, Kwon has lived for most of her life in the United States.

Born in Korea, raised in Malaysia and China, and currently based in Los Angeles, **Jiwon Lee** is a transnational Korean writer-director. Her latest short film, *Call for Cassie*, has screened at film festivals around the world, and she is currently developing her feature with CJ ENM through the CJ & TIFF K-Story Fund. Jiwon has also worked as a translator for leading voices in Korean cinema, including Park Chan-wook, Song Kang-ho, and Lee Jung-jae.

Kyle Carrero Lopez's debut full-length collection, *Party Line*, will be published by Graywolf Press in 2026. He's the author of the chapbook *Muscle Memory* and serves as editor of *The Poetry Project Newsletter*. His poems appear in *The Nation*, *Guernica*, *The Yale Review*, *Poetry*, *The New Republic*, and elsewhere.

Saffron Maeve is a Toronto-based critic, editor, and film curator. Her writing has appeared in *The Globe and Mail*, *Film Comment*, *Sight and Sound*, MUBI's *Notebook*, *Reverse Shot*, *Hyperallergic*, *Screen Slate*, *Cinema Scope*, the *Toronto Star*, *Le Cinéma Club*, and *Documentary Magazine*.

Born in Chicago, **Peter Orner** is the author of eight books, including *Maggie Brown and Others*; *Esther Stories*, a finalist for the PEN/Hemingway Award for Debut Novel; and *Am I Alone Here?*, a finalist for the National Book Critics Circle Award. A new novel, *The Gossip Columnist's Daughter*, will be out this August from Little, Brown and Company. His work has appeared in *The New Yorker* and *The Paris Review*, and has been awarded four Pushcart Prizes. A Guggenheim fellow and recipient of the Rome Prize, Orner is chair of the Department of English and Creative Writing at Dartmouth College. He lives with his family in Norwich, Vermont, where he's also a volunteer firefighter.

Soham Patel is the author of the poetry collections *to afar from afar*, *ever really hear it*, *all one in the end—/ water*, and the forthcoming *The Daughter Industry*, where "Sai's Closet" will appear next. They serve as associate editor at *Fence*.

Meghan Racklin is a writer and editor with work in *The Baffler*, *The New Republic*, the *Los Angeles Review of Books*, and many other places. She is based in Brooklyn, New York.

Nathaniel Rich is the author, most recently, of *Second Nature: Scenes from a World Remade*, and is a 2025 Guggenheim Fellow.

Ash Sanders is a writer who can't decide whether she lives in Brooklyn or Utah, and likely never will. She's currently rafting the Green and Colorado Rivers from Wyoming to Mexico for a documentary podcast called *Mirage* about the future of water in the West—and as a flimsy excuse to get invited on other people's boats. Her writing and audio pieces have appeared in *Atmos*, *Dark Mountain*, *Rolling Stone*, *Buzzfeed*, *Stitcher*, and elsewhere. She's also working on a book about Mormonism, climate change, and the end of the world.

Sam Sax is the author of *Yr Dead*, longlisted for The National Book Award, and *PIG*, named one of the best books of 2023 by *New York* magazine and *Electric Lit*, among other books. They live in Oakland, California, and lecture in an interdisciplinary arts program at Stanford University.

Katherine Seligman is a journalist and author who has been a reporter for *USA Today*, the *San Francisco Examiner*, and the *San Francisco Chronicle Sunday Magazine*. Her work has been featured on NPR, and in *Life*, *Redbook*, *The Sun* magazine, *The Best American Essays*, and elsewhere. Her novel, *At the Edge of the Haight*, won the PEN/Bellwether Prize for Socially Engaged Fiction.

Wallace Shawn is an award-winning playwright and a noted stage and screen actor. His plays include, among others, *The Fever*, *The Designated Mourner*, *Marie and Bruce*, *Aunt Dan and Lemon*, and the upcoming *What We Did Before Our Moth Days*, scheduled to open in New York in 2026. He is also the author of two nonfiction books, *Essays* and *Night Thoughts*, as well as the coauthor and star of the widely acclaimed film *My Dinner with André*.

Michael Snyder is a freelance reporter and contributing editor at *T: The New York Times Style Magazine*, with a focus on architecture, design, travel, and food. He has been based in Mexico City since 2016, and his work has appeared in a range of publications, including *The Architectural Review*, the *Los Angeles Times*, *Saveur*, *Smithsonian Magazine*, and *The Nation*.

OUT NOW IN PAPERBACK

LONG-LISTED FOR THE NATIONAL BOOK AWARD

NAMED A TOP DEBUT NOVEL OF 2024 BY *KIRKUS*

★★★★★
THE TELEGRAPH

"*Yr Dead* is a propulsive read, wildfire writing leaving nothing behind."

ERIN VACHON,
THE RUMPUS

"A kaleidoscopic wonder here to help us see this broken world anew."

R. O. KWON,
AUTHOR OF *EXHIBIT*

"A singular, titrated, indelible debut."

ALEXANDER CHEE,
AUTHOR OF *HOW TO WRITE AN AUTOBIOGRAPHICAL NOVEL*

GOLD MEDAL WINNER OF THE INDEPENDENT PUBLISHER BOOK AWARD

A FOREWORD INDIES BOOK OF THE YEAR FINALIST

"It's super f*cked up and I loved it"

ANTHONY JESELNIK,
THE JESELNIK AND ROSENTHAL VANITY PROJECT

"Stylistically inventive and provocative, Sax expands on their poetry with a blazing novel."

SAM FRANZINI,
OUR CULTURE

"Sax has produced a work that is meditative, deeply humane, and profoundly original."

KIRKUS,
STARRED REVIEW

AVAILABLE AT BOOKSTORES, AND AT STORE.McSWEENEYS.NET

McSWEENEY'S

OUR NEXT ISSUE WILL BE SPORTS-THEMED

Not all contents are guaranteed; replacements will be satisfying

The Worst Shot Ever Taken . . . . Kiese Laymon
A formal analysis of Steph Curry's shot at the Paris Olympics as an art object, and its implications for the history of basketball.

Rule Breakers . . . . Laura van den Berg
On-the-ground coverage from the Katie Taylor–Amanda Serrano fight, in which two of the world's most decorated female fighters square off for one final history-making bout.

Stolen Promise . . . . Rob Curran and Andrew Nelson
The story of Amane Dramera, who, like an increasing number of young West African soccer prospects, was smuggled into Europe and abandoned in an elaborate and cruel confidence trick.

SOLUTIONS TO THIS ISSUE'S GAMES AND PUZZLES

CROSSWORD
(Page 118)

A	L	L	I	E	S		T	P	S		G	M	C
W	I	I	N	U	N	C	H	U	K		F	E	A	R
A	G	E	S	P	O	O	R	L	Y		I	N	C	A
Y	A	S		H	O	P	U	P		E	L	E	G	Y
			C	O	Z	Y	M	Y	S	T	E	R	Y	
	L	A	U	R	E	L		O	C	T	A	V	E	
S	A	U	D	I		E	T	S	Y		S	L	E	D
P	B	R		C	A	F	E	C	A	R		T	R	I
I	P	A	D		U	T	A	H		I	N	S	E	T
T	A	P	E	O	N		U	N	G	O	O	D		
	R	O	C	K	T	H	E	B	O	A	T			
S	T	I	R	S		A	V	E	R	T		U	S	E
A	N	N	E		O	V	E	R	M	O	R	R	O	W
F	E	T	E		F	O	N	T	A	N	E	L	L	E
E	R	S		A	C	T		L	I	L	S	I	S	

JACKET CAPTCHA
(Page 119)

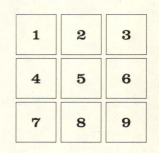

1. *The God of the Woods* by Liz Moore
2. *To the Lighthouse* by Virginia Woolf
3. *Kindred* by Octavia E. Butler
4. *Wandering Stars* by Tommy Orange
5. *Sea of Tranquility* by Emily St. John Mandel
6. *The Emperor of Gladness* by Ocean Vuong
7. *Crook Manifesto* by Colson Whitehead
8. *The Use of Photography*
   by Annie Ernaux and Marc Marie
9. *A Book of Days* by Patti Smith

COPYEDITING THE CLASSICS *(Page 120)*

Darkness had now fallen, and an early moon was sending its faint light to cast strange, grotesque shadows among the dense foliage of the forest.

Here and there the brilliant rays penetrated to earth, but for the most part they served only [1] to accentuate the Stygian blackness of the jungle's depths.

Like some huge phantom, Kala swung noiselessly from tree to tree; now running nimbly along a great branch, now swinging through space at the end of another, only to grasp that of a further [2] tree in her rapid progress towards [3] the scene of the tragedy her knowledge of jungle life told her was being enacted a short distance before her.

The cries of the gorilla proclaimed that it was in mortal combat with some other denizen of the fierce wood. Suddenly, [4] these cries ceased, and the silence of death reined [5] throughout the jungle.

Kala could not understand, for the voice of Bolgani had at last been raised in the agony of suffering and death, but no sound had come to her by which she possibly could determine the nature of his antagonist.

That her little Tarzan could destroy a great bull gorilla, [6] she knew to be improbable, and so, as she neared the spot from which the sounds of the struggle had come, she moved more warily and at last slowly and with extreme caution she traversed over [7] the lowest branches, peering eagerly into the blackness [8] for a sign of the combatants.

Presently she came upon them, lying in a little open space full under the brilliant light of the moon—little Tarzan's torn and bloody form, and beside it a great bull gorilla, stone dead....

Tenderly she bore him back through the inky jungle to where the tribe laid [9], and for many days and nights she sat guard beside him, bringing him food and water, and brushing the flies and other insects from his cruel wounds.

Of medicine or surgery the poor thing knew nothing. She could but lick the wounds, and thus she tenderly [10] kept them cleansed, that healing nature might the more quickly do her work.

[1] only served: This is a subtle one, because on close examination the *only* should modify both *served* and *to accentuate*—not just *to accentuate*.
[2] farther: *Further* is for metaphorical distance and *farther* for measurable distance.
[3] toward: This spelling is preferred by *MW*; *towards* is generally British.
[4] Delete the comma after *Suddenly*, as it undercuts the "suddenness."
[5] reigned: These are two commonly confused verbs: *to reign* is to rule over; *to rein* is to check or pull in by using reins.
[6] Delete comma: If this sentence is flipped around, it would read: "She knew it to be improbable that her little Tarzan could destroy a great bull gorilla"—no comma needed.
[7] traversed: *over* is implied by *traversed*, which means "to go or travel across or over."
[8] moon-splashed blackness: Either this or another correction is needed here, because per the above, the moon has been rising throughout this scene, and in the next sentence its light is "brilliant," so "blackness" doesn't make sense at this point.
[9] lay: *Lay* is the past tense of *lie* (as is meant here); *laid* is the past tense of *lay*. The conjugations of these verbs cause confusion even among seasoned copy editors.
[10] Suggest deleting *tenderly* or replacing it with another word, as *tenderly* is also used in the previous paragraph. Not all repeated words need to be queried—only those that might stick out to a reader.

124